THE ECCENTRIC REALIST

THE ECCENTRIC REALIST

*Henry Kissinger and the Shaping
of American Foreign Policy*

MARIO DEL PERO

CORNELL UNIVERSITY PRESS
ITHACA AND LONDON

© 2006, Gius. Laterza & Figli SpA. This translation of *Henry Kissinger e l'ascesa dei neoconservatori* is published by arrangement with Gius. Laterza & Figli SpA, Roma-Bari.

Copyright © 2010 by Cornell University

First published 2010 by Cornell University Press
Printed in the United States of America

ISBN 978-0-8014-4759-4

Book Club Edition

CONTENTS

THE ECCENTRIC REALIST

Introduction

On the night of September 26, 2008, during an otherwise predictable presidential debate, Henry Kissinger—his thoughts, his words and, more importantly, their true meaning—suddenly became a heated topic of discussion between the two candidates. Barack Obama and John McCain were discussing the possibility of the United States engaging in high-level talks, "without conditions," with some of America's most loathed enemies, including Mahmoud Ahmadinejad's Iran. Drawing a historical parallel, McCain claimed that the opening to China in 1972, one of the most renowned examples of U.S. engagement with a hitherto absolute enemy, had been carefully planned. Richard Nixon's visit, McCain claimed, "was preceded by Henry Kissinger, many times before he went." (Both claims were inaccurate: there was an element of improvisation during the entire process, and Kissinger had visited China only twice prior to Nixon's trip to Beijing.) Obama did not miss the opportunity: "I'm glad that Senator McCain brought up the history, the bipartisan history of us engaging in direct diplomacy," the soon-to-be-elected president argued. "Senator McCain mentioned Henry Kissinger, who's one of his advisers, who, along with five recent Secretaries of State, just said that we should meet with Iran—guess what—without precondition." "When we talk about preconditions—and Henry Kissinger did say we should have contacts without preconditions," Obama continued, "the idea is that we do not expect to solve every problem before we initiate talks." "My friend, Dr. Kissinger, who's been my friend for 35 years," McCain retorted "would be interested to hear this conversation and Senator Obama's depiction of his...positions on the issue. I've known him for 35 years."[1]

It mattered little to the two contenders that during those thirty-five years, Kissinger's view of world affairs had rarely been presented as an enlightened model for U.S. statesmen and that many, on the Right and the Left, had often lambasted Nixon's former national security czar for promoting and justifying a foreign policy devoid of moral scruples and humanitarian concerns. In many ways it also mattered little what Kissinger had actually said or suggested. (Despite Kissinger's successive semantic acrobatics to help McCain by claiming he supported negotiations with Iraq that were "geared to reality," Obama was largely right.)[2] The contest was not so much over the merit of the issue or the strength of Kissinger's argument, but its symbolic value. What both Obama and McCain sought was the mantle of Kissinger-the-symbol rather than the endorsement of Kissinger-the-expert. By invoking Kissinger's authority and claiming his support, whether willing or unwilling, the presidential candidates looked to justify their positions and emphasize who was the greater realist.

During the first term of the George W. Bush presidency (2001–5), some neoconservative intellectuals and senior advisors to the president scorned and derided the so-called reality-based community: those naïve people who "believe that solutions emerge from your judicious study of discernible reality." "We're an empire now," one aid to the president confessed to the author and journalist Ron Suskind: "when we act, we create our own reality. And while you're studying that reality—judiciously, as you will— we'll act again, creating other new realities, which you can study too, and that's how things will sort out. We're history's actors...and you, all of you, will be left to just study what we do."[3]

That was said, however, during a period of almost unprecedented imperial hubris in the United States. Fears and ideology stimulated this hubris and the ensuing dream of transforming the world, beginning with the Middle East. Facts, or rather "reality," forced a rapid retreat and the abandonment of such dreams. After the Iraqi fiasco, the most extreme neo-conservative fantasies were confined once again to their proper place in intellectual circles, think tanks, in-house magazines, Fox TV, and the Internet. People capable of studying "discernible reality," members of the "reality-based community," were back in demand.

Whatever Bush's advisors may have argued during the post-9/11 ideological hangover, in the end politicians, statesmen, and common people alike are always required (and always believe) to be "realistic" in their choices and behavior. When it comes to foreign policy, however, being realistic does not necessarily mean being a realist. In the post-1989 age of humanitarian wars, liberal interventionists and neoconservatives made frequent appeals to being realistic without falling into the trap of classical realism. Pondering her experience in the Clinton cabinet, former secretary of state Madeleine Albright said that "she hoped never again to hear foreign policy described as a debate between Wilsonian idealists and geopolitical realists. In our era," Albright maintained, "no President or Secretary of State could manage events without combining the two." In the middle of the 1990s, proclaiming the decade a "situation reminiscent of the mid-1970s," neoconservative gurus William Kristol and Robert Kagan claimed that "a neo-Reaganite foreign policy of military supremacy and moral confidence was needed" and urged fellow conservatives to stay aloof from the "neoisolationism of Pat Buchanan," but also from the "conservative 'realism' of Henry Kissinger and his disciples." According to Thomas Carothers, a Carnegie Endowment expert on democracy promotion, "Americans are so used to debating foreign policy from positions of realism and idealism, in which America's interest and capabilities are either systematically understated or overstated, that it is hard to avoid discussing democracy promotion in these terms. A position based on idealistic aspirations tempered by deeply realist considerations makes both sides uncomfortable. For democracy promotion, however, it is the only real choice."[4]

That politics, policy and, indeed, life often compel us to temper values with reality, ideals with possibilities, and goals with means, is a truism. It is nevertheless interesting to consider the parable of realism in U.S. public and political discourse since the great realist moment of twentieth-century U.S. foreign policy, Nixon and Kissinger's détente, and the much more restrained realist appendix of George H. W. Bush (1989–93). In the past three decades, realism and realpolitik have at worst been outright rejected, particularly in the early Reagan years, and at best qualified and consequently adjectived, as if unable to stand on their own. This trend has been particularly true for the past few years, when this sort of qualified realism has made a comeback, in some cases to support and justify Bush's choices—presenting them as not only just and bold, but also realistic—more frequently to denounce those same choices as hazardously unrealistic. Among the many illustrative examples are Charles Krauthammer's "democratic realism," Charles Kupchan and John Ikenberry's "liberal realism," Condoleezza Rice's "American realism," Francis Fukuyama's "realistic Wilsonianism," John Hulsman and Anatol Lieven's "ethical realism," and Bill Richardson and John McCain's calls for "a new realism" and a "realistic idealism," respectively. In recent years, particularly after 2003, everyone seemed increasingly compelled to present himself or herself as a realist. Everyone, however, also seemed obliged to qualify his or her realism. Even "balances of power," the quintessential realist mantra, could not stand alone as a category of analysis and, more so, a political prescription. To be meaningful, such "balances" had to at least "favor freedom," as reiterated several times in the U.S. National Security Strategy of September 2002.[5]

Qualifications notwithstanding, realism has thus made something of a comeback in U.S. political discourse. The connection of such a comeback with the stunning failures of George W. Bush and the difficulties the United States is currently facing is quite evident. In times of crisis, and of diffuse pessimism, it becomes convenient for policymakers and statesman to present themselves not just as realistic (which they always must be) but also as "realists." When it comes to foreign policy, being a realist means being cognizant of power realities, the unalterable structural features of the international system, the rules and practices of such a system (devoid of any meliorist utopia or missionary impulse), and placing the national interest above any other concern.

All of which leads us back to the Obama-McCain quarrel on Kissinger and his "real" position on negotiating with the enemy, with or without preconditions. Before 2008 it would have been hard to imagine two presidential candidates, or for that matter two U.S. political leaders, seeking legitimacy and political cover in what Kissinger did or did not say. This year, however, was different, a time of a perceived deep crisis, which in many ways evoked memories of 1929 and also the 1970s. It was a time that seemed to demand not only pragmatism, concreteness, and sobriety, but also realism. After almost two decades of global interventionism, nation building, regime change, and democracy promotion (policies, strategies, and discourses, incidentally, that Kissinger the public pundit rarely condemned or contested), the time had come for a return to a "Kissingerian" foreign policy, or even a "Kissingerian" president.

Despite being surrounded by liberal interventionist experts and advocates such as Susan Rice, Samantha Power, and Anthony Lake, Obama was increasingly portrayed (and, it must be said, ably represented himself) as the true realist in the presidential face-off: a man whose "reasonableness and balance," Michael Fullilove of the Brookings Institution claimed, contrasted sharply with McCain's "unrealistic proposals" and the "baroque inconsistencies" of the Arizona senator's speeches. *Philadelphia Inquirer* columnist Trudy Rubin proclaimed herself horrified by how "sharply" "Kissinger's sobriety...contrasted with McCain's emotive appeals" and McCain's Bush-like "preference for illusions over facts." "It was a reminder," Rubin claimed, of "how badly this country needs a dose of realism in the White House." "Look at where the grand pubahs of Republican realism," Kissinger among them, "stand on pretty much all the foreign policy issues of our day," progressive commentator Ilan Goldenberg argued, "and it becomes pretty obvious that McCain is no realist." The canonization of Obama as the realist that the America of 2008 badly needed was completed when one of the most influential foreign policy pundits, Fareed Zakaria, declared the Illinois senator "the true realist in the race." "In terms of the historical schools of foreign policy," Zakaria maintained, "Obama seems to be the cool conservative and McCain the exuberant idealist....Obama's response to McCain's proposals on Russia and China could have been drafted by Henry Kissinger."[6]

This discussion says more about U.S. political culture than Obama's or McCain's worldview or future foreign policies, let alone their realist credentials. In periods of difficulty, critical introspection, and domestic division, realist and anti-utopian formulas and codes tend to become more popular and acceptable. In such periods, offering the public an ostentatiously realist discourse can be highly profitable and convenient for politicians and aspiring statesmen—the first argument I advance in this book on the rise and fall of Henry Kissinger's fame and influence. During his tenure as national security advisor and secretary of state in the Nixon and

Ford administrations, Kissinger succeeded in presenting himself as the no-nonsense hard-nosed realist who could finally teach naïve and immature America the timeless (and indeed European) rules and practices of international politics. Educating America and fast-forwarding it to responsible adulthood were presented by Kissinger as bold tasks that ran counter to a deeply entrenched political culture, which only the sophisticated and heretical German-born intellectual, turned improbable "American hero," could achieve. The United States, Kissinger claimed in retrospect, "possessed neither the conceptual nor the historical framework" for "cold-blooded" policies. The "many different strands that make up American thinking on foreign policy" had "proved inhospitable to an approach based on the calculation of the national interest and relationships of power." Nevertheless, in the late 1960s and early 1970s, the time had come to "face the stark reality" and "learn to conduct foreign policy as other nations had to conduct it for so many centuries—without escape and without respite."[7]

The time had come, however, because a majority of Americans were urging such a change—a fact that Kissinger and many commentators often failed to mention. Disillusioned with a policy of global containment of the Soviet Union and bewildered by the consequences of the modernizing crusades of liberal administrations in the 1960s, Americans were asking for a change of course, political as well as discursive. Far from being a bold and idiosyncratic response to the crisis—in part real, in part exaggerated—that the United States faced, Kissinger's prescription was a mostly conventional one. The realist discourse of limits adopted by Nixon's advisor was not just in tune with the mood of the country; it was a product of such a mood and an attempt to exploit it, to forge a new consensus around a foreign policy whose contents (détente, the opening to China, and the end of intervention in Vietnam) were obligated, but whose basic narrative was to undergo a drastic change. This inclination to feign eccentricity and idiosyncrasy, where conformism was dominant, was not new in Kissinger's career. On the contrary it had already been a distinctive mark of a brilliant pre-governmental intellectual parable, where Kissinger had frequently offered analyses—on nuclear weapons, transatlantic relations, limited war, and the like—that pretended to be ahead (and outside) of time, and instead rephrased in rich and baroque prose conventional wisdom and orthodoxy.[8]

This concept leads to the second argument I make in the book: that Kissinger carefully considered, sometimes to the point of obsession, the

domestic repercussions of his words and deeds. Using previously inacces-
sible documents, recent books such as Robert Dallek's *Nixon and Kissinger*
have highlighted in great detail the attention paid by Nixon and his national security advisor to the internal political and electoral implications
of their foreign policy choices.[9] Such attention is normal, if not inevitable,
in any democracy, particularly the United States. Yet, to date, the most
popular argument put forward by Kissingerologists of all stripes has been
a different one, namely, that Kissinger was insufficiently aware of the interaction between foreign policy and domestic politics, and showed little
or no concern for U.S. democratic procedures as well as America's cultural
and political transformation during the 1970s.[10]

This lack of respect, it is claimed, was one of the main factors behind his
political defeat in the 1970s. Armed with this uncontested truth, I first approached this topic a few years ago during archival research on the United
States' reaction to the 1974 Portuguese revolution. Skimming through
various archival records and memoranda of Kissinger's conversations with
his staff, I discovered, to my great surprise, that Kissinger spent an inordi-
nate amount of time speaking to journalists and senators. In short, he paid
paramount attention to how his declarations and actions were presented
and received domestically.

Again, this sort of diligence was almost inevitable in the U.S. political
system, especially during the 1970s, when U.S. foreign policy was subject to
unprecedented public scrutiny and a "new internationalist Congress" tried
to reaffirm its constitutional prerogatives after almost thirty years of acquiescence to executive primacy in foreign affairs.[11] Furthermore, Kissinger
enjoyed the fame, popularity, and, in the end, influence he gained by successfully selling his and Nixon's foreign policy to the American public. But
Kissinger's attention to the nexus, and interdependence, between foreign
policy and domestic politics did not simply stem from the different political climate in the United States or his ambition and notoriously narcissistic
ego. There was something more. From the second half of the 1960s onward, the crisis of Cold War internationalism, if not of the Cold War itself,
had opened a heated discussion in the United States on the foreign policy
the country should promote: on its goals, means, and practices. Nixon and
Kissinger's proposals and strategies must be considered within this discussion. Realism was the discursive medium they used to convey such proposals and strategies to the American public. The aim was to forge a new,

broad internal consensus around a proactive and internationalist, although formally less ideological, foreign policy. Only by achieving this goal, Nixon and Kissinger reasoned, would it be possible to contain the "limitationist" requests to reduce U.S. international commitments as well as the politically impracticable demand of relaunching the Cold War as it was before Vietnam and the crisis of containment.[12]

In 1972–73, Kissinger and Nixon thought they had achieved this objective. According to many polls, U.S. public opinion appreciated the realist turn in American foreign policy and the "Europeanization" of its modus operandi. A new, lasting consensus appeared to have been forged. It was not so. Kissinger mistook a temporary and contingent transformation in the mood of the country as a permanent one. Beginning in 1972, Kissinger's critics, on the Right and the Left, began to condemn the European, and consequently un-American, matrices of Kissinger's political culture and strategic vision. Denunciations of Kissinger's amoral approach and calls for a new moralization of American foreign policy became more and more frequent. Détente with the Soviet Union was presented as a new form of appeasement. The New Right and many liberal hawks, led by Senator Henry Jackson (D—Washington state), presented negotiations on arms control and the 1972 SALT agreements as a capitulation of the United States that would lead to its strategic inferiority vis-à-vis the USSR. Kissinger's opponents considered nuclear interdependence and security based on the logic of deterrence and mutually assured destruction (MAD) as unacceptable, both strategically and morally. Finally, dialogue with a totalitarian and expansionist Soviet power, which violently crushed any form of political dissent within its borders, was presented as a violation of American principles, ideals, and values. "This country has not prevailed for two hundred years," Henry Jackson proclaimed in 1975, "only to have its chief foreign policy spokesman side with the Soviet rulers against the American commitment to freedom."[13]

Kissinger had attempted to de-exceptionalize the way in which U.S. foreign policy was conducted and, even more so, was narrated. His critics, particularly the future neoconservatives, instead proudly proclaimed America's uniqueness and exceptionalism, rejecting his calls for the United States to be a country among others whose position in the international system was measured solely by the merits of power and diplomatic prowess.

Confounded by his own success and fame, Kissinger did not fully comprehend the political strength of his domestic adversaries. Nor did he understand the power and resilience of an exceptionalist and nationalist view of America's role in the world—a notion he believed had been silenced for good by Vietnam and the crisis of Cold War liberalism. It was not the nature and functioning of U.S. democracy that Kissinger did not grasp: in fact, these he understood far too well and he had ably exploited them in his own political ascent. What he underestimated and failed to anticipate was the rapid reemergence of an exceptionalist, and soon hegemonic, political culture. By thinking that a realist transformation in U.S. foreign policy discourse was possible and that a new domestic consensus would be attained through it, Kissinger proved to be singularly unrealistic.

The unrealistic nature of Kissinger's realism, however, was not limited to his lack of understanding of domestic U.S. realities. It also applied to his reading of international affairs and to his geopolitical vision, which is the third and final argument of the book. Both at the time and later, Kissinger presented his efforts as an attempt to deal with the objective multipolar evolution of the international system. Yet Kissinger's diplomacy and actions often reveal that he paid little more than lip service to the notion of multipolarism. As I show in chapter 3, from the opening to China to relations with European allies, the paramount consideration was repercussions on the competition and balance of power between the United States and the Soviet Union. Kissinger looked at the world through a bipolar, albeit nonideological, prism. What is more interesting is that for Kissinger, bipolarity as an analytical category—his way of defining power relations in a specific historical juncture—produced bipolarism as a policy prescription. The preservation of such bipolarity was the primary objective for détente and the way it was conceived in Washington. Through détente and negotiations with the former absolute enemy, Nixon and Kissinger hoped to achieve a variety of goals: reduce the risk of a devastating nuclear conflict; preserve the U.S.-USSR duopoly of power; co-opt the Soviet Union to jointly discipline the system, particularly in Europe; facilitate an evolution of the USSR from a revolutionary power bent on destabilizing the system into a status quo actor devoted to its consolidation; and reduce the costs of U.S. primacy. "There can be no peaceful international order," Kissinger proclaimed in a statement delivered to the Senate Foreign Relations Committee in 1974, "without a constructive relationship between the

United States and the Soviet Union. There will be no international stability unless both the Soviet Union and the United States conduct themselves with restraint and unless they use their enormous power for the benefit of mankind."[14]

Détente was therefore an attempt to co-manage bipolarism in order to consolidate and uphold it. As such it was geopolitically conservative because it sought to preserve the status quo and keep in check the many forces that were instead eroding the bipolar discipline.[15]

Such an approach, however, opened up a series of inescapable dilemmas that revealed how Kissinger's realism lacked, ultimately, the necessary dose of realism. Kissinger's was in fact an attempt to safeguard and prop up bipolarism while delegitimizing its basic ideological underpinnings; his was a bipolarism without the Cold War. This contradiction was one Kissinger was never able to come to terms with. The consequences were fully on display in Europe, particularly in countries such as Italy, where détente threatened the political rigidities and divisions that the Cold War had produced and perpetuated. Lacking the ideological justifications of the past, pro-Western Italian Christian Democrats considered it possible and convenient to form a governmental alliance with the Italian Communist Party. Kissinger, however, harshly rejected such a possibility. Similarly, in postrevolutionary Portugal in 1974, Kissinger lambasted the Socialist Mario Soares (whom he nicknamed "the Portuguese Kerensky") for his initial policy of cooperation with the Portuguese Communists. There was an element of intellectual sloppiness in Kissinger's reaction to what was going on in Italy and Portugal: he never fully grasped the political intricacies of the two countries nor made an effort to study and comprehend them. He preferred to apply outdated as well as rigid bipolar models to the two cases, rejecting invitations from local interlocutors as well as from his staff to adopt a more nuanced approach. This stance was ironic in a man who had frequently invoked the need for greater "nuance" in the United States' approach to world problems. It was also a consequence of the fundamental contradiction concerning how détente was defined and promoted: a strategy aimed at imposing bipolar discipline and stability, but one that was also eroding some of the elements on which such stability had been based.[16]

This book offers an unconventional explanation of a crucial passage (and a crucial character) in U.S. history and solves some of the incongruities that still characterize historical interpretations of Henry Kissinger, détente, and international relations during the 1970s. The book takes the form of an essay, and its mode of presentation is interpretative rather than narrative. The 1970s are now recognized by many scholars as a watershed in world history.[17] During the decade, several factors and processes converged. As a result the nature of the international system was altered, powers relations were transformed, and the successive reaffirmation of America's world primacy was facilitated. In the United States we witnessed the return of American exceptionalism, which embraced the notion that the United States was bound to lead the world. This revival of American exceptionalism challenged Kissinger's realism and reaffirmed once again America's greatness and uniqueness. The new American consensus was that the United States, in Ronald Reagan's words, was still "the exemplar of freedom and a beacon of hope...a magnet for all who must have freedom, for all the pilgrims from all the lost places who are hurtling through the darkness, toward home."[18]

Kissinger's realist moment revealed itself as a parenthetical period in the history of the United States. In the 1980s and afterward, Kissinger vainly tried to render himself acceptable to the neoconservatives and the New Right, even embracing some of the critiques they had originally formulated of him and his détente.[19] He had to wait for more than three decades, however, for an extreme radicalization of U.S. nationalism and a consequent major crisis of U.S. hegemony before becoming the quintessential symbol of a form of realism that an embattled America once again invoked and seemed to need.

1

The Crisis of Containment

During the first two decades of the Cold War, the United States promoted a mostly coherent and unitary foreign policy. Washington did not always achieve its goals and occasionally suffered symbolic and practical defeats, the most significant of which came in October 1949 with Communist victory in the Chinese civil war and the subsequent birth of the People's Republic of China. The fundamental objective of giving form to a U.S.-dominated "international liberal order" was, however, consistently pursued, whereas the necessity to limit the influence of the Soviet Union and the spread of Communism was rarely questioned.[1]

The Nature and Objectives of Containment

This "international liberal order" was less global and universal than originally hoped for in Washington. The projects elaborated during World War II, and the optimistic vision of Franklin Delano Roosevelt that underpinned them, proved to be impracticable. Cooperation with the Soviet Union did not survive the end of the war and the disappearance of the forced, if highly effective, bond provided by the common Nazi enemy. Both Roosevelt and Winston Churchill recognized the Soviet sphere of influence in central Eastern Europe, although the fact this sphere was constructed through brutal and coercive practices provoked the protests and indignation of the U.S. public. Contrary to Roosevelt's auspices and predictions, the Soviet Union did not undertake a process of gradual and inexorable liberalization, which over time might have determined a progressive evolution in the Soviet system, a consequent convergence—of interests, but also of policies and models—between the two superpowers, and the inevitable extension of a U.S.-led liberal global order.[2]

Not only did the expected convergence not take place, but the Soviet Union also attempted to challenge this order by projecting an alternative universalism. The Soviet-socialist vision offered the world a counterteleology, amid a renewed global ideological dispute, that replicated some features of the one between Wilsonianism and Leninism thirty years earlier. Therefore, what came to be known as the Cold War also represented an ideological conflict between two universalisms and two progressive and finalistic views of modernity. The ideological dimension of the antagonism thus complemented the geopolitical competition between the United States and the Soviet Union, sharpening the antagonism and making it almost impossible to heal the fracture between the two sides. This ideological component rendered the post–World War II epoch a peculiar and unique period in the history of international relations.[3]

The objective of integrating the Soviet Union into the liberal order was rapidly substituted with that of excluding the Soviet regime to avoid the possibility that Moscow could somehow "influence" the foundational and structural features of this order. The Soviet Union was therefore excluded and "externalized." Yet because of the nature of the Soviet Union and its challenge to the international system, this exclusion was not enough. Moscow's influence had to be constrained and limited to counter the spread and appeal of Soviet socialist universalism, but also to lay the foundations for a liberal evolution of the Soviet regime that would, over time, remove the challenge it posed to U.S. world hegemony. The transformation of the USSR through collaboration and convergence—the highly unrealistic goal of Roosevelt—was therefore replaced by a new strategy of transforming the

Soviet Union through confrontation, rejection, and the exercise of constant pressure, all intended to exhaust the Soviet regime over time. U.S. policy vis-à-vis the USSR shifted from dialogue and interaction to "non-dialectical" rejection, producing a binary and nondialogic form of foreign policy.[4]

This new approach was synthesized in the metaphor of "containment": the term used from 1946 onward to summarize U.S. post–World War II global strategy toward the Soviet/Communist enemy. The term was popularized by the historian and diplomat George Kennan, one of the figures who contributed most, during the early Cold War years, to defining the new U.S. attitude toward world affairs, and its conceptual and theoretical underpinnings. In the famous Long Telegram sent from the U.S. embassy in Moscow in February 1946 and in an article published in the journal *Foreign Affairs* in July 1947, Kennan discarded the idea that any dialogue or collaboration with the Soviet Union was possible or, indeed, desirable. Intrinsically aggressive, opportunistic, and unscrupulous, the USSR could only be contained, in anticipation that its numerous internal contradictions and flaws would lead to its crisis and eventual transformation. For this reason, Kennan argued, the United States had to promote a "firm and vigilant containment" of the Soviet Union and its expansionistic tendencies, nipping the latter in the bud wherever they manifested themselves.[5]

The *Foreign Affairs* article "introduced the term 'containment' to the world." Authorship of the article, which had been published anonymously, was immediately attributed to Kennan, transforming him into a sort of celebrity and, for a brief period, allowing him to exercise a telling influence over Truman administration foreign policy. From 1947 onward, U.S. global Cold War strategy would be characterized as a strategy of containment: "George Kennan," Henry Kissinger later maintained, "came as close to authoring the diplomatic doctrine of his era as any diplomat in our history."[6]

Truman and his chief advisors enthusiastically accepted the prescriptions of Kennan's containment: firmness, a rejection of dialogue, the construction of alliances, promotion of various "measures short of war," and economic and political support to states menaced by Communism. For a couple of years, Kennan was an influential political advisor and led the Policy Planning Staff at the Department of State. His authority, however, rapidly waned, and during the rest of his life (which ended in 2005 at the age of 101) Kennan became a severe critic of U.S. foreign policy and the frequent misapplications of "his" containment.[7]

Two objections that cut across political and cultural lines were initially raised to the strategy of containment from those who preferred the preservation of dialogue with Moscow, and from those, on the opposite side of the political spectrum, who urged instead a more resolute attitude and, possibly, the "liberation" of central Eastern Europe from Soviet domination. The first critique was more incisive and popular in the early postwar years, with famed intellectual and columnist Walter Lippmann presenting the argument in a series of articles, later collected in a single volume that popularized the other famous metaphor of the time: the Cold War.[8] In particular, Lippmann denounced the paradoxically apolitical logic of Kennan's containment and the abdication of diplomacy it entailed: because "the history of diplomacy," Lippmann wrote, "is the history of relations among rival powers, which did not enjoy political intimacy...for a diplomat to think that rival and unfriendly powers cannot be brought to a settlement is to forget what diplomacy is all about."[9]

The second critique enjoyed a certain political success in the late 1940s and early 1950s. The Communists' victory in China, the successful nuclear explosion by the Soviets, and the onset of the Korean War seemed to question the ability of the United States and its allies to face down the challenge of international Communism. Consequently, the practicability and wisdom of Kennan's analysis and prescription were explicitly doubted. The alleged passivity of the doctrine of containment came under attack on the grounds that it limited Washington's policy to the mere defense of a status quo severely threatened by Soviet activism. Many commentators and politicians urged the replacement of an approach that was presented as both strategically self-defeating and morally reprehensible, in favor of a more dynamic stance that could destabilize the existing order to the advantage of the United States and its allies. Containment, it was argued, had to be substituted with a more assertive strategy of rollback, a policy whose first objective was the liberation of peoples still "in captivity" behind the iron curtain. For a brief period this position was explicitly supported by John Foster Dulles, the first secretary of state to Dwight Eisenhower (president from 1953 to 1961). Moreover, the rhetoric of rollback and liberation was embraced by various conservative intellectuals. Among the most prominent was the former Trotskyite James Burnham, who in the early 1950s dedicated a significant amount of his prolific intellectual production to the denunciation of the policy of containment.[10]

The abandonment of a strategy of containment in favor of one of "liberation" soon proved unfeasible. The construction of a protective sphere of influence beyond its western borders represented the primary element of Moscow's security strategy. Challenging this sphere, as Burnham and others requested, threatened to provoke a new and devastating conflict. Despite a clear U.S. superiority, nuclear war would have intolerable costs for all involved. That rollback was little more than an electorally convenient rhetorical formula became clear during the first opportunity to "liberate" a slice of the Communist bloc in Hungary in 1956. In spite of the appeals and requests for help from Budapest, the Eisenhower administration was careful not to challenge the Soviet right to harshly silence any form of dissent in its own sphere of influence. Some of those who dreamed of putting an end to Hungarian "captivity," such as CIA chief of operations Frank Wisner, would never recover from the delusion. From then on, Burnham and others would turn their brilliant pens to other causes, aside from a retrospective yearning twenty years later for the firmness and clarity of that very strategy of containment that had originally been the target of their sharp criticism.[11]

The consistency of Burnham and Dulles's critique of containment was impaired not only by the impracticability of the proposed alternative. The deficiency of their critique was analytical as well as prescriptive. Whatever one thought about its merits, the strategy of containment did not represent a static response to the challenge of Communism. In fact, it reflected an awareness of the insurmountable structural constraints—both military and geopolitical—to which U.S. foreign policy was subject, whatever administration was in office. And it stemmed from a realistic appraisal of the features of the international situation (starting with the preservation of a sphere of influence in central Eastern Europe), which Moscow considered nonnegotiable and for whose preservation it was willing to risk a new war. Within these constrictions, however, containment represented a maximalist and dynamic response.

The various U.S. administrations of the first twenty years of the Cold War (those of Truman, Eisenhower, Kennedy, and Johnson) interpreted the strategy in different ways but never reduced it to a literal interpretation of its explicit and proclaimed objective: to impede further expansion of the area controlled by the Soviet Union and international Communism. The objectives of containment were, instead, much more ambitious. To stop the USSR and Communism at the point they had reached in 1949 meant projecting Western and U.S. influence (and hegemony) into new theaters, which were still extraneous to the bipolar competition. Extending the global presence of the United States entailed the strengthening and consolidation of the almost unchallenged primacy the United States had developed during World War II. Containment and its progressive globalization thus represented a strategy oriented at conserving and widening what historian Melvyn Leffler has called a "preponderance of power," which the United States had enjoyed since the end of the war.[12] Despite Burnham's claims, containment did not represent a tacit acknowledgment of Soviet might and the consequent acceptance of some future, inevitable equivalence between the two sides. On the contrary, containment constituted an attempt to amplify and possibly crystallize the post–World War II asymmetric balance of power. Containment served to render the power disequilibrium in favor of Washington structural and irreversible. In the short term, this arrangement would moderate the behavior of the Soviet Union and restrain its capacity to project a counter-universalism. It was in the mid- and long term, however, that containment revealed its maximalist and dynamic face. To impose a condition of unalterable inferiority on the Soviet Union was the essential precondition for slowly wearing down the enemy. Frustrating Moscow's innate expansionism, which was considered the natural and qualifying trait of the Soviet regime, would debilitate the USSR and catalyze the explosion of its inner contradictions. As Kennan predicted in 1947, "Soviet power," just "like the capitalist world of its conception," bore "within it the seeds of its own decay." Through containment, therefore, it would be possible "to force upon the Kremlin a far greater degree of moderation and circumspection" and "to promote tendencies which must eventually find their outlet in either the breakup or the gradual mellowing of Soviet power."[13]

The Preconditions of Containment

Like any ambitious strategy, containment proved to be extremely costly and demanding. To build a global defensive perimeter around the Soviet bloc imposed huge military investments and the construction (and maintenance) of a growing number of bases all over the world. Propping up its own allies, economically and militarily, required a policy of aid and financial support without precedent in the history of any great power. To create a network of regional alliances obliged the United States to spend immense political capital, which was eroded daily by the demands of leadership and the necessity to frequently compromise with quarrelsome and unruly allies.[14]

International mobilization had to be matched by a similarly intense and permanent domestic mobilization because containment required the preservation and reinforcement of internal cohesion. It quickly catalyzed a call to arms, both private and public, to serve the national security state that had been created to pick up the gauntlet. The tasks and structure of the federal state, as well as its reach and intrusiveness, were immensely expanded in the name of containment and its requirements. New institutions—such as the Department of Defense, the CIA, and the National Security Council—were established. Military strengthening was pursued through an exponential growth in expenditures and the acceptance of a permanent budget deficit, which up to a few years earlier would have been unthinkable and politically unacceptable. A deficit-spending policy in the name of national security, and the ensuing indiscriminate distribution of federal subsidies, contributed to nourishing economic growth and making rising levels of taxation tolerable and acceptable. Entire regions of the United States—chiefly the Sunbelt—were transformed (and enriched) by public investment in the military sector and its various appended industries. The "military-industrial complex" was much more decentralized and fragmented than described in the phobic fantasies of its critics. These critics had a point, however, when emphasizing the relevant and enduring convergence of interests between the government and many large corporations stimulated by the Cold War's national security state.[15]

Four factors permitted the total mobilization, domestic and international, required by containment: strategic superiority; the conviction (and, in part, awareness) of possessing unlimited means and resources; accepted primacy and leadership in one's own sphere of influence; and, finally, domestic consensus and subsequent support for an ambitious and interventionist foreign policy.

Strategic Superiority

Throughout the first phase of the Cold War, the United States enjoyed a clear and undisputed strategic superiority. The U.S. nuclear monopoly was, however, short-lived; the Soviet Union tested its first nuclear weapon in the summer of 1949, much earlier than had been predicted by the most pessimistic of U.S. intelligence estimates. (The projected date of a Soviet atomic explosion was 1951–52.)[16]

The Soviets' possession of the ultimate weapon damaged U.S. confidence and exacerbated a strong sense of insecurity and vulnerability, which contributed to the anti-Communist hysteria that pervaded the United States during the early 1950s. Nevertheless, the strategic superiority of the United States was not in question; on the contrary, it continued to increase during the first years of the Cold War. The technological gap between the two superpowers was never entirely bridged by Moscow, guaranteeing the United States a clear nuclear supremacy. High and increasing military investment further bolstered this gap. Between 1952 and 1964, the defense expenditures of the United States as a percentage of gross national product (GNP) never fell below 9 percent, reaching a peak of almost 14 percent in 1952 and 1953. During this period, the United States' total defense expenditures were always higher than those of the Soviet Union, which certainly did not hold back on arms spending. In the early 1960s, the ratio between American and Soviet nuclear warheads was approximately eight to one. For a long time, the USSR limited its strategic arsenal to costly, if not always reliable, long-range missiles, whereas U.S. nuclear arms were distributed on different transportation modalities (missiles, bombers, and later, submarines). Some scholars have gone so far as to claim that for almost twenty years the United States enjoyed a first-strike capability: the ability, in other words, to preemptively eliminate any Soviet nuclear retaliatory potential.[17]

The United States was not always aware of this superiority, however. Proclamations by the Soviet leadership, and Nikita Khrushchev in particular, and the propagandistic exploitation of some Soviet technological progress in the field of rocketry fueled U.S. fears and anxieties. Such alarms were mostly unfounded, but political expediency induced many to refer to them. Accusing the sitting administration of not doing enough to safeguard the security interests of the country became a frequent, as well as instrumental, political practice. This accusation was made particularly during the Republican administration of Dwight Eisenhower, the president who most reluctantly persevered on the road of high military expenditure in that it compromised the preservation of (or rather, return to) a balanced budget. Eisenhower's fiscal conservatism was bitterly denounced by his political opponents, who accused the president of having accepted the development of a "missile gap" in Moscow's favor.[18]

The Soviet test of an intercontinental ballistic missile (ICBM) and, moreover, the launching of *Sputnik,* the first artificial satellite, in 1957, contributed to the missile gap phobia. According to physicist Edward Teller, the father of the hydrogen bomb and a strong supporter of a policy of high military investment, *Sputnik* represented for the United States a defeat "more important and greater than Pearl Harbor." The idea that a missile gap had developed was in fact groundless. Some Democrats, including senator and presidential candidate John Kennedy, however, tried to ride the wave of the missile gap controversy in light of the electoral returns it promised. Eisenhower was only partially able to resist the pressures to augment military spending. In spite of his goals and efforts, defense expenditures remained at 9 percent of GNP or higher. This situation was not only the result of political or electoral convenience, however. Accepting the analytical and prescriptive premises of containment made it almost impossible to limit the arms race: superiority and preponderance of power constituted the essential and unavoidable preconditions of the strategy. The United States had to be free to act on a global scale without fear of reprisals. This strategy was conceivable only if U.S. supremacy, in terms of hard military power, was neither contested nor defied.[19]

(Almost) Unlimited Means and Resources

The scant and decreasing appeal of Eisenhower's conservatism was also the result of the belief, diffuse at the time, that the possibilities available to the United States were almost unlimited. Objective data—structural and contingent—fueled such belief. It was also nourished by gross misinterpretations, shaped by the highly ideological optimism that dominated U.S. public discourse and informed many political and economic analyses.

During the first twenty years of the Cold War, the relative superiority of the United States vis-à-vis the rest of the world, including the USSR, was undisputable and unprecedented. Post–World War II bipolarism was acutely asymmetric and imperfect: no matter the parameter chosen to measure power (economic, military, cultural), there was not even a semblance of equivalence between the two poles—the United States and the Soviet Union—that dominated the international system. U.S. nuclear superiority, exercised as a monopoly for four years, was complemented by America's financial and industrial primacy. While the USSR, Japan, and all the main European powers had been destroyed and devastated by the war, the United States emerged from the conflict richer and more prosperous than before. In 1946, the United States possessed 60 percent of the gold reserves in the world. Only three years later, this amount had increased to 72 percent, mostly as a consequence of the onerous forms of payment attached to loans granted to Great Britain. The Bretton Woods system had transformed the dollar into the main reserve currency of the capitalist system. Foreign investments and American exports increased exponentially after 1945 (the latter augmented four times between 1950 and 1970), although, as in the past, it was the domestic market that represented the main driving force behind U.S. economic growth. In 1950, the total GNP of the United States was greater than those of the USSR, Great Britain, France, the Federal Republic of Germany, Japan, and Italy combined. This wealth contributed to an extraordinary increase in the level of individual prosperity and welfare: in 1950, per capita GNP in the United States was twice that of Great Britain and almost four times that of the Soviet Union.[20]

The economic superiority of the United States was largely artificial and transient. It was destined to diminish once other countries had recovered from the devastation of the war and reaped full advantage of the network of financial and commercial interdependences the United States itself had created and expanded. Despite fears and predictions of a bitter postwar recession, the U.S. economy (and the absolute, if not relative, wealth of the United States) continued to grow, suffering only occasional, as well as short and physiological, difficulties. This expansion was enabled by the constant increase in productivity, at a rate of 1.6 percent a year between 1948 and 1962—itself a consequence of unprecedented technological development. Growth, higher productivity, and technological progress allowed a constant increase in the level of prosperity and individual well-being. The "politics of productivity" facilitated a redistribution of wealth among most segments of the population through higher wages and rising consumption. Between 1945 and 1970, real per capita income increased 55 percent; in 1955, 95 percent of American families owned a refrigerator and 70 percent a car (in France there was just one car for every thirteen inhabitants). A society of mass consumption progressively took form in early Cold War America. It was a society in which widespread affluence and wealth contributed to reducing many social conflicts and facilitating a vast domestic consensus on various governmental choices, including those related to international affairs.[21]

Particularly in the 1950s, development, growth, and a broad consensus stimulated the fideistic belief, embraced by many social sciences of the time, that the U.S. model of capitalism had finally been able to square the circle; that, when sagaciously administered and piloted, growth and economic advance would proceed in a linear and progressive manner, eliminating social and political tensions; and that the Western and liberal model was destined to spread and triumph.

It was in many ways an *ante litteram* version of the "end of history," an idea that would powerfully resurface in the early 1990s with the implosion of the Soviet Union and the end of the Cold War. The United States, it was then argued, represented a more advanced evolutionary stage in a process that other countries, beginning with Western Europe, could and should follow and emulate. This belief represented the key conceptual pillar of Cold War liberalism, which dominated post–World War II U.S. ideology and political discourse. To the rest of the world, the United States offered a universal model of development and modernization. Such a model was ineluctably progressive and, most of all, offered an alternative to the equally modern model represented by Marxism and projected by the Soviet Union.[22]

The ideology (and practices) of modernization had a relevant impact on the foreign and national security policy of the United States. Modernization justified and legitimated an interventionist, liberal, and anti-Communist form of internationalism, which found expression in various development schemes for less affluent countries and in the attempt to lay the conditions for exporting and universalizing the American model. In theory, this liberal internationalism—which saw its apogee and the beginning of its crisis with the administrations of Kennedy and Johnson (1961–69)—allowed the conciliation of interests, ideals, and a self-congratulatory U.S. identity. In short, it could be used to contain the diffusion of Communism, expand Western-style capitalism and democracy, and reaffirm the superiority of the American model. U.S. Cold War liberalism represented, therefore, the latest incarnation of an exceptionalist self-representation, simultaneously nationalist and universalistic, that had characterized the historical experience of the United States.[23] It also justified high investments in the fields of defense and national security. With the partial exception of Eisenhower, all administrations during the 1945–69 period embraced the idea that high military expenditure represented not a burden imposed by the Cold War but a tool available to promote, fine-tune, and regulate economic growth, thus making it de facto constant and permanent. The domestic counterpart of modernization theory was a military Keynesianism, as a consequence of which, budget deficits ceased to be cyclical and instead became a structural element of the U.S. economic system. Security and development, economic growth and anti-Communism, deficits and rising military investments represented the interdependent and correlated fundamentals of the strategy of containment. It was a global and ambitious strategy that necessitated unlimited resources in order to overpower—militarily, economically, and technologically—the adversary.[24]

The actual and symbolic zenith of military Keynesianism also occurred in the 1960s, particularly under the Kennedy administration. A prominent role was played by Keynesian economists (such as Walter Heller, chairman of the Council of Economic Advisers from 1961 to 1964), who rejected the concern with high inflation and permanent deficit that had marked the Eisenhower era. From 1960 to 1970 the deficit increased constantly, reaching a record-breaking $25 billion in 1968 (with the rising costs of the Vietnam War obviously contributing to this amount). The deficit of the balance of payments rose from $3.4 billion in 1960 to $10.7 billion in 1970. During the same period, defense expenditures doubled, from $92.2 billion to $196.6 billion, although—as Keynesian theorists assumed—the high level of domestic growth produced a reduction in the level of defense expenditures as a percentage of GNP.[25]

The legitimization of a policy of deficit spending in the name of security imperatives and economic growth actually preceded the election of Kennedy by at least a decade. As we saw, the idea represented one of the fundamental elements of the strategy of containment. The first proclamation of the "unlimitedness" (and potential multiplicability) of the means the United States had at its disposal was contained in the famous document NSC 68, a broad and comprehensive study of U.S. national security strategy, elaborated between 1949 and 1950 by an ad hoc committee of State and Treasury officials under the guidance of Paul Nitze, Kennan's successor on the Policy Planning Staff. NSC 68 constituted one of the most relevant and paradigmatic documents of the Cold War and of post–World War II U.S. security policy.[26] Its formulations were bombastic and apocalyptic: "The issues that face us are momentous, involving the fulfillment or destruction not only of this Republic but of civilization itself." It employed ideological caricatures of the enemy, who was accused of calling "for the complete subversion or forcible destruction of the machinery of government and structure of society in the countries of the non-Soviet world and their replacement by an apparatus and structure subservient to and controlled from the Kremlin." It promoted the exceptionalist representation of the United States and its ability to make use of any instrument to face the challenge: "The integrity of our system will not be jeopardized by any measures, covert or overt, violent or non-violent, which serve the purposes of frustrating the Kremlin design."[27] And it described the existing bipolar competition as global, epochal, and universalistic: "The assault on free institutions is world-wide now, and in the context of the present polarization of power a defeat of free institutions anywhere is a defeat everywhere."

Most of all, NSC 68 offered a justification for the high level of military expenditures that the national security state imposed. The document underlined not only the necessity and affordability of such expenditures, but also their utility and beneficial effect for the economy and the society of the United States. High investments in the field of defense and security had not just a strategic, or at most an anticyclical, function; they could also offer a permanent stimulus to the economy. "One of the most significant lessons of our World War II experience," the document claimed, "was that the American economy, when it operates at a level approaching full efficiency, can provide enormous resources for purposes other than civilian consumption while simultaneously providing a high standard of living."

Guns and butter were not incompatible; they were, in fact, complementary and interdependent. Intensifying the production of the former guaranteed a multiplication of the latter. The immense cost of containment was not only bearable but also beneficial because the United States had unmatched means and resources, because these means and resources were increasing, and most of all, because tools had been designed to render this increase permanent and perpetual.

The Nature of U.S. Hegemony

The Cold War was also an ideological competition, which helps us understand why the strength and attractiveness of the American economic, political, and cultural model came to represent a further element of asymmetry and disequilibrium in the highly imperfect post-1945 bipolarism. The circulation of U.S. productive practices and cultural models—the so-called process of Americanization—was neither straightforward nor devoid of resistances, national adaptations, hybridizations, and distortions. According to some scholars, this interaction between the United States and the rest of the world influenced and transformed American culture and lifestyles too. Certainly, it did not represent a univocal and unambiguous process easily imposed by the American "center" onto the global "periphery." The Soviet Union and international Communism were unable, however, to match the magnetism and fascination projected by the American model globally. During the first two decades of the Cold War, the United States, and the capitalist form of modernity it embodied, became the point of reference and benchmark for all other countries—including the Soviet Union in certain aspects—to measure their development and progress.[28]

Thanks to its unique ability to build and spread hegemony, the United States gained an additional advantage vis-à-vis the Soviet Union. This advantage was reinforced by the way the United States promoted its policy of alliances: by the modalities used by Washington to construct a U.S.-led Western and Atlantic bloc, by the nature of the relationship between the United States and its lesser allies, and, finally, by the influence the latter were frequently able to exert on U.S. foreign policy choices. The Western bloc built by the United States after 1945 was probably not an "empire by invitation," in historian Geir Lundestad's immensely fortunate but simplistic slogan. The invitation, if it actually existed, was formulated by specific national elites, constantly renegotiated, and on a few occasions, even withdrawn. The U.S.-led Atlantic Community was the product, nevertheless, of a "consensual" (and therefore proper) "hegemony," based on an intense level of negotiation between the United States and its junior European partners, and on the willingness and ability of the former to accommodate, and when possible satisfy, the requests of the latter and their ruling classes. Far from casually, it was Western Europe, and Great Britain in particular, which started the process that eventually led to the creation of the Atlantic Alliance—a structure unprecedented for the level of institutionalization it was destined to achieve, the intense collaboration among its associates, and the constraints it imposed on the defense and security systems of its members, including the United States itself.[29]

Multilateral (or bilateral) compromises and accommodations within the U.S. sphere of influence were particularly remarkable when compared with the coercion and unilateral dominion imposed by the USSR within its bloc. These compromises made the Western bloc more coherent, well organized, and, in the end, stronger than its Communist counterpart, and allowed the United States to exercise greater influence over its allies and manage crises within the alliance more flexibly (and effectively) in the long term. The different features of the two blocs and respective alliance systems added a further element of asymmetry to the bipolar imbalance of power. The greater strength and cohesion of the U.S.-led alliance was indispensable in meeting the costs and commitments of containment. This strength guaranteed the United States an additional advantage in the ideological competition with Moscow in front of world opinion, as the continuing expansion and enlargement of the Atlantic Alliance still reveals. Yet it also allowed Washington to socialize most of the costs of containment with its allies, obligating them (not always successfully) to assume part of the common defense burden and to accept greater commercial and financial interdependence, which, at least in its first stages, primarily advantaged the United States. During the first two decades of the Cold War, the difference between "irresistible" U.S. hegemony and brutal Soviet domination often symbolized the contrast between a true and effective universalism, the liberal and Western/Atlantic one, and another that was such only in aspiration. It was a contrast between the global projection of the United States (and of its strategy of containment) and the much more limited, and in many ways regional, projection of the Soviet Union.

Domestic Consensus

The high costs of global containment were sustainable only as long as there was broad domestic support for its means and objectives. This support had to be built and preserved, despite the open challenge that containment and the national security state posed to some of the sacred and inviolable principles (and myths) of U.S. political culture: low military expenditures; refusal to join permanent alliances in times of peace; a limited and nonintrusive role for the federal government; protection of individual liberties; and a balanced budget and low taxation.[30]

During the first years of the Cold War, one or more of these principles were frequently invoked to resist containment and its implications at home. Resistance came both from progressives and conservatives. The latter denounced the national security state as another example of federal centralization and the extension of the public sector, which logically followed the social programs of the "quasi-socialist" New Deal of Franklin Roosevelt. The warfare state was thus presented as the logical and inevitable appendix of the welfare state. Curiously, given its later fame, the Central Intelligence Agency was primarily opposed by part of the American Right, which accused it of being an "American Gestapo" at the service of invasive federal power. In addition to criticizing the abandonment of wartime collaboration based on anti-Fascist principles, the Left denounced the excessive militarization of U.S. foreign policy and the severe impact of anti-Communism on political liberties and freedom of expression. Both conservatives and progressives frequently embraced isolationist points of view that opposed increasing U.S. participation in world affairs.[31]

A majority of Americans supported this participation, however. During the two decades following the end of World War II, greater U.S. international involvement was rarely questioned. Cold War centrist liberalism became culturally and politically hegemonic, despite its violation of some sacred topoi of American political culture. Why were the critiques of containment incapable of offering alternatives and building a counterhegemony? Various and equally valid answers can be given to this question.

First of all, Soviet behavior and the brutal way in which Moscow imposed its dominion in central Eastern Europe aroused criticism and genuine dismay in the United States. Roosevelt's projects for the postwar international order, based on the continuation of wartime collaboration with Moscow, rested on a certain degree of ambiguity and wishful thinking. Within the government, particularly in the State Department, more than one high-ranking official opposed the partnership with Moscow and believed a partition of Europe to be almost inevitable. Stalin did not want a Cold War, but his own responsibility—which stemmed from an impossible pursuit of total security and the resulting imposition of authoritarian and absolute control over his sphere of influence—must not be underestimated. In U.S. society, where prejudicial anti-Communism and anti-socialism had profound roots that had never been entirely severed, Soviet conduct stirred up old fears and paranoias, legitimated a diplomatic hardening, and facilitated the adoption of an interventionist and global strategy such as containment. Not casually, some of the most important U.S. foreign policy choices of the early Cold War followed Soviet actions. The coup in Prague of February 1948 induced Congress to accelerate the approval of a massive program of economic aid for Western Europe (the Marshall Plan), whereas the inception of the Korean War persuaded Truman to approve NSC 68 and implement some of its recommendations.[32]

One might add that the main alternative to containment was often represented by a politically and culturally heterogeneous isolationism, embraced by parts of the Right and Left, that had been permanently discredited, however, by the experience of World War II. Such isolationism had not been able to offer a response to Nazi expansionism, had embraced a policy of appeasing Hitler that proved strategically ineffective as well as morally repugnant, and, with the neutrality laws of second half of the 1930s, forced the country to abandon venerable foreign policy traditions and historical claims (the protection of neutral rights among them).[33] Moreover, such isolationism rested on a basic assumption, which the extraordinary technological breakthroughs of the modern age rendered less and less plausible: the idea that geography could guarantee the United States "free security," thus allowing the country to isolate itself from the rest of the world and concentrate exclusively on the consolidation and improvement of its own form of democracy.[34]

A third element that explains the domestic popularity of containment was that it promised unprecedented levels of wealth and prosperity. The period labeled the "age of consensus," particularly the 1950s, was also an age of anxiety and fear: of atomic war, of Communist subversion, of the alleged threat to the American way of life. For a vast majority of Americans, however, it was also a period characterized by increasing salaries, diminishing unemployment, unparalleled access to higher education, and social ascent. Furthermore, with the notable exception of African Americans, groups and minorities who until then had been on the fringes of American society also participated in (and benefited from) these processes. For many, the restrictions to political liberties generated by the Cold War and by anti-Communism were offset by the prosperity that containment stimulated. Governmental intrusiveness could be presented as the magnanimity of a state that distributed its investments almost indiscriminately and expanded, although often in an incoherent and uncoordinated way, social protection and public welfare on a scale without precedent in U.S. history.[35]

Finally, the broad support for containment and its rapid globalization also derived from its presentation as the latest incarnation of a historical mission the United States once again embraced. The defense of the "free world" against Communist obscurantism was presented (and conceived) as part of a historic burden that the United States—the unique and exceptional country—had to bear. Probably for the first time in its history, America was not just proclaiming this destiny but also fulfilling it. Containment expressed a deep-seated messianic tendency, which recovered and adapted certain Wilsonian assumptions, in particular the idea that the diffusion of U.S.-inspired market democracy was not only beneficial to the United States and its economy, but also vital to its security. In a global system whose various parts were increasingly interdependent and interconnected, it was crucial for the United States to extend its hegemony (and to spread its values) in order to defend and safeguard its interests and identity. "We are now at a moment in history when, under God, this nation of ours has become the mightiest temporal power and the mightiest spiritual force on earth. The destiny of mankind—the making of a world that will be fit for our children to live in—hangs in the balance on what we say and what we accomplish," proclaimed Dwight Eisenhower in accepting the Republican presidential nomination in 1952.[36] In the U.S. political imagination of the time, the containment of the Soviet Union and international Communism allowed to mesh interests and ideals. Marrying idealism and realism, containment appeared to the vast majority of Americans as a perfect foreign policy model and the best response, morally as well as strategically, to the challenge posed by Communism.[37]

Containment in Crisis

The strategy of containment and its various applications rested on a profound faith in the ability of the United States to achieve its fundamental objectives: broaden its hegemony and power preponderance; block the growth of the USSR and Communism at the point they had reached in the late 1940s; and pave the way for the implosion of the socialist Soviet regime, an implosion made inevitable in the long term by the regime's intrinsic contradictions. The Cold War liberalism that buttressed the philosophy of containment expressed, therefore, a deep-rooted optimism in the ability of America to be up to the task that destiny had reserved for her, and in the ineluctability of a naturally progressive course of history that was on the side of "freedom," not oppression. Sporadic stumbles and temporary setbacks occasionally marred this optimism, which was also contradicted by the tendency to overrate Soviet power and the capacity of Communist ideology to penetrate globally.[38] Nevertheless, this optimism represented the distinguishing mark of early Cold War liberalism. As stated by Henry Jackson, the quintessential liberal Cold Warrior and Democratic senator from Washington State, a liberal "was essentially an optimist."[39]

From the early 1960s, and increasingly throughout the decade, the foundations of this optimism began to crumble, however. The United States entered a deep, and until then completely unexpected, crisis—a crisis with multiple faces that converged to corrode the four essential and interdependent prerequisites of containment. Suddenly, it seemed that "few of the certainties of American Cold War policy remained intact." As Henry Kissinger would later emphasize, after two decades the "foreign policy capital" of the U.S. government had been "virtually exhausted."[40]

The End of Strategic Superiority

During the 1960s the concept of strategic superiority became more and more hollow. Many in the United States began to contest the policy of high military expenditures aimed at preserving a nuclear superiority that appeared increasingly meaningless politically, militarily, and strategically. Given their destructive potential, nuclear arms seemed to reduce the freedom of action for those nations that possessed them in vast and growing quantities, as was the case with the United States and Soviet Union. Atomic weapons increasingly revealed their nonmodern and non-Clausewitzian face: by virtue of their almost unlimited power to destroy and devastate, they had become unmanageable by the very politics they were supposed to be the continuation of and under whose control they theoretically fell. Through the application of nuclear power, the genie of war had escaped the political bottle from which it had been contained. It would take almost twenty years before a large, transnational movement for the abolition of nuclear weapons acquired a relevant political influence. Already in the early 1960s, however, influential voices criticized the arms race and the logic behind the competition for strategic superiority. In 1963, Kennedy's secretary of defense, Robert McNamara, remarked during a hearing before a House committee that the idea of "nuclear superiority" had a "declining relative value": a "fact of life," McNamara claimed, that could be ignored only "at great peril to" U.S. "national security." "Neither side" possessed a "force which" could "save its country from severe damage in a nuclear exchange" anymore, nor could either "realistically expect to achieve such a force in the foreseeable future." George Kennan went as far as urging the U.S. government to publicly, and unilaterally, surrender its first strike option—the principle of first use being "a pernicious one, incompatible with" U.S. "ideals and not conducive to the ultimate removal of the weapons of mass destruction from national arsenals." While the search for nuclear primacy had lost its rationale, the risk of nuclear proliferation appeared ever more likely in that many other countries outside the nuclear trio (the United States, the Soviet Union, and Great Britain) wanted to create their own atomic arsenals.[41]

Such danger represented the basic catalyst to a convergence of interests, unexpected although deep and structural, between the two great Cold War rivals. Both the Soviet Union and the United States faced a challenge to one of the fundamental features of their superiority: the possession, almost duopolistic, of nuclear arms. Uncontrolled proliferation could facilitate the rise of other power centers and further increase the danger of a nuclear conflict. A positive interest (to conserve a privilege and preserve the superiority and power hierarchy it created) and a negative one (to control the diffusion of atomic arms and the risk of a conflict) paradoxically transformed nuclear weapons from an antagonistic and competitive issue into one that stimulated, albeit forcedly, Soviet-American convergence and dialogue. In the summer of 1963, the United States and the Soviet Union ratified the Partial Test Ban Treaty, which banned nuclear experiments in the atmosphere, in outer space, and under water—tests that were indispensable to those countries seeking to develop their own nuclear weapon. The Partial Test Ban Treaty, which Khrushchev defined as "a turning point in the history of contemporary international relations," was not signed by China and France, both of which were desperately eager to join the nuclear club (and which they promptly did soon after). Yet the treaty revealed the convergence under way between the United States and the Soviet Union, which would become the platform of the successive process of détente between the two superpowers. This convergence rested on a fundamental and overdetermining Soviet-American interest: to preserve nuclear primacy, avoid proliferation, and limit the possibility of an atomic conflict. Against their will, the United States and the Soviet Union found themselves tied in an inexorable strategic interdependence; "our most basic link," Kennedy proclaimed a few days before his death, "is that we all inhabit this small planet. We all breathe the same air. We all cherish our children's future. And we are all mortal."[42]

The Cuban Missile Crisis of October 1962 had stimulated awareness of what strategic interdependence was truly about. On that occasion, the two powers found themselves as close as ever to nuclear war. The crisis rang an alarm bell for the United States and for those officials who, unlike Kennan and McNamara, believed strategic superiority still meant something and should be pursued. The near deployment of Soviet medium- and intermediate-range ballistic missiles (MRBMs and IRBMs) on the island of Cuba revealed the vulnerability of the U.S. deterrent. According to some intelligence estimates, the missiles would have allowed the Soviets to partially fill the still immense quantitative and technological nuclear gap with the United States. With limited costs, but at high risk, Moscow could have increased its first-strike capability by an impressive margin (up to 80 percent according to some estimates).[43]

The Soviet missiles were never installed, and after some tense days the crisis was resolved. The potential vulnerability of the United States, however, which the Cuban drama revealed, was considered intolerable by many U.S. politicians and commentators, and anticipated a situation Washington would have to face by the end of the decade: meaningful or not, the United States would no longer enjoy the privilege of clear nuclear superiority. Throughout the 1960s the Soviet leadership undertook a vast and ambitious program of nuclear rearmament. The stated objective was to achieve a degree of military parity, which subsequently would allow Moscow to redress one of the fundamental asymmetries of the Cold War and lay the premise for truly equal and bilateral negotiations over arms.

The Soviet budget destined for defense expenditures began to grow yearly at the rate of 4–5 percent, a clear demonstration of the priority the Soviets assigned to military production over civilian spending. In 1963, for the first time in twelve years, Soviet defense investments exceeded those of the United States in absolute terms. The nuclear and missile gap that had for so long favored the United States was largely (although never entirely) filled. Moscow concentrated its investments in heavy, long-range rocketry (intercontinental ballistic missiles, or ICBMs). In such category, the Soviet Union matched and outpaced the United States. By 1971 the Soviet ICBM-based nuclear yield surpassed the American; Soviet production of new, heavy SS-9 missiles went from a mere 30 to more than 300 in just five years (1966–71); total Soviet ICBMs increased five times in the second half of the 1960s. Concurrently, the USSR intensified its efforts in other fields—in particular, submarine missiles (SLBMs), which more than doubled during 1966–71, and antiballistic defense (ABM)—with the goal of reducing the technological hiatus that still existed with the United States.[44]

This effort was never crowned with success, however. Ultimately, U.S. technological superiority and the ability of the American capitalist system to generate the wealth necessary for large military investments prevailed. The fictitious parity achieved by the Soviet Union in the late 1960s and early 1970s was little more than a parenthesis in the history of the Cold War. Despite the phobias it contributed to breed, Soviet rearmament produced only a partial and illusory alteration of the bipolar asymmetry of power. From a strategic perspective, the United States preserved a clear advantage in other modalities of transporting nuclear warheads and delivery devices (MIRV). Moreover, nuclear weapons represented just one of the many variables that defined the actual power of a state. Although the Soviet Union had been able to gain ground on the United States in terms of military might, it still lagged far behind in many other determinants of power. High investments in nuclear weapons, the growing weight of the military sector, the consequent contraction of domestic consumption, and the bureaucratization of Soviet society instead reduced the appeal and diffusion of the Soviet model, making heterodox variants of Marxism-Leninism—be it Maoism, Castroism, or other revolutionary and third-world alternatives—more appealing.

There was, however, limited awareness of such an evolution in the United States. In addition to nourishing old fears, Soviet nuclear empowerment put an end to an era of undisputed U.S. strategic primacy. If evaluated unidimensionally, the preponderance of American power had been defied and outdone by the ideological, and total, Cold War adversary. The straightjacket provided by containment experienced its first, although partial and insufficient, loosening.

Means Are Not Unlimited

In 1950, the former undersecretary of state and banker Robert Lovett had claimed that "there was practically nothing that the country could not do if it wanted to do it." Twenty years later such a statement was unthinkable. Dreams and predictions notwithstanding, the resources available to the United States proved to be neither unlimited nor infinitely multipliable. The beginning of a complex transition to a postindustrial and post-Fordist society questioned the applicability of the economic formulas that had dominated U.S. Cold War policies and discourse. In its swapping of inflation with employment, the famous Phillips Curve did not seem to work anymore: the increase of the former was not matched by an equivalent reduction of unemployment. The considerable costs of the domestic reform programs promoted by the Kennedy and Johnson administrations collided with those imposed by the continuation of ongoing military plans and, especially, intervention in Vietnam. Suddenly, it became necessary to make those very choices that many had previously deemed possible to avoid. Contrary to the claims of adherents to military Keynesianism, guns did not generate butter but rather reduced it.[45]

The war in Vietnam caused the deflagration of yet unexploded contradictions, exposing some of the fundamental limits of Cold War liberalism and the model of development it proposed. "The Democratic Administrations of 1961–69," the journalist Martin Walker has emphasized, "financed—all on deficits and credit—their rearmament boom, their domestic welfare reforms and 'Great Society' programs, as well as the Vietnam War and their growing private investments in Japan and in Western Europe." Quite simply, "it was too much."[46]

In the Johnson years alone, the approximate cost of intervention in Vietnam exceeded $100 billion; the United States found itself with more than 500,000 men on the ground in Southeast Asia and facing forms of domestic protest and discontent unimaginable only a few years earlier. The Vietnam War crucially, although not exclusively, contributed to the large U.S. budget deficits of the second half of the 1960s: in the fiscal year 1968 alone, the deficit reached $25 billion. Inflation was, at 4 percent, the highest level since the Korean War. It would continue to grow in the following years, but not in inverse proportion to unemployment as it had in the past. The war—as had been stressed back in 1966 by State Department official William Bundy while examining its cost—could become "an albatross around the administration's neck."[47]

These problems accelerated the erosion of the economic superiority of the United States, a superiority that itself was artificial and transient, at least in its dimensions and relative range. Freed from the costs of power politics, still protected by the United States, and benefiting from the relative advantages enjoyed by all late comers, Washington's allies had undergone a process of economic (and technological) development that now made them competitive with the United States. In the 1950s and 1960s, the industrial productivity of many capitalist countries, West Germany and Japan in particular, had been far superior to that of the United States. The U.S. share of manufactured exports decreased 4.6 percent within a decade (1963–73), from 17.2 percent to 12.6 percent. In the same period, Japan doubled its exports, and many Western European countries improved their trade balances. Meanwhile, the United States' GDP represented a declining percentage of world GNP (from 25.9 percent in 1960 to 21.5 percent in 1980). The per capita GDP of Japan and some Western European states approached, and sometimes surpassed, that of the United States. The absolute GDP of these countries increased at double the rate of the United States' GDP. Surpluses in the trade balance of West Germany and Japan occurred at the same time that the United States was having increasing difficulties with its trade balance, which in 1971 experienced its first deficit in over thirty years.[48]

Trade and balance deficits, high inflation, and the loss of international competitiveness in the industrial sector intersected with the difficulties the dollar was facing and contributed to their exacerbation. The Bretton Woods system, on which post-1945 U.S. hegemony was largely based, had transformed the dollar into the international reserve currency, convertible into gold. During the 1960s, an overvalued dollar, exporting inflation to the rest of the world, was increasingly unable to fulfill its role as the pivotal international currency. U.S. gold reserves were reduced from 68 percent to 27 percent of world reserves (excluding those of the Soviet bloc countries).[49]

At least economically, the international system was evolving toward multipolarism, as many commentators obsessively emphasized at the time: "In the military sphere, there are two superpowers," Kissinger stressed a few years later. "In economic terms there at least five major groupings. Politically many more centers of influence have emerged."[50]

U.S. preeminence was no longer unquestioned. The costs of global containment were proving insupportable. U.S. administrations began to discuss the possibility of implementing previously approved defense programs.

Such a decision would have been unthinkable a few years earlier, but now it signaled the rejection, although *sub silentio,* of the search for dominance that had distinguished the Cold War security policy of the United States. Economic difficulties and the relative decline of the United States vis-à-vis several allies also contributed to render relations within the U.S.-led Western bloc increasingly tense and bitter. U.S. hegemony became more controversial and less consensual. Another of the preconditions of containment began to vanish.

Rejection of U.S. Hegemony

Trade and economic competition within the Western bloc damaged its cohesion and unity, nurturing recriminations and reciprocal accusations. During the first phase of the Cold War there had been several moments of tension and drama between the United States and its junior partners, particularly the Europeans. A distinctive trait of the alliance led by the United States (and of the hegemony Washington had constructed) had been its capacity to act as a clearinghouse where disputes could be mediated and compromises found. Almost all scholars of transatlantic relations during the early Cold War have underlined this aspect, emphasizing the flexibility and adaptability of the anti-Soviet bloc.[51]

During the 1960s this flexibility, and the possibility of consensually overcoming crises among countries of the Western alliance, witnessed a dramatic reduction. Many in the United States denounced what they considered unfair economic competition from Western Europe and Japan, which, they argued, benefited from U.S. foreign investments and, at the same time, were free from the burdens of ensuring global stability, which fell almost exclusively on American shoulders. U.S. allies, led by Charles de Gaulle's France, contested the choices of the Kennedy and Johnson administrations and their management of the difficult economic transition, which exported U.S. inflation to Europe and made allies pay for Washington's mistakes in a devious and surreptitious way.[52]

Economic strains intersected inextricably with military and strategic tensions, making them sourer and more difficult to resolve. The United States, and Congress in particular, accused the allies of not contributing adequately to the common defense effort. Containment had rising costs that could not fall solely on the United States. Many of these were old accusations that had marked the history of transatlantic relations, particularly in the early 1950s. U.S. problems and the war in Vietnam, however, had conferred unprecedented importance to them. Beginning in 1966, the Democratic senator from Montana, Mike Mansfield, began to periodically submit resolutions calling for a significant reduction in the number of U.S. troops stationed in Europe. These proposals combined a growing antimilitary sentiment, stemming from the difficulties the United States was encountering in Vietnam, a willingness to reduce military expenditures during a period of economic difficulty, and the conviction that European allies were not doing enough and had to accept greater responsibility. With their greater prosperity, Europeans, it was argued, had to take up a greater share of the costs of containment. Meanwhile, European members of the alliance were preoccupied with the possibility of a partial U.S. troop withdrawal from Europe and harbored doubts, particularly France, about the credibility of the U.S. deterrent. Such doubts were aggravated by the Soviet nuclear reinforcement and the greater power Moscow now had at its disposal. Washington's allies could only wonder whether the United States would ever accept the risk of a nuclear attack on its own territory just to defend Western Europe.[53] Simultaneously, however, many Western European members of the alliance invoked, and often practiced, a more autonomous foreign policy that was justified and fueled by the loosening of bipolar systemic constraints and by current U.S. difficulties. Other factors also contributed: the aforementioned European skepticism about the U.S. commitment to protecting Western Europe; the hostility of many Western European countries to the rigid U.S. attitude toward the Soviet Union and its satellites, with which potential trade opportunities were opening up; European perplexities about U.S. intervention and conduct in Vietnam; and the recurrent, and certainly overambitious, European dream to return to a national (and nationalist) form of power politics, which were less feasible in the bipolar Cold War era. Hypocrisies and legitimate criticisms, reasonable requests for greater autonomy, and wishful thinking—all contributed to European choices that contrasted with U.S. ones and whose first (and most glaring) example was the French decision to withdraw from NATO's integrated military structure in 1966.[54]

These tensions in European-American relations were both a symptom and a cause of the mounting U.S. hegemonic deficit, of a crisis of Atlanticism and of its institutions, to which many scholars and international relations experts of the period, including Henry Kissinger, were dedicating their ruminations.[55] The disappearance of one of the crucial preconditions of containment was caused not only by the misunderstandings between governments and elites on both sides of the Atlantic, but also by protests from citizenry who denounced and rejected American hegemony. Indeed, the latter intensified the former, since it was often politically expedient for Western European political forces to distance themselves from Washington's decisions and thus satisfy broad segments of their national electorates.

The crisis of U.S. hegemony was also a crisis of the model of development and modernization that it had tried to offer to the world. Challenged on the domestic front, where it was unable to satisfy many of the promises it had fueled, the liberal and progressive model appeared less appealing and applicable abroad. Tested with scant success in Latin America and with dramatic results in Southeast Asia, the strategy of modernization was denounced as the last incarnation of liberal imperialism (from the Left) and as a form of shortsighted universalism that aimed at homologating national peculiarities and hampering autonomous patterns of development (from the Right).[56]

The war in Vietnam, and the manifest "illiberal consequences" resulting from the actions of a "liberal empire," was the primary factor behind the denunciation of the American model. Mass protests took place in the streets and squares of major Western European capitals, where U.S. intervention in Vietnam and the alleged acquiescence of West European governments were harshly denounced. The student and labor protests during the second half of the 1960s had multiple national and international matrixes; their global and interconnected character, however, stemmed also from an attack on the rigidity of an international system that inhibited change as well as on the hypocrisies of U.S. and Soviet foreign policies.[57]

The rejection, or at least the critique, of the American and Western economic and cultural model was frequently matched by a growing and naïve fascination with mythogenic third-world alternatives that would soon reveal their limits. Yet it was also matched by a more concrete, although equally ideological, search for a European alternative to the Cold War and the liberal U.S. model. Such "third-forcism" stressed (and tried to exploit) the difficulties experienced by the United States, while offering a less radical and more feasible option to Guevarism or Maoism. It arose as a consequence of a situation in which bipolarity (the presence of only two powers "which [had] the potential to become poles for the international system") was less likely to automatically produce bipolarization ("the extent to which actors are clustered into [two] mutually exclusive camps").[58]

In reality the advanced industrial societies of Western Europe were facing a crisis not dissimilar from, and in some aspects even more profound than, that of the United States, whereas European integration progressed slowly and contradictorily. In the crisis of American hegemony and the earliest attempts at an autonomous European foreign policy—best symbolized by West Germany's *Ostpolitik*—it was nevertheless possible to identify the first attempt to give form and substance to a Europeanism that aimed at being different from, and in part an alternative to, Cold War Atlanticism.

Domestic Consensus in Pieces

The crisis of U.S. hegemony reflected the broader and more general crisis of Cold War international liberalism that had dominated the practice and discourse of U.S. foreign policy since 1945. The international attack on American primacy was matched by a denunciation from within the United States. The age of consensus had come to an end, and many postulates of post-1945 U.S. foreign policy were now openly challenged. Anti-Communism was no longer capable of providing the glue to bind the multiple centrifugal tendencies operating within U.S. politics and society.[59]

The opposition, just as the one developing outside the United States, was politically and culturally heterogeneous. The challenge to the consensus of the previous twenty years stemmed from two main threads: the New Left and a disillusioned strand of U.S. liberalism. To these, one might add the rancorous, if politically less incisive, critique from an Old Right (à la Burnham), which saw in an ineffective and limited war in Vietnam the umpteenth example of the self-defeating timidity of containment.[60]

In the New Left that emerged during the 1960s, the political and cultural dimensions were strictly intertwined with a generational one. It is difficult to find common intellectual foundations in the New Left, with the heterogeneity of its cultural and political references, which ranged from the critical sociology of Charles Wright Mills, to French existentialism, to Frantz Fanon's anticolonialism, to purely American forms of egalitarian communitarianism. In the apt synthesis of historian Van Gosse, the New

Left was a "movement of movements…a constant efflorescence of sub-movements, temporary coalitions, breakaway factions and organizational proliferation."[61] One of the unifying traits of this multifaceted and boister-ous "movement of movements" was its critique of U.S. actions abroad: its presentation of American intervention in Vietnam not just as an aberra-tion, or at most a mistake, but as the inevitable outcome of the philosophy and inner logic of U.S. Cold War foreign policy. The New Left reread the history of this foreign policy, identifying long-term continuities that the Cold War had only redefined and remodulated. The political and historio-graphical revisionism of the New Left, itself not devoid of exceptionalist references to a truly egalitarian and now betrayed American past, there-fore questioned the foundational pillar of liberal internationalism: the idea that the United States was a progressive force in the international system. The New Left challenged the moral and political certainties of liberal in-ternationalism and repudiated its intrinsic universalistic aspirations. It re-jected the notion that it was necessary to export democracy in the name of security not because of its impracticability, but because it considered democracy and the model of development the United States intended to export as rotten at its core. For the New Left, in Vietnam the U.S. foreign policy was revealing its true face: it was just an updated form of imperi-alism. This imperialism was peculiar and unorthodox in its means and manifestations ("open door" imperialism in the famous formula of histo-rian William Appleman Williams and other revisionists), but nevertheless exploitative and destabilizing. For the New Left, the United States did not represent a potential solution to world problems; on the contrary, it was one of their main causes.[62]

The New Left offered a powerful, and often intellectually sophisti-cated, critique. It was a minority movement, however: raucous, brilliant, but also composite, diverse, and lacerated by quarrels and divisions. A dif-ferent critique of containment came from those sectors of the liberal and Democratic establishment that had supported the main Cold War policies of the United States and approved its ends, instruments, and often, com-promises. Once again the trauma of Vietnam constituted a crucial wa-tershed. The idea that it was necessary (and, indeed, right) to devastate a country in order to save it from Communism revealed all the contradic-tions and absurdities of a coherent and linear application of containment. In this case, however, critics did not assail the assumptions and goals of liberal and progressive internationalism but rather the idea that it could be promoted and achieved unilaterally and solipsistically by the United States, without the cooperation of other countries and strengthening global institutions and international law. According to liberal critics of containment, multilateral cooperation amid empowered international institutions was necessary because of the interdependent nature of the international system, the destructiveness of nuclear arms, and the constraints with which even the unique American superpower now had to abide.

Interdependence, many liberals argued, imposed collective solutions on problems that could only be solved through negotiations with friends and enemies alike. Furthermore, not only did it force the United States to curb the unilateralism of its actions but also to limit its global interventionism. Such interventionism inhibited the development and consolidation of multilateral modalities of crisis management, relieved Washington's allies of responsibilities and deterred them from acting, corrupted the U.S. political system by militarizing American society and centralizing power in the hands of the executive branch, and finally loosened the control and transparency on which American democracy allegedly relied.[63]

The chairman of the Foreign Relations Committee, William Fulbright (D-Arkansas), was among the first liberals to dissociate themselves from Johnson's foreign policy. He did so by denouncing the structural crisis of containment and its malicious effects on U.S. democracy. The United States, Fulbright proclaimed, had become the victim of an "arrogance of power." "Power," he bluntly stated, "confuses itself with virtue and tends also to take itself for omnipotence"; America was now "at that historical point at which a great nation is in danger of losing its perspective on what exactly is within the realm of its power and what is beyond it." The Senate majority leader, Mike Mansfield (D-Montana), who had urged for a reduction in U.S. military commitment abroad, was another emblematic example of a disillusioned Cold War liberal engaged in self-critical introspection, which supporters of containment presented as a retreat. In Kissinger's words, Mansfield "was not a member of a radical fringe, but a charter member of the Senate establishment." He was also, however, "an isolationist, eager to reduce all American overseas commitments, reflecting the historical nostalgia that sought to maintain America's moral values uncontaminated by exposure to calculations of power and the petty quarrels of short-sighted foreigners."[64]

Kissinger's was very much a stereotyped caricature of Mansfield and the possible political consequences of a successful liberal critique of containment. In reality, old-style isolationism had been discredited for good and would never return. Nevertheless, the risk that many, including Kissinger, perceived was that the United States would opt for a drastic limitation of its global commitments. Such a choice would undermine U.S. credibility vis-à-vis allies and enemies. The peril, a sophisticated 1969 report by the NSC staff argued, was the potential popularity of a "limitationist" reaction to the difficulties the United States was facing. Such "limitationism" did not "spring from the traditional isolationist disposition to remain aloof from the world," but reflected "a mood of doubt and frustration," whose impact "upon the position of the U.S. in the world could be no less significant than the impact of isolationism before World War II."[65]

Containment, a strategy that by definition rested on the belief that there were no limits to the projection of U.S. power, suddenly faced a diffuse "limitationist" sentiment. This sentiment was manifested in the request, from different sectors of domestic public opinion, to devote less time and resources to international affairs (in order to concentrate on domestic matters) and calls to modify the practice and discourse of foreign policy. In different ways, the New Left and the disenchanted strand of U.S. liberalism urged a retreat from containment. Meanwhile, part of the Republican Right and the military apparatus pleaded once more to go beyond containment and accelerate a final showdown with the Soviet Union and international Communism. The crisis of containment, and of the consensus that had buttressed it, opened an intense and agonizing discussion regarding the kind of foreign policy and strategy the country should adopt. As stressed by political scientist Robert W. Tucker, for the first time in twenty years "the scope, ideological temper, means and purposes of American foreign policy" were open to discussion. It was a discussion involving various foreign policy proposals and different responses to the crisis. Richard Nixon and his main foreign policy advisor, Henry Kissinger, entered the debate with their own proposal, and with a discursive frame through which to convey it and make it hegemonic in the political and cultural debate. The proposal and discourse of Henry Kissinger were markedly realist in their outlook and inspired by the necessity to rebuild the broad domestic and international consensus needed for an active and global foreign policy.[66]

2

KISSINGER AND KISSINGERISM

Most studies of Henry Kissinger tend to present him as the quintessential exponent of a continental European realism that became popular in Cold War America. According to this established interpretation, Kissinger's approach to world affairs was always distinguished by an attempt to oust the extreme moral and ideological traits, which had made the Cold War a peculiar and unique period in the history of modern international relations. The popular historian and pundit Walter Russell Mead has claimed that for Kissinger, "the United States and the Soviet Union" were simply "two great powers like Prussia and Austria." According to one biographer, Kissinger adhered to a flexible and uninhibited realpolitik that rejected "moral absolutes." Such an approach left little or "no room for idealism." As a scholar, and even more so as a statesman, Kissinger has therefore been described (and sometimes stereotyped) as the last, great adept of a realist tradition that adapted to the changed structure of the world system but was careful to respect the basic rules of international politics. His "reliance on great power diplomacy, his assumption of unquestioned priority of international over domestic politics, his Weberian conception of the statesman's personal responsibility for the ethical dilemmas of foreign policy—all these tenets of realism," political scientist Michael Joseph Smith has argued, "informed Kissinger's approach."[1]

The Education of Heinz Kissinger

This reading of Kissinger as an unreconstructed archrealist is one that needs to be challenged or at least qualified. Kissingerian realism has been (and still is) far from linear, coherent, and doctrinally orthodox. A good dose of opportunism and unscrupulousness induced Kissinger to adapt his realism to the spirit of the times and to U.S. Cold War political culture (if not to politics tout court). As underlined by one of the intellectual fathers of U.S. realism, political scientist Hans Morgenthau, one of Kissinger's greatest skills has been his ability to "adjust" from time to time "intellectual conviction to political exigencies." In government as well as in academia, Morgenthau critically maintained, Kissinger operated as a "many-sided" Odysseus, a *"polytropos"* with multiple faces, whose intellectual peripateticism was rarely disinterested. "Kissinger," Morgenthau argued in 1975, "is a good actor who does not *play* the role of Hamlet today, of Caesar tomorrow, but who *is* Hamlet today and Caesar tomorrow."[2]

Various elements contributed toward making Kissinger a supposed Metternich of the nuclear era and fueled his reputation as "the European mind in American policy," capable of invoking and successfully determining a "Europeanization" of U.S. foreign policy: his biography and background; his academic experience; his pressing, but never truly heretical or outside the zeitgeist, criticism of U.S. foreign policy; and his role in the administrations of Richard Nixon (1969–74) and Gerald Ford (1974–77), when for two years (1973–75) he was simultaneously secretary of state and national security advisor.[3]

Kissinger's biography, even more than his scholarship and policy, was crucial to his image of a learned European who taught young and immature Americans how to act and behave in the international arena. Over time, Kissinger incessantly promoted himself as the sophisticated, historically cultured, and intellectual European guiding a naïve, optimistic, and superficial America, only to see it used against him during his last years in office.

A German Jew raised in the city of Fürth, Bavaria, Heinz Kissinger, in 1938 at age fifteen, fled Germany with his family to escape Nazi persecution. In the United States the Kissingers soon joined the large New York Jewish community, and Heinz became Henry. His full integration into American society would take a few years, however, and include a world war and a cold war before being completed. After attending secondary school and one year at the City College of New York, during which he also worked at a brush company, Kissinger was able to exploit the opportunities offered by World War II, as did many other young, talented members of religious and national minorities in the United States. In 1943 he was drafted and was soon made a U.S. citizen; no longer was he a German Jew living in New York's Washington Heights, but an American of Jewish origin, European heritage, and a thick, unmistakable, German accent.[4]

His experience in the U.S. Army was crucial in many ways and not only because it offered rapid political and social integration into his adoptive country. Kissinger spent three years in Europe (1944–47), the latter two in occupied Germany, where he worked as a translator and, at the age of twenty-one, administrator of the city of Krefeld. During this period Kissinger met his first mentor, the flamboyant and intellectually sophisticated Lieutenant Fritz Kraemer, who took the "little Jewish refugee" under his wing. It was Kraemer who stimulated Kissinger's curiosity for the study of history, philosophy, and international relations. Moreover, it was Kraemer who advised Kissinger to go back to the United States and enroll in a finer and more prestigious university than the one he had briefly attended in New York: "A gentleman," Kraemer claimed, "does not go the College of the City of New York."[5]

Once back in the United States, Kissinger, benefiting from the educational opportunities offered to war veterans, decided to study at Harvard over Princeton and Columbia. At Harvard, the young Kissinger read philosophy, history, and political science with enthusiasm, passion, and ambition in a highly selective and competitive academic environment. Excelling as a student represented the second instrument of Kissinger's social ascent. During his time at Harvard, Kissinger progressively built a social and power network that he would exploit in the following years. More significantly, he wrote two long manuscripts—his senior thesis and his Ph.D. dissertation—on which many exegetes and philologists of Kissinger's thought would concentrate in later years in their search for the fundamental elements of his realism.

Kissinger's senior thesis became legendary for its length (at almost four hundred pages, it was the longest in the history of Harvard) and, moreover, for the nature of its topic. Through a comparative analysis of an unlikely and heterogeneous trio, the thesis, titled the "Meaning of History," examined the works of Immanuel Kant, Oswald Spengler, and Arnold Toynbee. In this piece of unpublished research, which historian Bruce Kuklick considers Kissinger's "most intellectually creative and sustained piece of work," Kissinger dealt with an issue to which he would return in his later, more mature works: the relationship between choice and necessity; structure and individual freedom; free will and historical and cultural constrictions. In "The Meaning of History" Kissinger discussed the possibility of the individual imposing his mark on history, with the objective of "assert[ing], against Spengler and Toynbee, both free will and historical meaning." In his discussion, the young scholar rejected deterministic and rigid historical approaches, which were popular in academic as well as public discourse at the time. Although expressed in different ways, these two elements—the creative potential of the individual (and of the statesman) and the refusal of linear and evolutionary models of political and historical analysis—would recur frequently in Kissinger's scholarship and statesmanship. In "The Meaning of History," Kissinger claimed that it was man, with his intrinsic limits, who ultimately "imparts his own meaning to history," through "an inward experience which teaches man his limits and his intrinsic worth." The "condition of mankind's self-transcendence" was therefore "the ultimate basis of human freedom."[6]

Kissinger's second manuscript was his doctoral dissertation, written under the supervision of William Yandell Elliot in the Department of Government. The dissertation, eventually published as *A World Restored: Metternich, Castlereagh, and the Problems of Peace, 1812–1822,* dealt with the European balance of power after the end of the Napoleonic Wars and the Congress of Vienna, and the emerging multipolar order.[7] While most of his contemporaries at Harvard were busy working on coeval political issues, Kissinger immersed himself in nineteenth-century international relations. He did so, however, in the belief that such study offered tools and categories to understand, decrypt, and possibly manipulate, contemporary events. "I have chosen for my topic the period between 1812 and 1822," Kissinger candidly admitted in the preface of his dissertation, "partly, I am frank to say, because its problems seem to me analogous to those of our day."[8]

In *A World Restored,* Kissinger engaged once again with the fundamental relationship between possibility and necessity, choice and circumstance. This relationship is presented, however, as more complex and contradictory than it had been described in "The Meaning of History." As a consequence, the position of the individual who tries to make his mark upon history, while recognizing his inner limits, becomes even more heroic: for whereas "only a shallow historicism would maintain that successful policies are always possible...men become myths not by what they know, nor even by what they achieve, but by the tasks they set themselves." The objective of Kissinger's analysis—which is never fully accomplished—is therefore "to find a way for individual freedom and creativity in an apparently determined universe." History, instead of "overwhelming statesmen," presented them "with moments when they [can] impose their will on its progress."[9]

A World Restored was also concerned with the most fundamental problem of international politics: how to establish and preserve order and stability, which for Kissinger represented "the supremely carried value in the world." Stability, Kissinger stated in the opening page of the book, "has commonly resulted not from a quest for peace but from a generally accepted legitimacy," intended "as an international agreement about the nature of workable arrangements and about the permissible aims and methods of foreign policy." Thus, stability should not "be confused with justice," nor did it necessarily derive from peace. On the contrary, seeking peace for its own sake risked putting the "international system...at the mercy of the most ruthless member of the international community." The basic distinction was therefore not between just and unjust states, peaceful countries and war-prone ones, but between revolutionary states (like Napoleon's France) that did not respect the rules and states committed to legitimacy and, by default, order and stability.[10]

As Kissinger himself implied, *A World Restored* was also a book about the Cold War and the challenge posed by the revolutionary Soviet Union to the legitimate international order. A second, less noticed, theme made *A World Restored* a book about contemporary events as much as nineteenth-century diplomacy: the nexus between domestic politics and foreign policy; internal consensus and international legitimacy. This problematic was destined to mark Kissinger's journey as an intellectual and a statesman. Indirectly, Kissinger confronted the thorny subject of the pernicious influence that a country's institutional and bureaucratic structure exercised on its external relations. Specific attention was placed on the suitability (and preparation) of a national political culture to absorb and interiorize the inescapable laws of the international system and the weight that domestic public opinion—unprepared, inflammable, and emotively manipulable—could bear on diplomacy. In different ways, these factors influenced the choices and actions of the two protagonists of *A World Restored*. For Castlereagh and Metternich, political, cultural, and institutional constraints limited their creativity and ability to operate. They succeeded in putting an end to the Napoleonic revolutionary experiment and molding a new, stable international arrangement, but they proved unable—particularly Metternich—to "contemplate the abyss, not with the detachment of a scientist, but as a challenge to overcome" and to creatively operate for "a task of construction" and not just "to deflect" the "inexorable march of the forces at work." In the end "the two statesmen of repose were... both defeated... by their domestic structure: Castlereagh by ignoring it, Metternich by being too conscious of its vulnerability."[11]

The importance of "The Meaning of History" and *A World Restored* should not be exaggerated. They do not offer original historical interpretations nor make the young Kissinger an already relevant figure of contemporary realist thought. Nevertheless, Kissinger's early works are particularly significant for the message they try to project. Within them are some of the theses and conceptual and discursive tropes that would distinguish Kissinger's later production and realist-like discourse. A more systematic consideration of these connections are presented at the end of the chapter. For now a less manifest aspect of Kissinger's heterodox dissertation's topic, as well as archaic, pompous, and often convoluted writing style, is worth emphasizing. The impression one draws from reading *A World Restored* is that it also allowed the young Kissinger to transmit a precise image: to convey a message more than offer an analysis. It represented, in other words, the first step in a process of self-representation that would prove to be highly expendable both academically and politically. In studying a key period in the history of modern Europe, which anticipated an era of undisputed European domination in world affairs, Kissinger seems already intent on teaching the rules of international politics to a United States still unprepared for the task that destiny had apparently set it. Kant, Spengler, and Toynbee offered a first response to the naïve and superficial inner American optimism: a retort to the progressive, ineluctable, and paradoxically apolitical view of historical process that had become popular in Cold War America. Castlereagh and, even more so, Metternich showed how such awareness could be translated into policy and diplomacy by the statesman willing to learn and practice the ahistorical and amoral codes and rules of the international system. The United States was to look at the Europe that faced and defeated Napoleon's revolutionary challenge if it wanted to learn how to face the new, radical threat to order and legitimacy brought by China and the Soviet Union. This Europe, Kissinger argued, must be known, studied, and understood. It was necessary to penetrate its arduous and complex political discourse, to comprehend its conceptually difficult and sophisticated categories (indeed, "conceptualization" would become one of the key terms of the rich Kissingerian vocabulary), to learn its practices and methods, complicated and unscrupulous in their means as much as coherent and terse, even morally, in their ends (namely, the pursuit of order and the defense of national interest).

Even in his early works, Kissinger tries to spread this message. Far from casually, he resorts to an eccentric and cumbersome prose, which is hard to decrypt and accessible only to those willing to delve into the arcana of international relations and possessing the instruments to decode its argot. In some respect, it does not matter that this prose is also frequently confused and contradictory, while rich in semantic and conceptual "acrobatics," as recently asserted by political scientist Stanley Hoffmann. During the first years of the Cold War, the necessity of a quick-fire introduction to the (very European) laws of international politics was considered indispensable, indeed vital, by a vast majority of U.S. elites, pundits, and experts. The discursive practices and historical analogies on which Kissinger relied, which he himself crucially contributed to shaping, were unique (i.e., studying Metternich instead of Roosevelt, the Congress of Vienna rather than the Marshall Plan), but perfectly congruent with the discussion of the day. Indeed, they were perfectly suited to what a young, ambitious Harvard graduate student, who aimed at a career—political or academic—in the field of international relations, could be asked. With *A World Restored,* Kissinger began to consolidate his image as "the European mind" in U.S. politics, as the realist in the land of an idealism that was unsuitable for the global challenges the country faced. Kissinger's incessant cultivation of this image would prove extremely beneficial for his career. Yet it was an image that revealed the historically determined and, paradoxically, quintessential American nature of Kissinger's realism: a realism that found its ideal environment and cultural medium in the Cold War.[12]

Kissinger as a Cold War Intellectual

After completing his doctorate, Kissinger did not receive from Harvard the job opportunities he had expected and hoped for. He considered offers from other prestigious universities (Chicago and Pennsylvania) but decided to leave academia temporarily. Kissinger subsequently accepted an invitation from the Council on Foreign Relations to become staff director of a study group on nuclear weapons and their impact on foreign policy. That an important, influential, and mainstream institution as the Council on Foreign Relations would offer such an opportunity to a young and untested scholar indicates that, claims to the contrary notwithstanding, Kissinger's thought was not truly unorthodox in comparison with that within the (high) political culture that hegemonized U.S. public discourse at the time. Indeed, during the early Cold War, this political culture was characterized by a strong fascination with war and "dominated by the rhetoric, symbols, and issues of national security."[13]

At the Council on Foreign Relations Kissinger worked with some of the most important and influential members of the U.S. foreign policy establishment: Paul Nitze; his successor at the State Department's Policy Planning Staff, Robert Bowie; the former undersecretary of state, David Rockefeller; former CIA director and undersecretary of state Walter Bedell Smith; the former head of the Atomic Energy Commission, Gordon Dean; and many others. Kissinger's study group concentrated on two interrelated aspects that characterized post-1945 strategic thought in the United States: the effective use of nuclear arms and the ways to exploit such a possibility politically and diplomatically. The catalyst for discussion was the enunciation of the doctrine of "massive retaliation" in 1954 by the Eisenhower administration. Theoretically, "massive retaliation" implied the possibility of using nuclear weapons even in response to a conventional military attack, with the objective of enhancing the U.S. nuclear deterrent and avoiding a costly rearmament process. Leaving the enemy uncertain about the United States' reaction to military action, "massive retaliation" also looked to seize the initiative from the adversary and prevent it from deciding the location, time, and form of engagement.[14]

Kissinger used the work of the council's study group to write a book, which appeared in 1957 under the title *Nuclear Weapons and Foreign Policy*. The book proved surprisingly successful and sold more than 17,000 copies in just one year. Read and debated in specialized journals as well as magazines and newspapers, *Nuclear Weapons and Foreign Policy* allowed Kissinger to establish himself as one of the leading experts in the field of strategic studies, despite his limited knowledge of technical details and the evolutions in nuclear technology.[15]

The book, and the discussions of the study group before it, aimed at understanding the political and diplomatic use of nuclear weapons, which had come to define the relative and absolute strength of a state. The relationship between force and diplomacy, politics and war, represented a classic issue of the realist reflection on international relations, which for Kissinger had not lost its relevance amid the Cold War and Soviet-American nuclear duopoly. Indeed, Kissinger argued, it was of paramount importance to understand how to "translate power into policy," avoid "doctrinal rigidity," and accept "the ominous assumption that any [future] war" was "likely to be a nuclear war." Force, particularly those components of force (i.e., atomic) through which the United States still retained the edge, could not be renounced: "in a society of 'sovereign states'" Kissinger stated, "a power can in the last resort vindicate its interpretation of justice or defend its 'vital interests' only by the willingness to employ force." A "renunciation of force, by eliminating the penalty for intransigence," would "place the international order at the mercy of its most ruthless or its most irresponsible member."[16]

Yet the will to use these instruments required a new strategic doctrine based on possible use of this "awesome" technology, and an understanding of "whether the nuclear age" presented "only risks" or "also offer[ed] opportunities." To acquire such an understanding, one had to think "conceptually" and overcome quintessential U.S. cultural limits, in particular the "reluctance to think in terms of power" and strategy. These limits were particularly evident in the doctrine of "massive retaliation," which was one of the main targets of Kissinger's critique. Eisenhower's approach, Kissinger argued, suffered from two fundamental deficiencies. The first was its patent rigidity, by virtue of which there appeared to be no alternative to inaction or total retaliation. The second was that it expressed the naïve and superficial hope that it was possible to find a definitive solution to the problems the United States faced, including its antagonistic relationship with the Soviet Union. According to Kissinger, "massive retaliation" constituted the latest manifestation of the United States' inclination to seek all-out victories, which were simply impossible in the nuclear age. "Disgusting" as it may be for U.S. military thought, "the renunciation of total victory" had to be accepted. "Far from being the 'normal' form of conflict," all-out war constituted, instead, a "special case." Deluding oneself with the idea that total victory was achievable risked generating the reaction of an absolute refusal of force and a self-destructive search for peace at any cost. The problem was therefore political and psychological more than strategic. "The dilemma of the nuclear period," Kissinger maintained at the beginning of the book, "can therefore be defined as follows: the enormity of modern weapons makes the thought of war repugnant, but the refusal to run any risks would amount to giving the Soviet rulers a blank check."[17]

How could one run such risks without falling into the abyss of total nuclear war? How could nuclear weapons be put, in Clausewitzian fashion, at the service of diplomacy and the statesman? The answer—not particularly original and already introduced by other analysts—lay in the concept of limited nuclear war. As the only choice between all-out nuclear conflict and absolute passivity, limited war could be nuclear, Kissinger confidently claimed, before he went on to propose a series of rules that belligerents would have to abide by. Limited war represented "the form of conflict" that enabled the United States "to derive the greatest advantage from" its "industrial potential," because "a war of attrition is" precisely "the one war the Soviet bloc could not win." To wage such a war, it was necessary, however, to improve and diversify the U.S. nuclear panoply by strengthening its still vaguely defined tactical components.[18]

Akin to the work of other nuclear strategists of the period, that of Kissinger represented an attempt to think the unthinkable: to imagine and visualize the cuckoo's nest of a self-contained and not-too-destructive nuclear war; to normalize nuclear weapons and cicatrize the wound they had inflicted on the modern and Clausewitzian view of war and its relationship to policy and diplomacy. The book aimed, first and foremost, at challenging the "apocalyptic talk about nuclear weapons" that at the time tied the hands of those in power. "The willingness to engage in nuclear war when necessary is part of the price of our freedom," Kissinger wrote in another essay. Not casually would Kissinger—with his German accent and strange haircut—be one of the figures who inspired Stanley Kubrick's *Dr. Strangelove.*[19]

To normalize the nuclear era, Kissinger emphasized an aspect that had been at the core of his previous works: the central role of the statesman and expert. *Nuclear Weapons and Foreign Policy* denounced American naïveté in foreign affairs and took a stance against both the bombastic rhetoric of total war and the irresponsible irenic escapism of those who believed that the advent of nuclear arms made war among major powers meaningless and implausible. It challenged, in other words, the notion that the cogent nexus between force and diplomacy, violence and policy, had been inexorably altered by the destructiveness of atomic weapons. Kissinger denounced such maximalist and impulsive visions, and presented them as hysterical and irrational reactions to a transformation in the tools of war that needed to be studied and understood. Politics was still in charge of war, and its fundamental tasks—the preservation of an advantageous balance of power, the maintenance of stability, and the promotion of the national interest—had not changed. The social sciences of international relations and strategic studies had a responsibility to assert knowledge, sobriety, and reason where phobias, hysteria, and irrationality currently prevailed. "The core of *Nuclear Weapons and Foreign Policy,*" historian Robert Schulzinger convincingly argued, "was not about the atomic bomb, but a plea for the contribution of serene and imperturbable experts to direct foreign policy."[20]

Widely discussed and reviewed, *Nuclear Weapons and Foreign Policy* was also severely criticized. Many commentators did not miss the opportunity to emphasize the basic "illogic of Henry Kissinger's nuclear strategy."[21] Kissinger's nuclear war was criticized on practical and technical grounds. Paul Nitze took particular pleasure in highlighting some of Kissinger's grossest mistakes: "there are several hundred passages" in *Nuclear Weapons and Foreign Policy,* Nitze argued, "in which either the facts or the logic seem doubtful or at least unclear." Furthermore, Nitze took issue with Kissinger's attack on "the over-all approach of the United States as a nation to international politics and military strategy"; by so doing, he anticipated the kind of criticism Kissinger would face fifteen years later. Morgenthau praised Kissinger for offering "a program of action" that appeared "to be both militarily and politically feasible and biologically tolerable," as well as a Clausewitzian "judicious adaptation of what [was]...technologically possible" to what was "politically desirable and tolerable." He posed, however, one fundamental and pertinent question: how could one prevent a "limited atomic war" from moving "step by step" toward an "all-out atomic war?" This was the crucial issue that no one had yet grasped: how to keep a nuclear war limited and to avoid an escalation to a total thermonuclear exchange. The temptation for the losing side to escalate the conflict, many argued, would be irresistible. Furthermore, the "fog" of a chaotic and uncontrollable war would make Kissinger's rules and limits almost impossible to respect. "Limiting a nuclear war," historian Campbell Craig underlined, required "a uniquely precise collaboration between the belligerents," a reciprocal willingness to "offer generous terms of surrender," and a strict and disciplined "collaborative process" between the two sides, not only in setting the regulations for such a war, but also in stopping the fighting and accepting a cease-fire. In order to work, Kissinger's limited nuclear war had to be conceived and waged as an Ivy League fencing match.[22]

Ultimately, the idea of limiting a nuclear war was a contradiction in terms, as Kissinger himself would later implicitly admit. A further contradiction to Kissinger's analysis, which has been less scrutinized than the oxymoronic category of "limited nuclear war," is also worth examination. Behind Kissinger's pragmatic strategic prose and his denunciation of America's inherent unsuitability to play great power politics lay, in fact, an unrealistic position that was characteristic of U.S. foreign policy in the twentieth century, particularly during the Cold War. The issue was one of credibility and the tacit recognition of the largely symbolic nature of the competition between the Soviet Union and the United States. By theoretically inflating the possibility of a total war, Kissinger presented the option of "massive retaliation" as lacking credibility. According to Kissinger, this credibility gap devalued the immense capital provided to the United States, both politically and diplomatically, by its nuclear superiority. The inability to better exploit nuclear arms had been evident during the United States' brief atomic monopoly (1945–49): "whatever the reason," Kissinger maintained, "our atomic monopoly had at best a deterrent effect. While it may have prevented a further expansion of the Soviet sphere, it did not enable us to achieve a strategic transformation in our favor."[23] This credibility deficit allowed the Soviet Union to partially fill the power gap, while diminishing the utility of the costly process of U.S. military rearmament. Lowering the "usability threshold" of nuclear arms from total to limited war, however, allowed the potential use of atomic weapons. Contemplating their use put such arms back in the service of politics; U.S. nuclear superiority could thus reacquire a political and strategic meaning. As stressed by historian Jussi Hanhimäki, Kissinger believed that "only by embracing a strategic doctrine that assumed a limited nuclear war as a realistic option could the United States derive the necessary diplomatic leverage from its military arsenal."[24]

The imperative to state and constantly reassert the credibility of the anti-Communist position, toward friends and enemies alike, contributed to the indiscriminate globalization of U.S. commitments. The ensuing inability to distinguish between primary and secondary interests—between the theaters that were vital for the security of the United States and those that were not—would be severely criticized from a realist and particularistic perspective. The two famous American realist thinkers George Kennan and Hans Morgenthau, for instance, would denounce U.S. intervention in Vietnam (a conflict that had been promoted also, if not primarily, in the name of credibility) as the inevitable outcome of a superficial, irresponsible, and inevitably unrealistic universalism. Kissinger considered instead the problem of credibility one of the central issues U.S. foreign policy had to face. Even when in power, he took (and justified) many choices in the name of symbolical imperatives and the obligation to preserve the prestige and honor of the United States, to the extent of sacrificing strategic coherence and ethical rigor.

In adopting this position, Kissinger proved to be an intellectual and aspiring statesman molded within (and by) the Cold War. Kissinger interiorized—for choice, conviction, and convenience—Cold War categories and cognitive frames, particularly what historian Frank Ninkovich has called the "obsession for credibility." As a consequence of this obsession, "few places in the world" could be "automatically ruled out as unimportant," while a "continual use of force, and not simply the constant assertion of a ready willingness to use it" was required.[25]

Although Kissinger pretended otherwise, his analyses and categories were part and parcel of a discourse (and in a sense an ideology) that was hegemonic in post–World War II U.S. political culture. They concurred to shape this discourse and ideology, but were also a product of them. It is not by chance that Kissinger's theses echoed similar ones of the period, or that the shift from a strategy of "massive retaliation" to one of flexible and elastic response was soon adopted by the new Democratic administration of John Fitzgerald Kennedy.

The success of *Nuclear Weapons and Foreign Policy* propelled Kissinger into the U.S. foreign policy establishment, in which he became one of its most influential experts. Kissinger returned to Harvard to become deputy director of the newly established Center for International Affairs and serve as a lecturer (by 1962 Kissinger was granted a full professorship). He also became an assiduous commentator on international affairs in specialized journals such as *Foreign Affairs,* as well as in more popular and broadly circulated magazines such as the *New Republic,* the *Reporter,* the *New York Times Magazine, Harper's,* and others. He was subsequently able to gain a certain, although frustratingly limited, proximity to power centers. Kissinger became advisor to Nelson Rockefeller—the grandson of oil ty-coon John Rockefeller, future governor of New York (1959–73), and, for a short time (1974–77), vice president of the United States—and obtained some minor posts, which proved far from satisfying, in the Kennedy and Johnson administrations.

Above all, Kissinger continued to write, consolidating his fame as an expert in strategy and international affairs and an implacable critic of the vices and defects of U.S. internationalism. In 1961 he published another major work, *The Necessity for Choice.*[26] In tortuous and often puzzling prose, Kissinger reaffirmed and qualified some of the theses he had first put forward in *Nuclear Weapons and Foreign Policy.* Although he did not entirely abandon his theory of limited nuclear war, he recognized some of the dilemmas and contradictions he had conveniently avoided four years earlier. In particular, he admitted the practical and conceptual difficulty in defining the mechanisms of bipolar discipline and self-regulation that could prevent the escalation of a limited war into a total conflict. The problem was not moral but practical. Partially accepting Nitze's objec-tions, Kissinger admitted that the difference between nuclear and conven-tional wars was easier to define than that between total and limited nuclear wars. Nevertheless, a strategy of limited war was still preferable because it "strengthen[ed] deterrence and . . . if deterrence should fail . . . provide[d] an opportunity for settlement before the automatism of the retaliatory forces." Limited war, Kissinger reaffirmed, still offered "the possibility—not the certainty—of avoiding catastrophe." The United States should therefore continue to develop a tactical nuclear arsenal and not renounce its possible use. Credibility made this strategic posture necessary, and even though Kissinger himself appeared less certain about its practicability, he continued to advocate and rationalize it.[27]

Necessity for Choice was first and foremost a renewed attack on the strategy and foreign policy of the Eisenhower administration. It was also an endorsement of the strategic revision by John Kennedy and his secretary of defense, Robert McNamara, which favored a symmetrical and "flexible response" to Communist aggression. Such an approach had to be based on the development of a complex and articulated defensive panoply capable of offering the variety of instruments necessary to graduate and modulate the response to an enemy initiative. In times of crisis, "flexible response" was supposed to provide the United States with multiple options, thus avoiding the brutal and impracticable choice between inaction and total war.[28]

Kissinger criticized Eisenhower and John Foster Dulles for misapplying the original logic of containment. "As the containment theory came to be applied under Secretary Dulles," Kissinger argued, "what had originally been considered the condition of policy—security against aggression—seemed to become its only goal." Eisenhower's foreign policy "seemed unable to articulate any purpose save that of preventing an expansion of the Soviet sphere."[29]

These and other criticisms of Eisenhower's policies rendered *Necessity for Choice* a sort of "manifesto for the Democrats."[30] Several propositions advanced by Kissinger were in tune with the foreign policy platform of the Democratic Party. By suggesting the possibility of dispatching experts and military advisors to areas threatened by Communist subversion, Kissinger anticipated the action the United States would undertake in Indochina. By criticizing the "far too bipartisan" nature of recent U.S. foreign policy ("a democracy, to be vital, requires leaders willing to stand alone"), Kissinger adopted a partisan position, as Kennedy had earlier. He did so accepting the argument—unfounded but politically expedient—of the so-called missile gap: the alleged, but nonexistent, Soviet advantage in the field of missilery and rocketry.[31] Accusing Eisenhower of having sacrificed national security on the altar of budget imperatives, as Kennedy did instrumentally in the electoral campaign of 1960, proved politically advantageous at the time. Kissinger adhered, albeit with greater sophistication, to positions that had already been expressed by important Democratic senators, independent committees (such as the Gaither committee), and the former army chief of staff General Maxwell Taylor, who in a famous book (*The Uncertain Trumpet*) claimed that the United States was bound to suffer missile inferiority vis-à-vis the Soviet Union "in terms of numbers and effectiveness of long-range missiles unless heroic measures" were taken immediately.[32]

Analogously, Kissinger claimed that Moscow was developing a missile advantage, which the Soviets could exploit strategically and diplomatically: "the missile gap in the period 1961–1965," he confidently asserted, was "unavoidable." If U.S. "retaliatory force remains highly vulnerable or if the Soviet Union produces more missiles than now appears likely, the Soviet Union could be tempted to launch a surprise attack." "The United States," Kissinger claimed, could not "afford another decline like that which" had "characterized" the post-1945 period: "our margin of survival has narrowed dangerously... if these trends continue, the future of freedom will be dim indeed."[33]

These formulations were singularly apocalyptic and Kennedy-esque. They stemmed from the conviction, already expressed in *Nuclear Weapons and Foreign Policy*, that force and strategic superiority still meant something, that even in the nuclear age they guaranteed a political dividend to those who possessed them. According to Kissinger, the gap from which the United States allegedly suffered weakened the effect (and, again, the credibility) of the American deterrent and greatly increased the ability of the Soviet Union to exert pressure, extend its political influence, and "blackmail" the West.[34]

Necessity for Choice also introduced the issue of the decline of U.S. hegemony and relative power. The gloomy prophecies of future U.S. strategic inferiority, as well as the denunciation of Washington's growing inability to face the Soviet challenge, anticipated themes that later dominated public and political debate in the United States. The belief that the United States was in relative decline vis-à-vis allies and enemies would later induce Kissinger-the-statesman to urge a conceptual and practical change in U.S. foreign policy. In 1961, Kissinger-the-scholar instead offered an orthodox and conventional response: he recommended renewed military investment and the diversification of U.S. military instrumentation. (This recommendation was accompanied by the usual tirades against American naïveté and the United States' congenital unpreparedness for the great game of international politics.)

In this response to the alleged decline of the United States, one can see further proof of Kissinger's adherence to the categories, stereotypes, and topoi of the strategic culture of the Cold War. Wrapped in typical European realpolitik rhetoric, Kissinger's argumentation was filled with slogans, explanations, and operative prescriptions of a peculiar American globalism that other realists—particularly George Kennan—explicitly contested. Kissinger's positions included support for global interventionism, which was as inherent to a symmetrical and universalistic approach as "flexible response" was; a consequent refusal to limit the radius of action for U.S. foreign policy; the surreptitious, but strong, emphasis on the interdependent nature of the international system, nourished by an obsession for credibility that made it impossible to distinguish theaters central to U.S. interests from those that were less important; and a bipolar reading of the international context and the consequent underestimation of national and regional specificities.[35]

Nevertheless, Kissinger's Cold War globalism differed from that of Kennedy and his advisors, and this divergence prevented Kissinger from exercising the political influence he aspired to. Kissinger's was, in fact, mostly a strategic and geopolitical globalism. The global instrumentation the United States had to develop, according to Kissinger, was based on diplomatic and military tools, which entirely neglected the economic dimension, while dealing with ideology and culture in a patently superficial way.[36]

Furthermore, Kissinger's political and analytical focus was almost exclusively Atlantic and Eurocentric. The absence of the third world—the real core of the bipolar competition in the early 1960s—and scant interest in economic issues rendered Kissinger's geopolitical globalism incongruent with the topics that dominated coeval liberal Cold War discourse. As noted, Kissinger's thought was far from heretical or heterodox. Instead, it fit perfectly with the conceptual schemes and discursive practices of post–World War II U.S. internationalist culture. The result of educational deficiency, intellectual sensibility, and political calculation, it nevertheless lacked an essential element: attention to progress, economic growth, and the increasingly popular theories of modernization. Kissinger explicitly rejected progressive and teleological visions of history, preferring the analysis of structure and stability to that of transformation and evolution. In *Necessity for Choice* he made this preference abundantly clear. Choice was indeed necessary, because it was naïve and self-destructive for the West to be "waiting for history to do its work." Far too frequently, Kissinger maintained, "evolutionary theory" had been used by the West "as a bromide," in the unfounded and historically inaccurate belief that "democratic institutions developed *after* industrialization and *as a result* of economic development." "To rely on economic development to bring about enlightened political institutions" would be "to reverse the real priorities."[37] In adopting such positions, Kissinger neglected one of the core issues of early 1960s Cold War liberalism, which greatly impaired his desire to play a greater role in the Kennedy administration. Far from casually, the intellectual who exercised a greater influence on U.S. foreign and security policies at this time was the economist and historian Walt Rostow, the main theorist behind modernization and the structural interdependence between security and development, anti-Communism and social transformation.[38]

Rostow's name would be forever tied to the liberal foreign policy of the 1960s—its lofty ambitions and dramatic failures from Vietnam to Latin America. Kissinger, who had supported and justified many premises behind Kennedy and Johnson's globalism, emerged undamaged from the collapse of Cold War liberalism. As we shall see, he was able to build part of his political fortune upon that collapse. He did so by stressing those elements of his approach that distinguished him from the liberal modernizers: the primacy of geopolitics and the rejection of a progressive, and "economicistic," view of the course of history. Once appointed Nixon's national security czar, Kissinger would vent his frustration with the liberal theories that extolled a "necessary progression from economic growth to political stability," and lambasted the "Marshall Plan syndrome," which relocated too much power "into the hands of economists."[39] A successful policy of nation building in less developed countries—Kissinger would later argue—did not depend on the mechanisms of economic growth and the creation of an indigenous middle class as affirmed by liberal Cold War modernization projects. Much more important in this respect was the capacity to "establish political authority." Stability, the primary objective of politics, was actually threatened by policies of modernization and development that risked "accelerating the erosion of the traditional...order." According to Kissinger, through its ideology of modernization, the West had "bemused itself with economic and technical remedies" that were "largely irrelevant to the underlying political and spiritual problem."[40]

In the years following the publication of *Necessity for Choice,* Kissinger turned his attention to another issue that had forcefully reentered public debate and the political agenda of the Kennedy and Johnson administrations: the cohesion of the Atlantic Alliance and the relationship between the United States and European partners. This was obviously not a new problem. It experienced a significant transformation during the 1960s, however. The Cold War and anti-Communism represented weaker and less efficacious ties for the transatlantic relationship. The diffusion of power, new developments in Europe, and proto-détente between the United States and the Soviet Union were altering traditional Cold War partitions. In some instances, as with the Federal Republic of Germany, a new generation of political leaders challenged the idea that the fundamentals of the Euro-American relationship could not be modified. In other cases, as with de Gaulle's France, Atlantic unity was contested and subsequently weakened as nationalist formulas that rejected various manifestations of Atlantic interdependence—economic, strategic, and cultural—were asserted.[41]

As continues to be the case today, frictions within the Atlantic alliance worried those transatlantic elites that have historically represented the cultural, ideological, and political vehicles of U.S.-European relations, as well as of the institutions created to manage, promote, and intensify this interdependence. The Council on Foreign Relations was (and remains) one of the most important sites where discussions between established Atlanticists, Europeans, and North Americans took place. In the mid-1960s the Ford Foundation awarded the council substantial funding to undertake research on the transatlantic relationship and its future. Transatlantic crises have been one of the privileged topics of international studies in Europe and in America, and since 1949 libraries have been filled with volumes on the Atlantic Alliance, with the vast majority predicting its inevitable collapse. Legions of scholars, politicians, and students have been asked to reflect—rarely in an original way—on the past, present, and future of Atlantica. Kissinger was no exception. He had long dealt with Euro-American relations and was thus asked to participate in Council on Foreign Relations discussions, where he led a series of seminars and wrote *The Troubled Partnership,* which appeared in 1965—one of the ten books that emerged from the project.[42]

Formally, *The Troubled Partnership* put forward a typically Atlanticist stance, which criticized the United States and blamed it for most of the problems plaguing the transatlantic relationship. The United States, Kissinger claimed, "came to deal" with its European partners "paternalistically," with a "certain self-righteousness and impatience." Its leadership, however, was weak and confused. Washington paid insufficient attention to the requests of allies. Wavering and contradictory U.S. strategies were losing credibility with partners, who were rightly skeptical of the willingness of the United States to risk an atomic war to protect them. Washington's pathological preference for institutional and technical solutions obfuscated the primarily political (and "spiritual") nature of the tensions within the alliance and obstructed the development of a frank and productive dialogue. "The United States," Kissinger argued, had "fallen into the habit of dealing with its European Allies, except Great Britain, almost psychotherapeutically," confusing "periodic briefings and reassurance with consultation," and seeking "to muffle expressions of concern rather than deal with underlying cause." Drawing on his fame as the European wise man in the United States, Kissinger pulled no punches in highlighting to Americans the views, phobias, and also rights of the Europeans.[43]

A careful reading of *The Troubled Partnership,* however, reveals that behind the formal denunciation of U.S. unilateralism was a masked reaffirmation of it. Kissinger passionately discussed the unsuccessful project to create a NATO collective multilateral nuclear force. His criticism of the ambiguities and impracticability of such a force, and the incoherence of American negotiating tactics, combined with condemnation of the military unreliability of European allies, particularly over nuclear issues. The Europeans did not appear to possess the courage and determination to face the ideological and geopolitical challenge of the Soviet Union. Kissinger's criticisms looked to improve the consultation procedures within the Atlantic alliance and were expressed in a typically convoluted and opaque style. Consultation, Kissinger claimed, was "far from a panacea"; it was "least effective when it was most needed" and when there existed "basic differences of assessment or of interest." It worked "best in implementing a consensus rather than in creating it." The United States believed that "Alliance diplomacy" could be conducted "as if it were analogous to the domestic policy of stable societies" and that "all problems" were "soluble through goodwill and a willingness to compromise." Yet this "rationalistic streak" did not apply to international relations and alliance policy. And it did not apply to a Euro-American community where different approaches and interests among members were too deep and bitter to be reconciled through a simple reorganization of the methods and institutions regulating Atlantic interdependence. Consultations had to be improved, some European requests needed to be accepted, and a greater "equality" among the members of the alliance and "unity with respect for diversity" were necessary. Ultimately, however, U.S. objectives could not be sacrificed for allies whose power, while recovered from World War II, was dependent on and inferior to the United States. The United States could not allow Europeans requests for greater multilateral consultations to limit its sovereignty and freedom of action, particularly in the nuclear arena. Contrary to many Atlanticists, Kissinger did not believe Europeanism and Atlanticism to be necessarily complementary, and he expressed skepticism for the Euro-federalist projects: "while the United States should welcome any unified Europe that reflects the desires of the Europeans, it is doubtful that either our Atlantic or national interests require our passionate commitment to a supranational structure for Europe...a confederal Europe would enable the United States to maintain an influence at many centers of decision rather than be forced to stake everything on affecting the views of a single, supranational body." A united and strong Europe could be tempted to loosen its ties with the United States and subsequently emerge as a competitor. Although unlikely, the possibility had to be avoided, even if it required the expression of an "Atlantic commonwealth in which all the peoples bordering the North Atlantic" could "fulfill their aspirations." Tellingly, no mention was made of what those "aspirations" were or of members of the alliance that did not "border the North Atlantic."[44]

In *The Troubled Partnership,* Kissinger reaffirmed his bipolar vision of the international system and the need to prevent junior U.S. allies from impeding American freedom of action. Part of this vision, Argyris G. Andrianopoulos convincingly argued, was an "awareness of the degree to which Western Europe and Japan remained militarily dependent on the U.S." and the conviction that "as long as the defense of Western Europe depended on the American nuclear guarantee the Allies would acquiesce in the hegemonical position of the U.S." As such, greater consultation and equality could be invoked because of the structural inequality of transatlantic relations and Europe's inevitable subordination to (and dependence on) the United States. Kissinger would adhere to this belief once in power, when his "penchant for working unilaterally to set the framework for détente with the Soviet Union surely was based in part on these beliefs in the poverty of multilateral consultation and the need to retain maximum freedom of action for the United States."[45]

An issue that must be explained, however, is Kissinger's infatuation with de Gaulle—the U.S. Atlanticists' bête noire—and his ambiguous support of many of the French president's policies. Kissinger's Gaullism has been presented by many, and by Kissinger himself, as proof that he was sensitive to the exigencies of Western Europeans and aware of the multipolar evolution in the international system and of the inevitability of a greater European role in world affairs.[46]

Yet Kissinger's opinion of de Gaulle can also be understood as reinforcing his unilateralism (and bipolarism). First of all, Kissinger's celebration of de Gaulle and his foreign policy was never acritical. De Gaulle was praised for his conservatism, preference for a "Europe of States," and rejection of a technocratic and functionalist view of European integration, which was much in vogue in Washington and many European capitals at the time. De Gaulle was also praised for a historical awareness that remained alien to American political culture and U.S. leaders. "The art of statesmanship...was to understand the trend of history," Kissinger maintained. "The United States, with its technical, pragmatic approach, often has analytical truth on its side," but "de Gaulle, with his consciousness of the trials of France for the past generation, is frequently closer to the historical truth," argued Kissinger in a claim that was as elegant in form as it was Delphic in substance.[47]

Yet in Kissinger's pre–White House writings, praise and appreciation of de Gaulle were frequently tempered by bitter and caustic criticism. With his rigidity, de Gaulle was accused of nourishing an unnecessary Franco-American competition. "The irony of the Franco-American rivalry," Kissinger wrote, was that de Gaulle had "conception greater than his strength, while United States power" had "been greater than its conceptions." Most of de Gaulle's proposals were noble but impracticable and destined to fail. They were motivated by "psychological" factors and demonstrated that history was "made by men who" could not "always distinguish their emotions from their analysis." "By couching" the European challenge to the United States "so woundingly," the French leader had spurred "American self righteousness rather than the objective reexamination of Atlantic relationships which the situation" demanded. "By generating so much personal ill-will among American leaders," de Gaulle might "rend the fabric of illusions on which his policy" depended.[48]

Kissinger's opinion of de Gaulle was therefore far from unequivocal. Like no other coeval leader, de Gaulle was the embodiment of the heroic statesman making his mark on history—as celebrated in Kissinger's early writings—and rescuing independence of choice and action from circumstance. His was "no doubt...a heroic posture," yet it was also an irrational and overambitious one that produced unintended and counterproductive results.[49] For Kissinger, the fundamental point about the Cold War was that there were no alternative spaces between the two dominant poles, particularly in Europe. In his bipolar horizon, the "heroic" Gaullist illusion was preferable, however, to the petulance of those within Atlantic structures who proposed useless technical solutions to inescapable political problems and, consequently, disturbed U.S. military and diplomatic freedom of maneuver. The de Gaulle who pulled France out of NATO's integrated military structure, opened dialogue with Communist China, and provided his country with a limited nuclear arsenal was less annoying than those leaders who favored multilateral forces, recurrent consultations, and military integration. The latter constrained U.S. action, undermined the coherence of its general strategy, and limited its operational efficiency.

From this perspective, de Gaulle was the antidote to the Atlanticists' illusions of limited political, cultural, and strategic integration, embraced by those who believed that participating in the Atlantic Alliance was not dissimilar to "owning shares in a stock company."[50] Furthermore, the French experience proved that there was no place other than the Atlantic alliance for the country's protection. In short, there was no option to siding with the United States and the West, as some important crises of the Cold War had demonstrated. Bipolarism did not offer alternatives or an easy way out. Kissinger paternalistically tolerated de Gaulle, primarily because he preserved a faith in the structural steadiness of the bipolar system and American superiority that others, including Kennedy and Johnson, lacked. Nonetheless, this bipolar view also expressed a tenuous awareness of effective U.S. strength. This strength was the consequence of how U.S. hegemony had been wielded in post–World War II Europe. The most important element was the capacity of the United States to exercise (and extend) its primacy through negotiated and consensual practices. In this regard the transatlantic case was paradigmatic. U.S. leadership in the Atlantic bloc had been built via dialogue and accommodation rather than simple force or pure diplomacy. It was, in other words, a real hegemony that was capable of cementing the Western bloc and promoting a process of exchange and integration without precedents in history. This domination represented one of the greatest assets of the American empire throughout the Cold War and one of the fundamental matrixes of U.S. superiority over the Soviet Union. Kissinger's unilateralism and bipolarism, alongside the increasing difficulties encountered by the United States in the 1960s, prevented him from appreciating this view as a scholar and exploiting it—as would have been appropriate and necessary—as a statesman.[51]

The Four Basic Elements of Kissinger's Geopolitical Discourse

An examination of Kissinger's principal pre-1968 writings reveals two aspects. The first is the heterodoxy and ambiguity of his realism. Indeed, Kissinger's approach cannot really be qualified as classical realism. Strategic globalism, an emphasis on credibility and interdependence, and the geopolitical homologation of interests rendered Kissinger's realism a partial one, very much embedded in the hegemonic foreign policy culture of early Cold War America. Claims to the contrary notwithstanding, Kissinger-the-scholar operated within a culturally and historically determined environment. He absorbed its influences and paradigms, adopted its stereotypes and dogmas, and nourished its prejudices and misinterpretations.[52]

The second aspect is the persistence of themes, formulas, and slogans that became popular in the United States during the second half of the 1960s with a perceived crisis of the American political system and its values. More than a structured and coherent body of thought, Kissinger's writings appear as a discourse: a hieratic and pleonastic set of discursive practices repeated in the attempt to give shape to an ahistorical geopolitical vision that the United States had to learn and interiorize. This discourse was convenient, both academically and politically, and proved particularly useful for those taking advantage of the anxieties that emerged during the 1960s. It was a "crisis discourse" on which a new domestic consensus could be built. It was destined, however, to be short-lived, transitory, and unable—as we shall see—to stand up to other "crisis discourses" with deeper and more solid roots in U.S. political culture.[53]

There were four essential components in Kissinger's "crisis discourse" and the contradictions it generated.

The Emphasis on Limits

Much of Kissinger's scholarly production revolved around the dilemma of the limits that statesmen had to accept and confront: structural limits determined by the distribution of power in the international system; historical limits from processes not necessarily progressive and evolutionary, but nevertheless ineluctable; and cultural and political limits that originated from a nation's culture, spirit, and ability to pursue a coherent and effective foreign policy. On this last aspect, Kissinger was often critical of his adoptive country and surreptitiously embraced a form of cultural relativism that led him to consider some nations as more adept at great power politics. The heroic nature of the statesman lay in his capacity to transcend these limits in terms of the goals set and means used, if not of the results that were achieved. It lay in his effort to recover a "choice" that systemic and historical "circumstances" no longer seemed to offer. The historian, Kissinger argued, "has to be conscious of the possibility of tragedy," whereas the statesman "has the duty to act as if one's country were immortal." The statesman who took the reins of U.S. foreign policy in a period of crisis and decline—as Kissinger himself did—could not but adopt an intrepid and heroic posture, presenting decisions as original and courageous actions that challenged a disadvantageous international situation and a hostile and culturally ill-equipped domestic political culture.[54]

This position was constantly reaffirmed by Kissinger and contributed to his fame as a gloomy pessimist that discussed the twilight of the West and its latest bastion, the United States. On numerous occasions, Kissinger the statesman maintained that Americans lacked the vigor and the resoluteness to face down the Soviet Union—a "Sparta" compared to the weak and self-satisfied U.S. "Athens." The deficit was primarily spiritual and political—"philosophical" in Kissinger's words—and not purely military or economic. For historian Dana Allin, Kissinger's was a Spenglerian and pessimistic form of conservatism, founded on the belief that "the Western forces of order and stability were at odds with a disintegrating tendency as fundamental as entropy." According to the journalist Tad Szulc, Kissinger's diplomacy operated on the assumption that "the West's moral fibre was breaking down." Kissinger himself, in a famous interview with *New York Times* journalist James Reston, confirmed this pessimistic and declinist vision, arguing that a "historian had to be conscious of the fact that every civilization of the past had ultimately collapsed." History could only be "the tale of efforts that failed, of aspirations that weren't realized, of wishes that were fulfilled and then turned out to be different from what one expected." It was therefore impossible for any great power to indefinitely preserve a position of unchallenged preeminence, although the statesman "had to act on the assumption that problems could and must be solved."[55]

The emphasis on the rigid and intrinsic limits constraining the action of the statesman and the pessimism that derives from this view have represented strong and basic topoi of Kissinger's discourse. They dominated Kissinger writings (pre- and post-1969) as well as public speeches during the period when he was both national security advisor and secretary of state. The three, large volumes of Kissinger's memoirs overflow with "limitationist" rhetoric, as defined by one of his collaborators, Robert Osgood. The main task facing the United States in the late Sixties, Kissinger claimed, was "the realization—as yet dimly perceived—that" the United States "was becoming like other nations." The United States thus needed to recognize that its power, "while vast had limits." "Resources were no longer infinite in relation" to its problems, which meant that time had come to "set priorities, both intellectual and material."[56]

Nevertheless, this overcharged rhetoric of limits reveals many contradictions in Kissinger-the-scholar, as well as Kissinger-the-statesman, as made clear by recently declassified documents that frequently show Kissinger's paradoxical and self-deluding optimism during the years he served in the White House. This issue is discussed in the next chapter. Here, I emphasize two basic antinomies of Kissinger's "crisis discourse" and his rhetoric of limits.

The first is the importance Kissinger attributed to knowledge and historical awareness. Limits could be faced and possibly transcended only by those acquainted with the laws of the international system, the lessons of history, the concepts and categories of political philosophy, and the equilibria of geopolitics. When asked by a journalist about the personal qualities that were necessary for the conduct of a successful diplomacy, Kissinger replied that the most important was knowledge: "knowledge of what I am trying to do. Knowledge of the subject. Knowledge of the history and psychology of the people I am dealing with."[57] It was a kind of knowledge different from the one dominating U.S. academia at the time, and which had easy and preferential access to decision-making centers. For Kissinger, history and philosophy were more important than political science or economics. Kissinger's paraded realism was actually humanistic in its outlook. Yet it also pretended to possess scientist foundations when it was based on the assumption that it was necessary and possible to acquire the instruments and means for conducting foreign policy. Kissinger's point of reference was not the algid social science technocrat, to whom U.S. diplomacy and intelligence often deferred during the Fifties and early Sixties.[58] Rather, it was an idealized scholar who "knew" and, consequently, could act. Although delineated differently, Kissinger's ponderings contain traces of the optimism that dominated social science discourse in early Cold War America. Limits could be identified, examined, and therefore overcome. Consequently, the rhetoric of limits clashed with the possibility that knowledge and experience seemingly offered. It was a basic contradiction that returned during Kissinger's years at the White House, which undermined the coherence of his policies and weakened him politically.

The second incongruence concerned Kissinger's geopolitical globalism. This was encapsulated by the tactic of "linkage" adopted by Kissinger and Nixon: the attempt to link the evolution of the bipolar relationship and U.S. concessions to Moscow, to Soviet behavior in theaters where it was believed to exercise some influence.[59] Linkage was based on a one-world outlook that assumed the international system was increasingly interdependent and that all that occurred was inevitably interconnected, knowable, and thus manipulable. Kissingerian globalism, with its emphasis on interdependence, ended up nourishing a notion of possibility that clashed with the emphasis on limits of Kissinger's "crisis discourse." The optimistic rhetoric of possibilities that marked Kissinger's scholarly production was displayed in his work on the opportunities that nuclear weapons offered to creative (and knowledgeable) statesmen and intellectuals. It was also evident in his unilateralist faith in U.S. freedom of maneuver and its unquestioned primacy in the Atlantic community. Kissinger never embraced the optimism of social and economic liberal progressivism, which was politically and culturally alien to him and did not stimulate his intellectual curiosity and interest. Yet from the missile gap to flexible response, from intervention in Vietnam to the obsession for credibility, he endorsed all the major postulations of U.S. Cold War strategic globalism.

The Critique of Bureaucracy

The condemnation of bureaucracy—of its obtuse conformism, inability to think creatively, and conceptually inhibitory influence on the statesman—distinguishes most of Kissinger's writings. There is, of course, a Weberian element in Kissinger's aversion to bureaucracy. Kissinger relied on the ideas of Max Weber to denounce the chloroforming of policy affected by the elephantine apparatus of the modern-day state. According to Kissinger, these bureaucratic behemoths generate "mechanisms" and tend to "develop a momentum and a vested interest of their own" that are disconnected from the interests of the state they are supposed to serve. In the West, this process facilitated the advent of a leadership that Kissinger defined as "bureaucratic-pragmatic"—a leadership particularly adroit at identifying technical and mechanical solutions to the problems it faced, but entirely unsuitable for facing unexpected challenges. Committed as it was to reaffirming the primacy of routine over creativity, this sort of leadership would never "develop new political orientations" or catalyze the "major political shifts" circumstances sometimes called for.[60]

The critique of bureaucracy was intertwined with a denunciation of the moralist, legalistic, and overly pragmatic nature of what Kissinger considered the peculiar U.S. approach to matters international. Such denunciations would become especially bitter during Kissinger's tenure as national security advisor, when in tandem with Nixon he successfully stripped power from the federal bureaucracies in charge of foreign policy, particularly the State Department. This approach justified the centralization of the control and the conduct of foreign policy in the hands of the president and, by default, a disproportionate expansion of the power and influence of his main advisor. The centralization of the decision-making process provoked anger and irritation in increasingly sidelined agencies within the U.S. government. More importantly, it contributed to making U.S. foreign policy more erratic and incoherent. As Stanley Hoffmann rightly pointed out, Nixon and Kissinger's hostility to bureaucracy produced a "vicious circle" wherein the two "reserved more and more control over the key

issues to themselves, but this only compounded the problem, since the execution of policies had to be largely entrusted to departments that had not
been consulted or even informed." This rejection of centralized foreign
policy making was among the factors that stimulated Congress to try to
reaffirm its role and the reason behind profound political and institutional
crises in the United States in the 1970s.[61]

Leaving aside the political problems it exacerbated, Kissinger's dislike
of bureaucracy reveals a deep ambivalence. Indeed, one could provoca-
tively argue that Kissinger was himself a bureaucrat, or had longed to be
one all his life. As noted earlier, his intellectual production drew on the celebration of expertise and knowledge. In Kissinger's writings, however, a
critique of conformist bureaucrats was often, and incongruously, matched
by an attack on the superficiality and shallowness of politicians. The responsibility and competence of the former are juxtaposed with the impru-
dence and ignorance of the latter. The awareness of complexity and limits
is compared with the opportunistic and emotional volatility of Western democracies, especially the United States. Bureaucrats and politicians would
become the primary targets of Kissinger's criticisms, both during and after
his years in government.

The Hostility to Cold War Liberalism and the Relativism of Realist Culture

I have emphasized how Kissinger's thought, geopolitical vision, and rhetoric were consistent with the spirit of the time, the discursive canons and
strategic culture dominant in the United States. Nevertheless, Kissinger's
discourse was distinctive for its criticism of some of the assumptions, practices, and principles of Cold War liberalism. Such criticism became harsher
following the election of Nixon in 1968, when it was also more convenient
for Kissinger to distance himself from liberal globalism, which was challenged for having dragged the country into a useless war in Vietnam. A
similar critique can also be found in Kissinger's pre-1968 writings. Although not always in a direct and transparent fashion, Kissinger had criticized some of the uncontested axioms of U.S. liberalism, beginning with
its alleged cultural and ethical universalism. In Kissinger's discourse, statements about the diversity of national cultures and the inability to transform such cultures were strictly connected to the rhetoric of limits, in this

case domestic ones each country faced, as previously discussed. Such statements produced a relativistic attitude—culturally and politically, if not geopolitically—which was far from the liberal emphasis on individual rights that had been stimulated by the ideological dimension of the Cold War and was soon to be relaunched in the 1970s when the issue of human rights powerfully entered the arena of international relations.

Some scholars have argued that this relativism derived from Kissinger's personal experience and the inevitable sensibility of an immigrant toward cultural difference and national peculiarity. My view, however, is that it originated more from the modalities through which Kissinger's discourse had been built and presented. Power and the national interest were, at least in theory, the only effective common denominators that kept different units of the international system together. Invocation of an Atlantic commonwealth notwithstanding, there was no tangible civilizational, cultural, religious, or linguistic bond that tied states together. Far from casually did Kissinger express great admiration for Chinese Communist leaders (Mao and, even more so, Chou En-lai) and deep contempt for some important foreign allies (such as Aldo Moro, Willy Brandt, and Olof Palme) as well as domestic critics of his policies (such as the Democratic senator from Washington state, Henry Jackson, and future Republican president Ronald Reagan).[62]

Kissinger explicitly rejected the moralism, progressivism, and legalism that informed U.S. Cold War liberalism. The defense and promotion of the national interest, he claimed, constituted the key criteria in defining the morality of foreign policy initiatives. For this reason, Kissinger always discarded the idea that his was an amoral approach, as claimed by some of his critics. To figures like AFL-CIO leader George Meany, who urged that U.S. foreign relations be based on a solid "moral purpose," Kissinger replied by emphasizing the need to anchor U.S. policy on the more stable concept of national interest.[63]

Moralism's counterpart was, Kissinger argued, the legalistic infatuation of U.S. internationalists: the belief that it was possible to achieve a "juridification" of international politics and the consequent transformation of tensions into legal disputes that could be solved and overcome through international law. Kissinger denounced this vision, presenting it as apolitical, ahistorical, and finalistic, based as it was on the deceitful and complacent illusion that it was possible "to legislate an end to international conflict," as in the case of the Kellogg-Briand Pact of 1928.[64]

For Kissinger, liberal legalism reflected a more general, genetic flaw of U.S. liberalism and its foreign policy philosophy. It expressed a teleological progressivism and the consequent illusion that history, when adequately managed, could be brought to an end; that the problems facing the United States, beginning with the threat to its security, could find a final solution. This critique was the sort that Kissinger had levied against Eisenhower's "massive retaliation." More generally, it was also Kissinger's main objection to the logic of containment. Containment was based on the assumption that the bipolar system was abnormal and unhealthy. For Kissinger, instead, the post-1945 system was not only natural and physiologic, but commendable for the systemic stability it guaranteed. The problem was eminently "conceptual." "Because peace was believed to be 'normal,'" he maintained in his memoirs, "many of our great international exertions were expected to bring about a final result, restoring normality by overcoming an intervening obstacle...this definition of containment treated power and diplomacy as two distinct elements or phases of policy. It aimed at an ultimate negotiation" that was instead utopian and unattainable.[65]

The obsessive search for an unrealizable definitive solution characterized the liberal and progressive thought hegemonic in U.S. public discourse during the first two decades of the Cold War. Through a constant quest for chimerical international normalcy during the 1960s, however, this policy destabilized an international order that Kissinger had come to consider very advantageous to the United States' national interest.

Stability and Legitimacy

In one of his most famous and abused quotes, Kissinger, paraphrasing Goethe, claimed that if he "had to choose between justice and disorder, on the one hand, and injustice and order, on the other," he would "always choose the latter."[66] According to Kissinger, statesmen, particularly those in charge of dominant countries, must always aim at preserving stability. The objective was to create equilibrium among the units (the states) of the system, which was possible only when the superior powers—the United States and the Soviet Union during the Cold War—accepted the legitimacy of such a system and respected its rules. Revolutionary countries, such as Napoleon's France or the Soviet Union during the early Cold War years, tended to reject the legitimacy of the system and worked to undermine and destabilize it. International relations were therefore presented by Kissinger as a clash between revolutionary and conservative states. He declared great admiration for both, while reserving his most caustic criticism for the naïve progressive tendencies of U.S. liberalism.[67]

Order and stability through equilibrium and acknowledgment of the legitimacy of the system was the basic equation that defined Kissinger's geopolitical discourse. It is the formula that revealed the self-satisfied conservatism of Kissinger's vision of world politics. The problem, however, lies in the vague and oblique definition of legitimacy. The concept of legitimacy was defined, on occasions, as respect for a set of implicit rules by states. Yet such conventions were never clearly defined. To be legitimate, the international order must leave "no power so dissatisfied" that the state "does not prefer to seek its remedy within the framework" of such order and instead vents its discontent through a revolutionary foreign policy. Legitimacy has thus little or nothing to do with justice. Although legitimacy represented the indispensable precondition for dialogue among units of the system, and therefore for diplomatic interaction, it was nonetheless only a general agreement among subjects that continue to "have different ideas on what constitutes justice."[68]

The absence of more clearly defined mechanisms and instruments that described the rules among states made such a definition of international legitimacy extremely vague. This absence yet again illustrates a characteristic trait of Kissinger's work: his writings, in the end, look to nourish an image rather than offer an analysis and suggest a policy. The image is that of the expert who surpasses the naïve hopes of those who believe it possible to transform the international system by altering the nature of other states' political systems. The emphasis on stability and order placed Kissinger on a collision course with a Wilsonian tradition that was still well regarded by many U.S. internationalists, who suggested that the extension of U.S.-style market democracy was not only just and desirable but also vital for the security of the United States.[69]

In reality, Kissinger's supposed anti-Wilsonian stance was not as unequivocal as is often claimed. Globalism, interdependence, and the desire for credibility were quintessentially Wilsonian and modern traits, which Kissinger the scholar and statesman absorbed and adopted, as did any careful U.S. observer of twentieth-century world politics. The obsessive attention to order, stability, equilibrium and legitimacy in Kissinger's discourse expressed, however, a desire to escape the teleological illusion inherent in the Wilsonian dream of transforming the international system. Kissinger's argument against liberal internationalism was also an open argument against the influence of Wilsonianism over U.S. foreign policy and the consequent inability of American diplomacy to look to the lessons offered by European realpolitik. Wilson's "zealous idealism" provided a useless, if not dangerous, compass for navigating the turbulent waters of international politics. "Neither Wilson nor his later disciples," Kissinger would reflect, "have been willing to face the fact that, to foreign leaders imbued with less elevated maxims, America's claim to altruism" and "moral exceptionalism" evoked "a certain aura of unpredictability; whereas the national interest can be calculated, altruism depends on the definition of the practitioner."[70]

Finally, the emphasis on order and equilibrium clashed with the overall logic of containment. Even in Kennan's original and somewhat hazy formulation, containment suggested the transformation of the Soviet socialist system and considered it vital to the security of the United States and the well-being of the international community as a whole. For Kissinger, instead, the problem was not the domestic nature of the Soviet Union but its revolutionary foreign policy (with the latter not necessarily deriving from the former). From this perspective, the Kissingerian discourse represented the analytical and prescriptive antithesis to containment. It was a prescriptive antithesis to containment because the United States' objective was not to transform the Soviet Union or simply wait for the "seeds of its decline" to finally germinate (a task that was nevertheless beyond Washington's means), but rather to induce Moscow to abandon revolutionary projects that destabilized the international order. To achieve this goal it was necessary to convince the Soviet Union to accept the legitimacy of the system and commit to preserving its equilibrium and stability.

Although ambiguous, contradictory, and in many ways ingrained in U.S. Cold War strategic culture, Kissinger's discourse and rhetoric were well suited to justifying the change in U.S. foreign policy demanded by events in the late 1960s. As we shall see, the growing perplexity in American public opinion toward the costs of containment and the feasibility of U.S. policies found expression in Kissinger's proposals, which served to justify, albeit temporarily, a change in the methods, practices, and goals of U.S. foreign policy. Such a change was largely imposed by circumstances but was nevertheless traumatic and required the construction of a new, broad domestic consensus. Whoever was to direct U.S. foreign policy in the late 1960s would have to operate outside what Kissinger called the "simplicities of the Cold War" by abandoning the assumption that ultimate victory was possible. No one, however, could compete with Kissinger in offering a discourse that justified this turn and claiming to possess the necessary knowledge for the new era.[71]

3

Kissingerism in Action

The year 1968, the historian Melvin Small recently claimed, was "the foreign policy election of the twentieth century."[1] Foreign affairs played a central role in the presidential race between Richard Nixon and Lyndon Johnson's vice president, Hubert Humphrey. The crisis of containment and its most glaring manifestation, the Vietnam War, obliged Nixon and Humphrey to dedicate most of their speeches and interviews to international matters. The role of the United States in the world system, the new strategies necessary to face the Soviet challenge, and the way the United States could reaffirm and relaunch its leadership in the West were widely debated and discussed.

Justifying Détente

Most of the foreign policy decisions the Nixon administration would take were somewhat compulsory, nevertheless; they were choices that even a

Humphrey administration would have made and that had, in part, already been adopted by Johnson. There were, of course, more radical responses to the crisis the United States was facing. Alternative suggestions oscillated between those of the New Left to end involvement in Vietnam and drastically modify the methods and goals of U.S. foreign policy, to those from the Republican Right that supported a return to strategic and moral Cold War certainties and a revived containment strategy toward the Soviet Union and international Communism. In what was considered the legitimate political discourse of the time, options and possibilities were, however, much more circumscribed. The United States could not give up the international responsibilities it had acquired during the Cold War, but neither could it continue to promote an unsustainable strategy of global containment. A change was indispensable. The margins of change were nevertheless narrow. The crisis of containment was not matched by a structural transformation in the international system conducive to strategic innovations and turns. In spite of the dominant public rhetoric, the system continued to be bipolar, and thus it defined the parameters of any new U.S. foreign policy initiative. Dialogue with Moscow, rapprochement with the People's Republic of China, and exit from the Vietnam imbroglio—the cornerstones and supposed innovations of Nixon and Kissinger's strategy of détente— represented policies that had already been pursued, albeit intermittently, by the Johnson administration. As such, it was an approach capable of generating a much-needed consensus at home.

Negotiations with the North Vietnamese had officially begun in the months preceding the 1968 election. Indeed, Humphrey had hoped until the last minute to be able to strike an agreement that could have greatly benefited him at the polls.[2] An analogous possibility of an opening to China had been carefully explored by the Johnson administration and endorsed by some important advisors to President Johnson. The tensions between Moscow and Peking were increasingly evident, although their most graphic manifestation would come in 1969 when Soviet and Chinese forces repeatedly clashed along the Ussuri River. The stereotyped image of a Communist monolith, which had long influenced (and distorted) American strategies, could no longer be invoked to prevent the normalization of relations with China. Johnson would have probably sought such normalization, had it not been for the Cultural Revolution in China and the subsequent political and social turmoil it caused. Nixon himself had solicited a change in the U.S. approach toward China in a famous article that appeared in a 1967 issue of *Foreign Affairs*. Once elected president, however, Nixon proceeded cautiously on this front, influenced by domestic considerations and conditioned by the doubts and Eurocentric approach of his national security advisor.[3]

More important, détente with Moscow and the promotion of serious negotiations on nuclear weapons revealed continuity between the foreign policy of Johnson and Nixon. Dialogue with the Soviet Union had been ongoing, with inevitable ups and downs, for many years, at least since Stalin's death and the Soviet diplomatic offensive that followed.[4] The July 1963 treaty banning nuclear testing in the atmosphere, outer space, and under water had represented a crucial turning point. The treaty sanctioned the informal beginnings of détente and, in many ways, its institutionalization. It was the moment when the two superpowers finally recognized the existence of fundamental mutual interests, both in a negative sense (avoid a nuclear war) as well as a positive one (preserve a quasi-nuclear duopoly and the bipolar order that derived from it). After 1963, détente with Moscow had been pursued strategically but also economically because trade incentives represented one of the tools available to the United States to mollify and induce the Soviets to accept an agreement. In 1967, the U.S. ambassador to Moscow, Llewellyn Thompson, had convinced the Soviet Union to start a new round of talks on arms control. Many Democratic analysts and politicians assumed the time had come to modify U.S. trade policy toward the Soviet Union, proceeding to a liberalization and abolition of the stringent limits imposed on the transfer of nonmilitary items to the Soviet bloc. In 1968 this proto-détente had been temporarily halted by Soviet intervention in Czechoslovakia and the brutal crushing of the Prague Spring. It is historically plausible, however, to suppose dialogue would have resumed once shock over the violence used by the Soviets to preserve their dominance in central Eastern Europe had been overcome.[5]

"In America," Nixon claimed during his first meeting with Mao in February 1972, "those on the right can do what those on the left can only talk about." Much of the content of Nixon and Kissinger's foreign policy, including the opening to China, was however less innovative and heretical that has been claimed, both at the time and in retrospect.[6]

The real turnabout was not in actions or deeds, but in the discourse used to explain and justify them as well as in Nixon and Kissinger's efforts at geopolitical conceptualization. The ideology of U.S. foreign policy, and its discursive practices, underwent a radical and innovative change. What ensued was a drastic change in the representation and narrative of U.S. grand strategy, alongside the motives behind America's new choices. It is still debated as to who, between Nixon and Kissinger, was the true strategist of détente. Nixon was a cunning and acute politician with a deep knowledge of international affairs. Unlike many previous presidents, he had a strong passion and interest in foreign issues. At least until 1973, when the Watergate scandal began to ruin him, Nixon was clearly in charge, and decided the timing and content of U.S. foreign policy. But the author of the ideological, discursive, and strategic transformation of U.S. foreign policy—which was the true novelty of détente—was without doubt Henry Kissinger. It was Kissinger who articulated a new foreign policy discourse and who theorized the need for a new grand narrative. This discourse was mostly based on the intellectual assumptions that had defined his work as a scholar, but also stemmed from the crucial need to build a new domestic consensus to replace the now dissolved one that had buttressed containment during the previous twenty years.[7]

Three elements converged in the formally realist way that Kissinger used to present and sell détente to the American public: (1) the exigency for broad domestic support of a new internationalism capable of facing neo-isolationist and "limitationist" proposals that called for a considerable reduction in U.S. international commitments; (2) the necessity to confer new legitimacy on the bipolar international structure, whose strengthening and preservation came to represent both means and ends of U.S. foreign policy in the Nixon years; and (3) the need to justify, consolidate, and possibly expand U.S. primacy, even through unscrupulous and sometimes contradictory practices.

These elements were interconnected parts of a general approach that aimed at containing a twofold domestic challenge. The first challenge came from those who urged the return to the simple and clear logic of the early Cold War. Kissinger considered such thinking impractical because of its costs and new political conditions, but also counterproductive in light of the destabilizing effect a Cold War redux might have on the international equilibria. The second challenge emerged from those who believed it possible, indeed desirable, for the United States to gradually give up its quest for world leadership. Kissinger, in his response to this dual challenge, attempted to redefine the bases of the international system in order to endow it with a new legitimacy. For a brief time, as we shall see, Kissinger was able to ensure that U.S. foreign policy enjoyed a new domestic consensus, which rendered acceptable the bipolar system, and the costs and burdens necessary to preserve and strengthen it.

Kissinger's geopolitical vision was in many ways conservative and defensive: "It is extremely in our interest," he maintained in 1973, "to keep the present world going as long as possible." Moreover, it was a "maniacally bipolar" vision, which contradicted Kissinger's public posture and his rhetorical emphasis on the systemic transformation and alleged multipolar evolution in the international order.[8]

Kissinger's was an analytical as well prescriptive bipolarism. According to effective power parameters, primarily the military one, there remained two clearly superior subjects in the system during the late 1960s: the United States and the Soviet Union. As stated by the National Security Council in 1969, "in military power, geographical reach, and the global scope of their interests, the discrepancy" between the two superpowers "and the second rank powers" was "greater than ever." According to the analysis, "the structure of military power in the world" was "no less dominated by the superpowers than at the outset of the Cold War. The military balance between them" was "no less consequential for the security or insecurity of others. Consequently, more than twenty years after World War II, despite all the diffusion of political activity, U.S.-Soviet relations" continued "to dominate the center stage of international relations." For Kissinger, the relative decline of the United States in the economic realm and the decreasing attractiveness of Soviet socialism were counterbalanced by the strengthening and consolidation of the two countries' superiority in a more tangible index of power: possession of an immense nuclear arsenal.[9]

In a curiously circular process, bipolarism as an analytical and prescriptive frame reproduced bipolarism as a strategic objective: the system was bipolar, and it was convenient for the United States to consolidate and preserve it. This conservation was to become the objective of U.S. foreign policy and constituted the goal of Kissinger's diplomacy and strategy.

Various reasons contributed to Kissinger's belief that such an objective was not only desirable but also attainable. First of all, the Soviet Union had moderated its policies and rhetoric, and had come to recognize, like the United States, a commonality of interests with its Cold War archrival.

Kissinger explicitly acknowledged the cautiousness of the Soviet regime and its inclination to support the status quo. The Soviet Union had expanded its range of action well beyond its original sphere of influence, dramatically increased its military potential, and was concerned with the growing ideological and geopolitical antagonism with Beijing. As a result, the National Security Council claimed, Soviet leaders had "become more concerned with protecting their gains as opposed to simply stirring up trouble" and were now "more conscious of the limits and costs of their influence and of the hazards of becoming over-committed." According to Kissinger, the USSR had finally understood "the limitations of both its physical strength and of...its ideological fervor." Both sides, Kissinger claimed, were reducing the ideological antagonism between them. The United States was abandoning its immature and dangerous liberal universalism, founded on the naïve assumption that "all the peoples of the world" were "secretly American." This universalism, Kissinger maintained, had over-extended U.S. interest and engagement in the world, reaching a level that was beyond its resources "not only physically but also psychologically."[10]

In an analogous fashion, the Soviet Union was also tempering its ideological zeal. The ideological element that had marked the first phase of the Cold War, Kissinger argued, was diminishing. What remained was the geopolitical dimension of the antagonism, which stemmed from the objective bipolar character of the international system. From this perspective, the rivalry between the United States and the Soviet Union was both natural and physiological. The end of the Cold War (or at least a "first" Cold War) did not imply the end of the bipolar conflict as many wished and argued. In contrast to the past, such antagonism was nevertheless now disciplinable and manageable. It was a condition that the United States had to learn to accept, thereby abandoning the illusory and dangerous belief, as embodied by containment, that the competition between the two superpowers could come to a final solution *with the United States* triumphant. For this reason, Kissinger maintained, the Nixon administration believed it was facing "the end of the post-war era" and the time had come "to find conceptions" that were "appropriate to the realities of the '70s." The United States, Nixon argued in 1970, would continue to assist allies and friends, but it could not "and will not—conceive all the plans, design all the programs, execute all the decisions and undertake all the defense of the free nations of the world."[11]

Soviet moderation and the commonality of interests between the superpowers made the consolidation of the bipolar structure possible, with its legitimacy now accepted by the Soviet Union. Given that the Soviet-American antagonism was neither solvable nor winnable, the United States and Soviet Union could only acknowledge the situation and work together to preserve the equilibrium. A legitimate system required the acceptance of its traits by the main powers, who were asked to renounce the possibility of altering or overthrowing such a system. Kissinger believed that the U.S. strategy of containment as well as revolutionary Soviet internationalism had aimed at upsetting Cold War bipolarism. Through détente the United States would be able to control the Soviet Union by drawing it "into *de facto* acceptance of" and "assimilation into the existing world order."[12]

The inherently bipolar structure of the international system had to be backed up, and made stable and durable. To achieve this goal, it was necessary to confer legitimacy to this structure, making it acceptable and respected also by the Soviet Union. This objective was favored and helped by the moderation of the USSR and by its consequent inclination to share America's interest in preserving the bipolar order.

In addition to Soviet moderation and the bipolar commonality of interests, there was a final factor fueling Kissinger's belief that it was possible to fortify bipolarism. This factor was his inner optimism, and it worked on numerous levels. There was his optimism in the ability of the United States, and the Nixon administration specifically, to carry out a bold and complex grand design, while centralizing the decision-making process and evading pressure from Congress, other members of the administration, and domestic public opinion. There was also Kissinger's optimism in the willingness of Moscow to accept the legitimacy of the system as defined by Washington, in the limited influence that other subjects, such as China, could exert, and in the ability of the United States to condition those countries' choices and behavior. Finally, there was optimism that previous stereotypes and topoi of the Cold War could be abandoned and replaced by a new U.S. foreign policy discourse and ideology, which contained categories, concepts, and formulas—a new grand narrative in other words—very distant from the political culture that had been long dominant in the United States.

These were the motivations behind Kissinger's certainty that it was possible to abandon containment and elaborate a new strategic design. It is useful to recapitulate the ends this design was intended to meet—the reasons why the survival and consolidation of bipolarism were objectives of Kissinger's foreign policy. The first basic goal—repeatedly mentioned in Kissinger's memoirs—was to avoid war. On this goal, Kissinger-the-statesman was light years from Kissinger-the-scholar, who celebrated "limited war" and magnified the strategic possibilities the nuclear revolution offered to creative and courageous thinkers. "Until the beginning of the nuclear age," Kissinger argued, "it would have been inconceivable that a country could possess too much military strength for effective political use." "The nuclear age" had "destroyed this traditional measure": a country "might be strong enough to destroy an adversary and yet no longer be able to protect its own population against attack. By an irony of history a gargantuan increase in power had eroded the relationship of power to policy." Military might no longer provided great powers with the tools to "impose their will" even "against countries with no capacity for retaliation." Arms still represented the basic denominator of international hierarchies and defined the polarity of the system, but the destructive capacity developed by the United States and the Soviet Union, as well as the immense and increasing cost of the arms race, obligated them to negotiate over their numbers and achieve some sort of discipline.[13]

A legitimate and consensual bipolar order allowed the United States and the USSR to regulate rearmament. The first phase of détente, which had begun in 1963, crystallized bipolar nuclear preeminence and the power that derived from it. The test ban treaty and, more so, the 1968 Non-Proliferation Treaty canonized U.S. and Soviet atomic dominance. China and France did not sign the first treaty but proceeded to develop their own limited nuclear arsenal. Nevertheless, the 1963 and 1968 agreements acknowledged that the United States and the Soviet Union had a shared interest in sealing the power hierarchy produced by the original nuclear duopoly.

After 1968, and with the massive expansion of the Soviet arsenal, a further step had to be taken. Nuclear bipolarism had been accepted and common interests acknowledged, but it was also vital to discipline the nuclear balance by controlling it and defining a set of rules that would assure deterrence, upon which peace and stability ultimately depended. Stabilization of the bipolar relationship and recognition of the new power equilibrium were necessary to prevent either side from using the destructive capability available to them. "The solid basis of détente" was offered first and foremost by the "growing mutual recognition of the need to avoid war." The peaceful but competitive coexistence between the two powers had to be regulated and managed in order to avoid a nuclear war, while preserving and consolidating the "heavily militarized *modus vivendi*" and global "strategic stalemate" of the late 1960s and early 1970s. This dilemma represented, in the words of diplomat and historian Raymond Garthoff, "the common security interest of both sides" and thus "the basic motivating force" behind détente.[14]

In addition to preventing conflict and crystallizing nuclear parity, Kissinger's vision of détente and the legitimization of the bipolar system incorporated a further goal to promote order and consolidate the systemic equilibrium. This goal was represented by the control of centrifugal tendencies within the two blocs that endangered the bipolar structure. It was in this area that the conservative character of Henry Kissinger's strategy (as well as of that of the Soviet Union) was fully revealed. To discipline and regulate bipolarism also meant freezing the bipolar status quo on the European continent. The Soviets were particularly sensitive to this condition; for Moscow it was vital to definitively formalize the bipolar partition of Europe and recognize the intangibility of the borders produced by World War II. Once again, it was a condition on which Kissinger agreed. As such, Nixon's national security advisor opposed autonomous Western European initiatives and feared reduced U.S. influence over the political choices, international and domestic, of some of its European partners. In the words of one coeval commentator, John Girling, given the condition of the day détente represented "a more realistic method than 'containment' for preserving the essential: the *status quo* generally favourable to American patronage" and subsequent reassertion of U.S. "supremacy."[15]

During his tenure in the Nixon and Ford administrations, Kissinger frequently stressed this exigency and denounced, not always without reason, the propensity of many lesser U.S. allies to shirk Atlantic responsibilities and flirt with autonomist and third-force projects. According to Kissinger, Western Europe and the EEC countries had far too often sought and found an element of cohesion in their opposition to the United States and its policies: "with respect to the Europeans," Kissinger would claim during a meeting of his staff in December 1973, "the basic problem" was "the attempt to organize Europe, to unify Europe on an anti-American basis, or at least on a basis in which criticism of the United States" was "the organizing principle." The objective of the Europeans, Kissinger maintained, was to place the United States outside "any structural arrangement in which" it "might predominate" and to make resistance to the United States the basic catalyst for "European unity." In Europe, therefore, détente with Moscow and the legitimization of bipolarism aimed at keeping such pressures, which had intensified in the early 1970s, in check and thus preventing any opposition to the bipolar order and its implicit and explicit political rules.[16]

Consolidation of the bipolar structure and consensual negotiation with Moscow were vital to achieving two interdependent systemic objectives: to guarantee order and stability (which Kissinger-the-scholar had already defined as the primary objective of statesmen), and to establish a structure that contained and neutralized centrifugal strains within the two blocs. A third objective, more contingent but equally important, must be added: to overcome the domestic political crisis that lacerated the United States through a foreign policy capable of obtaining the support and endorsement of a vast majority of Americans. Building a new consensus over foreign policy, in its practice as well as goals, represented a crucial element of the Kissingerian strategy. Often neglected, or at least underestimated, this dimension emerges clearly in the rich archival documentation now available to scholars.[17]

Kissinger-the-scholar had already emphasized that domestic support represented the crucial precondition for a coherent and effective foreign policy. Internal consensus was the vital *conditio* of foreign policy and not just for U.S.-style Western democracy. According to Kissinger, "charismatic-revolutionary leaders"—such as those of emerging third-world nations, but also, one could add, leaders of a country amid crisis or difficulty—had a strong incentive "to use foreign policy as a means of bringing about domestic cohesion." In order to guarantee substantial domestic support for Washington's international choices—which had progressively eroded during the 1960s—Kissinger considered it fundamental to reorganize and relegitimize the bipolar order and co-opt the Soviet Union in its supervision. Erroneously, as we shall see, Kissinger believed that the country was no longer willing to sustain a costly policy of global containment, justified by an "evangelism of fear" of Communism, whose mobilizing power had greatly diminished. The evaporating Cold War consensus had to be replaced with a new consensus, whose basic catalysts were détente and cooperation among the great powers. The time had come to move from conflictual to consensual bipolarism.[18]

Consolidating and Legitimizing the Bipolar Structure:
The Diplomacy of Détente

For Kissinger, détente was fundamentally a bipolar strategy, both in the reading of the international system and the goals it set. It was primarily directed toward the Soviet Union and the possible impact of U.S. diplomatic choices on relations between the two superpowers. In spite of Kissinger's many realist-like proclamations, belief in the structural interdependence of the system was still dominant. Such a bipolar framework meant it was inevitable that an intimate connection would be established between individual events and the state of the relationship between the two main actors. This aspect was made explicit in Nixon and Kissinger's concept of linkage. Linkage stemmed from a conviction that problems and possibilities were strictly interconnected and that the behavior of the Soviet Union in a certain theater or over a specific issue was bound to have broader repercussions, whether positive or negative, on Soviet-American relations. Détente, Kissinger argued in 1974, was "indivisible" and could not be pursued "in one area or toward one group of countries only." According to this logic, the lack of Soviet collaboration over Vietnam or Moscow's action in the Middle East, to name but two famous examples, could induce the United States to halt negotiations on arms reduction (Strategic Arms Limitation Talks, or SALT) or suspend approved aid programs for the Soviet Union. According to Kissinger, linkage—the ability to "link events"—would finally provide U.S. foreign policy with a much needed "conceptual framework" grounded "in a firm conception of the national interest," which freed policy from the pressures of "parochial interests" and the quintessential U.S. propensity to oscillate "between overextension and isolation."[19]

In reality, linkage represented a less original and more rigid and conventional approach than was claimed at the time. It was less original because it had already been adopted, albeit informally, by most post–World War II U.S. administrations. It was more rigid because it locked processes and events that frequently had a tenuous connection with the superpower relationship within a "bipolar box," thus obstructing their normal and autonomous development. Moreover, linkage once again highlighted the Eurocentric and bipolar nature of Kissinger's vision and the strategy of détente. Relations with the Soviet Union and conservation of the European equilibrium represented the compass orienting Kissinger's analyses and policies, and conditioning times and contents of the main foreign policy choices of the Nixon administration.[20]

This characterization was particularly true of U.S. diplomatic initiatives toward the People's Republic of China, the American reaction to the parallel German attempt at détente represented by Willy Brandt's *Ostpolitik,* and in the way that Nixon and Kissinger dealt with the war in Vietnam. In all these cases, Nixon and Kissinger's decisions and choices, as well as their timing, were conditioned by the primary objective of maximizing the impact vis-à-vis the Soviet counterpart. Kissinger's was never intended to be a multipolar world made of variable and constantly renegotiated alliances. It was, on the contrary, a uniquely bipolar system in which everything was decided and calculated on the bases of the effect on the U.S.-Soviet competition.

The sensational opening to China, possibly the most stunning initiative of Nixon's foreign policy, can be read and understood in this light. The initiative did not constitute recognition of a new superpower on the world stage, nor did Nixon and Kissinger's successful promotion of trilateral diplomacy acknowledge that a systemic transformation toward tripolarism was taking place. The triangular United States-USSR-China arrangement was always unbalanced. As William Bundy rightly noted, from the very beginning it was based "not on equal treatment of the Communist powers but on a pronounced favoring of China."[21]

The opening to China did not reflect a new geopolitical awareness; it was, instead, functional to achieving two other objectives connected to the bipolar thinking orienting U.S. choices: avoid Soviet predominance in the Far East by co-opting China in the regional containment of the USSR, and thus reduce the burdens (and costs) of U.S. global primacy. A third goal can also be added that further emphasizes Kissinger's bipolarism as fundamentally Eurocentric. Kissinger's worries were primarily directed at the possible repercussions for Europe of Soviet dominion in Asia. A consolidation of Soviet hegemony in Eurasia risked altering the global balance of power and had the potential to drive Washington's European allies—many of whom Kissinger did not hold in high regard—to seek some sort of accommodation with Moscow. The consequent "Finlandization" of Europe, as it was called at the time, would have left the United States "isolated in an unfriendly world environment" and would have realized, without war, Washington's most dreaded geopolitical nightmare: the control of the Eurasian landmass, and of its immense resources, by a hostile and antagonistic power.[22]

For Kissinger the opening to China helped to prop up European bipolarism at a moment of extreme difficulty in that the United States lacked the resources and domestic support to continue a policy of global containment of the Soviet Union. Furthermore, rapprochement with Beijing offered an instrument to inducing Moscow to accept an agreement on arms control. Such an agreement was in itself essential to strengthening bipolarism by offering it further legitimacy and reducing the considerable costs it entailed.

The opening to China was thus planned and decided within an entirely bipolar mind frame. There was also the obvious corollary of Vietnam and the (unfounded) belief that Moscow and Beijing could pressure their North Vietnamese ally, thus helping the United States to get out of the quagmire. Historian Jussi Hanhimäki has convincingly argued that "ultimately it was the Soviet Union that represented the primary concern of Kissinger's foreign policy against which all other issues were weighed." Previously rejected because of the potentially negative effects on the bipolar relationship, the rapprochement with China was justified by Nixon and Kissinger for the precise impact it would have on the Soviet Union: it represented, in other words, a clear "anti-Soviet action." The conviction that the Soviets would be more conciliatory if they feared a United States rapprochement with Beijing reflected, Kissinger claimed, "a kind of Realpolitik approach" that would obviously have his support.[23]

After the military skirmishes on the Ussuri River, the Soviet ambassador to the United States, Anatoly Dobrynin, tried to verify the U.S. position with regard to the clash between the Soviet Union and China. The Soviets even suggested the creation of a bipolar axis against China and considered the possibility of a preemptive strike against Chinese nuclear facilities. Albeit slowly, Nixon and Kissinger began to consider the possibility of using the "China card," while also looking to exploit divisions within the Chinese leadership by aiding the ascent of moderate figures, such as the Chinese premier Chou En-lai, who favored the opening of a dialogue with the United States. In August 1969, during a meeting of the National Security Council, Nixon recognized that the United States had a strategic interest in avoiding a Chinese defeat. This decision, Kissinger claimed in his memoirs, represented "a major event in American foreign policy": the United States declared its interest in "the survival of a major

Communist country, long an enemy and with which" it "had no contact." Such contact would soon be established through the U.S. ambassador to Warsaw, Walter Stoessel, and through the Romanian government.[24]

In the following months, Stoessel met several times with a Chinese diplomat in Poland, and other channels of communication were opened before the U.S.-Chinese rapprochement became public. Detailed reconstructions of this tortuous and often Byzantine negotiation between China and the United States are now available. The Nixon administration always considered such negotiations a lever to be used in its relationship with the Soviet Union—leverage that could induce Moscow to moderate its behavior in the Far East, reduce its military support of North Vietnam, and, even more importantly, assume a positive and productive approach in the first round of SALT talks, which had begun in Helsinki in late 1969.[25]

This stance was the strategic horizon on which the opening to China took place. Between 1970 and 1971, however, the rapprochement was hindered and frequently suspended as a result of U.S. military operations in Indochina and China's fear that North Vietnam might adopt a more pro-Soviet posture, thus reducing Beijing's influence in the Indochinese theater. The Warsaw channel dried up, China's anti–United States propaganda became more intense and bellicose, and Mao, during a meeting with the North Vietnamese premier Pham Van Dong, defined Kissinger as "a stinking scholar...a university Professor who" did not know "anything about diplomacy."[26]

It took a few months before a new contact was established. This circumstance happened primarily because of domestic dynamics in China, particularly the weakened position of the main opponent of the Sino-American rapprochement, the minister of defense Lin Biao. Preceded by important decisions of high symbolic value—Nixon's decision to authorize the transfer of diesel engines to China, and Beijing's decision to invite the American writer Edgar Snow to China—talks between the two sides were reactivated in late 1970, this time under the direct supervision of Kissinger.[27]

A few months later, Chou En-lai sent a message to the White House which expressed China's willingness to "receive publicly in Beijing a special envoy of the President of the US...or the U.S. Secretary of State or even the President of the US himself for a direct meeting and discussions." The time for hidden back-channel diplomacy had finally ended. The Chinese believed the moment had come to cash in on the political dividend that a public rapprochement with the United States would guarantee.[28]

In the following months, Kissinger carefully prepared for his visit to China. On the one hand, it was necessary to avoid domestic pressures (particularly from the pro-Taiwan lobby) that could hinder reconciliation between the two countries. On the other, it was crucial to maximize the shock value of the visit so that it had the desired impact on relations with Moscow. In July 1971, during a trip to Asia, Kissinger and some of his collaborators visited Beijing in absolute secrecy. For the first time since 1949, a U.S. diplomatic mission set foot in China.[29]

The trip had a relevant symbolic function and was meant to prepare for the successive visit of Nixon. Kissinger and his Chinese interlocutor discussed two key issues: Taiwan and the admission of the People's Republic of China to the United Nations. Indochina was also at the center of the discussion. On this, Kissinger made explicit what the Nixon administration's fundamental objective was in Vietnam: to be certain there was a politically acceptable interval between the American withdrawal and the inevitable unification of the country under Communist rule.[30] Although discussions did not concentrate specifically on the Soviet Union, it was clear to both sides that the common Soviet enemy was the real catalyst of the rapprochement.

A detailed and convincing recent study of Kissinger's diplomacy has maintained that China, in Nixon and Kissinger's vision, represented "a strategic ally of the United States against the Soviet Union." Washington and Beijing, Kissinger claimed in retrospect, may have operated with different interests but developed "comparable analyses of what was needed to use the international equilibrium to" their "mutual benefit" at that "particular moment in history." The strategic partnership between the United States and the People's Republic of China did not rest upon formal agreements but rather an acknowledgment of their common interests and "tacit understandings based on parallel views regarding the details of the balance of power."[31]

The unstated but significant anti-Soviet element of the Sino-American entente was confirmed by successive trips to Beijing by Kissinger in October 1971 (a few days before the admission of the People's Republic of China to the United Nations) and by Nixon in February 1972. Both occasions illustrated the strength of the anti-Soviet glue for the strategic China-United States relationship, but also revealed the difficulty in achieving any real agreement. The Taiwan issue continued to divide the two sides and would in fact prove insoluble. Chou En-lai and Mao's requests that the Americans renounce their support of Taiwan and recognize Chinese claims over the island clashed with the vast support Taiwan enjoyed inside the United States and the commitments made by previous U.S. administrations. Similarly, U.S. requests that China reign in its North Vietnamese ally to help facilitate a solution to that conflict was not possible because Chinese influence over Hanoi was much more limited than Nixon and Kissinger considered, and, even if it feasible, such a gesture would have undermined Chinese credibility by pushing North Vietnam closer to the USSR.[32]

Nixon's visit—"the week that changed the world" in the rhetoric of the time and certainly the apex of the U.S. trilateral strategy—did not produce significant diplomatic results. This outcome was destined to characterize Sino-American relations during the 1970s and would frustrate the hopes and ambitions generated by Kissinger's first visit. The discussions between Kissinger, Chou En-lai, Nixon, and Mao covered most world affairs, and the transcripts of these meetings offer an extraordinary picture of international relations during the period as well as the cultural and geopolitical visions of Chinese and U.S. leaders.[33] Nevertheless, it is worth reiterating that these meetings and discussions produced few concrete results. Rather, they reaffirmed the bipolar matrix of the United States' strategic decision to "open" to China and, along with it, China's consciousness of the possibility of exploiting such bipolar logic. Nixon reasserted that he harbored no illusions with regard to the Soviet Union and emphasized the need to coordinate U.S. and Chinese policies toward Moscow. His visit ended with the release of a famous joint statement, the "Shanghai Communiqué," on the various aspects of the relationship between the United States and China. Although it was ambiguous and vague in several passages, particularly those regarding Taiwan, the communiqué was unequivocal in defining the anti-Soviet roots of the rapprochement. Indeed, the communiqué contained an explicit message to Moscow in its affirmation of the commitment of both sides to prevent "efforts by any other country or group of countries to establish... hegemony in the Asia-Pacific" and an implicit message that the Soviet menace represented the driving force behind the common strategic interest between Beijing and Washington.[34]

Promoted and managed in a bipolar fashion, the United States' opening to China was aimed at co-opting the latter in a policy of regional containment of the USSR, avoiding an alteration of the global balance of power

in Moscow's favor, and influencing Soviet leadership to show more pru-
dence and greater interest in reaching an agreement on nuclear weapons.
Through the rapprochement the United States also intended to consolidate bipolarism in Europe in the belief that it would be shaken by a clash
between the USSR and China, which, given the disparity of forces between
the two, would end with the inevitable capitulation of the latter.

Kissinger also believed, however, that Europe had to be saved from itself. Indeed Europe, and Western Europe in particular, constituted the second piece of Kissinger's strategy of consolidation and legitimization of the
bipolar order. The opening to China was a functional act to prevent alleged
Western European defeatism and any potential Finlandization of the Old
Continent. Preventing excessive autonomy and independence of Western
Europe was needed to fortify the bipolar division of Europe, which appeared threatened by the new diplomatic activism of various European
countries, including now the Federal Republic of Germany (FRG).

On this front, the U.S. strategy of détente opened up several dilemmas
and contradictions, as Kissinger himself was willing to admit. Negotiating
with the Soviet Union and cooling Cold War tensions had the effect of
loosening the bipolar straightjacket in Europe and de facto legitimizing
analogous initiatives by European countries. The risk was that in the name
of détente—a strategy that aimed at crystallizing the bipolar equilibrium
in Europe—the Europeans would feel justified in promoting initiatives
that had a different, if not opposite, goal, namely, exploiting the negotiations with the USSR and its Eastern European satellites in a bid to undermine and progressively unloose the bipolar structure. Two different and
noncomplementary visions of détente—the American and the Western
European ones—competed with one another, with the former involun-
tarily stimulating and legitimizing the latter.[35]

Kissinger was aware of this contradiction and troubled by it. He would
later maintain that the chief danger was that the Soviet Union could
take advantage of a "differential détente" by nurturing disagreements
and frictions between Washington and its lesser allies. Primary sources
show a different picture, however. Kissinger, in fact, feared that a Soviet-
Western European détente would reduce Moscow's incentive to proceed
with negotiations with the United States, in part thwarting the results
of the Sino-American rapprochement. Furthermore, a distinct Soviet-
European détente risked stimulating the Western European propensity

to act autonomously, thus reducing Washington's power in Europe and destabilizing the bipolar order that Kissinger wanted to strengthen and preserve. To those, such as the Italian Christian Democratic leader Aldo Moro, who argued that great power détente made it impossible to maintain rigid barriers in Europe, Kissinger replied that détente did not imply the end of bipolar antagonism and the geopolitical divisions that it had caused. On the contrary, détente looked to guarantee more effective regulation and control of such divisions. Détente was simply another way to manage and discipline bipolarism and not a process designed to bring it to an end; it was a different, albeit less ideological, way of waging the battle with the Soviet Union. For Kissinger the risk was that Western Europe would seek independence from the two blocs, which could derail the process of détente by drastically curtailing the United States' ability to pressure the Soviet Union.[36]

For this reason, Nixon's national security advisor looked on with perplexity, if not outright hostility, at Willy's Brandt Ostpolitik and the attempt by the FRG to promote a rapprochement with the Soviet Union and the Communist countries of central Eastern Europe. The primary objective of Ostpolitik was to unfreeze the rigid division of Germany and Europe. To achieve this objective Brandt was willing to abandon what had been until then one of the fundamental axioms of West German foreign policy: the refusal of diplomatic relations with East Germany (the German Democratic Republic, or GDR) and countries that recognized it, with the exception of the USSR (the so-called Hallstein Doctrine). West German Ostpolitik represented a shift from the long-term strategy—pursued until the mid-1960s by various Christian Democrat governments—of reunifying the two Germanys through rigidity and confrontation, to a longer-term strategy of reunification based instead on dialogue and interaction. These opposite perspectives reflected the fundamental geopolitical transformations that had taken place as a consequence of the evolution of the Cold War and of its nature. The former presupposed, just as the original U.S. strategy of containment had, that the end of bipolarism could only take place with the defeat of the USSR and the end of the Soviet bloc; the latter, considering this scenario unlikely, was instead based on the assumption that a gradual relaxation of the bipolar division of Europe could take place only with the intensification of exchanges between the two blocs and the two Germanys. According to this approach, the development of a growing web of commercial and diplomatic ties between the blocs would generate a mutual interest in rendering the division less rigid and impermeable.[37]

Brandt's and Kissinger's strategies were based on similar analytical premises: a recognition of the end of containment and the first Cold War; an acknowledgment that the costs of confrontation and nondialogue with the Soviet Union were impossible to sustain; and awareness that an accidental conflict was always possible and that it would almost certainly occur on European soil, and Germany in particular. These shared assumptions, however, generated dissimilar projects and designs. Kissinger wanted to preserve a bipolar order that guaranteed U.S. leadership in a key part of Europe. To maintain such leadership, Kissinger was "prepared to subordinate the long-standing relationship with the Allies to America's strategic interest in preserving its global position." West Germany, which had already renounced fundamental attributes of power (in particular, possessing its own nuclear arsenal), longed instead for the unloosening of a bipolar structure that limited its strength and freedom of action.[38]

Ostpolitik and, more generally, the various attempts by Western European countries to promote their own détente with Moscow were considered by Kissinger as an updated manifestation of unrealistic nationalism. "In less scrupulous hands," Ostpolitik could indeed "turn into a new form of classic German nationalism." "From Bismarck to Rapallo," Kissinger argued, "it was the essence of Germany's nationalist foreign policy to maneuver freely between East and West."[39] Kissinger's preoccupation did not stem from a belief that European allies could achieve their goals, but from the effect that these actions might have on bipolar relations and U.S. strategy. Europe was simply too weak and divided to negotiate by itself with the Soviet Union or to play a significant role in international affairs. European wishful thinking provoked, however, several negative repercussions that had the potential to compromise the success of American plans. The various agreements between the FRG, the Soviet Union, and other Soviet bloc countries made U.S. incentives, particularly commercial ones, less attractive and diplomatically usable. Furthermore, the allure of indirectly extending its influence in Europe through intra-European détente could limit Soviet interest in the U.S. proposal to jointly regulate European bipolarism. On this issue, Kissinger (and many others along with him) clearly misjudged Soviet eagerness to expand its sphere of influence and underestimated Moscow's preference for direct dialogue with the United States.

This preference also derived from the predisposition of Soviet leaders to adopt parameters of power not too dissimilar from those of Kissinger and from their conviction that U.S. support was essential to make the post–World War II partition of Europe permanent. Like conservative critics of the Nixon administration, Kissinger warned that Ostpolitik could develop into a new form of appeasement—an accusation that would soon be levied against Kissinger's own version of détente.

Brandt's strategy was aimed at transforming the FRG into a magnet for Communist central Eastern Europe. The problem, Kissinger later wrote, was to understand "which side of the dividing line would in fact be the magnet"; the fear was that "the Communist world would wind up in the stronger position," stimulating "a creepy dissociation" of the FRG "from Western policies except those for the physical defense of Western Europe." According to Kissinger, Brandt "possessed neither the stamina nor the intellectual apparatus to manage the forces he had unleashed" and had become the "prisoner" of such forces, "wallowing in their applause instead of disciplining it with a sense of proportion or a long-range policy." Ostpolitik could offer the Soviets "an asset...to be used to counter any leverage that the United States might get from improving relations with China."[40]

Thus, a parallel and uncoordinated détente threatened to diminish the credibility of the United States vis-à-vis allies and foes alike. The cohesion of the Western bloc and the uncontested U.S. leadership were essential preconditions of the Kissingerian design. Yet the United States seemed incapable of controlling its allies. Brandt's initiative offered Moscow the possibility of a selective détente through which it could diplomatically isolate the United States. As emphasized by Argyris Andrianopoulos, a fundamental element of Kissinger's bipolar strategy was the "continued and undiminished primacy—described by Kissinger as 'control' or 'hegemony'—of the U.S. in relationship with its principal Allies in Western Europe." Ostpolitik, just like other European diplomatic initiatives of the time, openly challenged such primacy.[41]

Finally, Ostpolitik, like bipolar détente, seemed to stimulate the evolution of certain Western European political systems that had been effectively blocked by the divisions of the Cold War. This was the case with Italy and, after successive transitions to democracy, Portugal and Spain: three countries with very different problems but united by the presence of strong Communist Parties that had the potential to enter government.

From Kissinger's perspective, hardening European bipolarity also curbed political processes that had the potential to allow Western European Communist Parties to play a more direct role in national policies and to exert greater influence over foreign and security matters. The contradiction was particularly acute: détente, a strategy to freeze the political and geopolitical makeup of Europe, also threatened to destabilize it. Kissinger was aware of this contradiction. Those within the United States sympathetic to a possible opening of the Italian government to the Communist Party (Partito Communista Italiano, or PCI) often claimed that the PCI and other Western European Communist forces were genuinely independent from Moscow and that such independence could only be fostered through governmental responsibilities. Kissinger did not share the view; even if it were true (he acknowledged it was possible) it was unacceptable in light of his basic strategic premises. The objective of détente was a consensual stabilization of bipolarism negotiated with Moscow. For both superpowers, national and independent Western European Communist forces represented destabilizing agents and thus were a nuisance for the strategy of a strengthened bipolar order. "When you imagine what communist Governments will do inside NATO," Kissinger erupted during a meeting of his staff,

> it doesn't make any difference whether they're controlled by Moscow or not. It will unravel NATO and the European community into a neutralist instrument. And that is the essence of it. Whether or not these parties are controlled from Moscow—that's a subsidiary issue....we keep saying that there's no conclusive evidence that they are not under the control of Moscow, implying that if we could show they were not under the control of Moscow, we could find them acceptable....A Western Europe with the participation of communist parties is going to change the basis of NATO....to bring the communist into power in Western Europe...would totally reorient the map of postwar Europe.[42]

Kissinger's initial hostility did not halt Ostpolitik, which in fact achieved some relevant results such as the Soviet-West German nonaggression treaty of August 1970, the Warsaw treaty between Poland and West Germany of December 1970 that recognized the Oder-Neisse border, and the basic treaty between the two Germanys in December 1972. Nor was Kissinger able, as he had hoped, to reverse the change in the political system of some U.S. allies in Europe. At most, he succeeded in influencing the timing and modality of such transformations. Through his hostility to these processes, however, Kissinger tested the commonality of vision between the United States and the Soviet Union, and ascertained scant Soviet interest in selective and competitive forms of détente that could damage the fundamental bipolar relationship with the United States.[43]

Its practical effects notwithstanding, Kissinger's approach toward European matters was paradigmatic of his strategic vision and the projects that stemmed from it. It was a bipolar vision both analytically and prescriptively. In this instance, bipolar analysis considered a relationship between the Soviet Union and Western Europe (or Germany) on equal terms as impossible. As a consequence, the development and intensification of such a relationship was believed to only benefit the Soviets. A bipolar prescription logically ensued: it was necessary to bloc or at least control the European initiative within the frames defined by Atlantic discipline.[44]

A similar bipolar dimension can be seen in a third example: the Vietnam War and the attempt of the Nixon administration to find an "honorable" exit. The course of the conflict had discredited the strategic justification behind U.S. intervention as well as the belief that the United States could tolerate the costs of the war (human, economic, and political) and emerge victorious. Crucially, Vietnam had contributed to the erosion of domestic consensus and the crisis of containment. The conflict also proved that the premise of American intervention in Indochina was without foundation. No regional domino would be triggered by a Communist victory. Over the years, the conflict catalyzed regional tensions between North Vietnam and China and fueled a competition between the two Communist giants, China and the Soviet Union. At the same time, a war that the United States had entered to reassert the credibility of its global anti-Communist commitment had the effect of drastically undermining such credibility, showing American fragility and inducing many European allies to question Washington's commitment to their defense.[45]

After 1968 it would have been unlikely for any administration to do anything but disengage from Vietnam. The belief that Nixon would end the war speedily and swiftly was one of the reasons for his electoral success. It proved to be a mistaken assumption. There was a gradual U.S. de-escalation, with American troops eventually brought home, and the number of casualties diminishing significantly as a result, but the war continued for four more years, devastating Vietnam in the process. The United

States promoted a "Vietnamization" of the conflict by training and support-
ing South Vietnamese armed forces with the intention of transferring most
of the burdens and responsibilities of the conflict to them. Vietnamization
was complemented by massive air raids on North Vietnam. Frequently, the
goal of such bombing was political rather than military: it aimed to make
Hanoi more flexible at the negotiating table and convince it to accept a final
settlement. Even more significantly, Nixon and Kissinger decided, against
the opinion of some advisors, to expand the conflict into neighboring states.
The president and his national security advisor approved the bombing of
North Vietnamese sanctuaries in Cambodia and Laos (formally neutral
countries) and the successive invasion of the two countries.[46]

Why did Kissinger and Nixon choose to prolong the war despite con-
ceding it could not be won? Once again, the answer can be found in bipolar
constructs and the obsession for credibility that they fed. Despite their acknowledgment of the marginal strategic value of Vietnam and, moreover,
the impossibility of reversing the course of the war, Nixon and Kissinger
tried to achieve "peace with honor" and use it politically with regard to
friends and enemies alike. Kissinger's fundamental objective was to make
sure there would be a "decent interval" between the final U.S. withdrawal
and reunification of Vietnam under Communist rule. The prolongation
of the war, the never-ending negotiating sessions with North Vietnamese
representatives in Paris, and the recurrent aerial bombings were meant to
secure this objective. Adopting a position that was anything but realist,
Kissinger argued that by intervening in the first place, the United States
had "created" an interest where one did not exist: military intervention
and U.S. casualties had "settled the issue of whether the outcome" of the
conflict was "important" for America and for those who "depended on
the United States." Kissinger admitted that the true relevance of Vietnam
might have been exaggerated and that the war was "draining" American
"national strength." In spite of everything, "the confidence in American
promises" remained, however, at stake in Vietnam.[47]

This emphasis on credibility revealed once more the bipolar prism
through which Kissinger observed (and misinterpreted) the international
scene. On the one hand, it made it impossible to deal with the specific
Vietnamese imbroglio without transforming it into a symbol of the more
general state of the bipolar relationship. On the other, the fixation with
credibility allowed Vietnam to hold several relevant issues hostage through

an inverted form of linkage. Nixon threatened to cancel the first summit with the Soviet Union after a North Vietnamese military offensive: "an honorable conclusion to the Vietnam conflict," the president argued, "far exceed[ed] the importance of the Soviet summit." Similarly, this bipolar perspective overestimated the limited ability of the Soviet Union to influence North Vietnamese choices and actions. Moreover, the Sino-Soviet rift had increased Hanoi's room for maneuver, allowing it to play one Communist power against the other, as it did aptly and with some success.[48]

Vietnam was important not in itself, but for what it symbolized from a bipolar perspective, where commitments (namely, "created" interests) had to be honored. A "peace with honor" and a (far from) "decent" interval were finally achieved when the United States, North Vietnam, and the provisional revolutionary government of the South signed an agreement in January 1973. It is debated (and debatable) whether four additional years of war somehow influenced the behavior of the USSR or strengthened the international credibility of the United States. At the time, however, the domestic impact of the end of the war and the effect on the consensus-building efforts of the administration appeared certain.[49]

Building and Articulating a New Domestic Consensus: The Discourse of Détente

The end of U.S. military intervention and the attainment of "peace" in Vietnam—cosmetic and fictitious as it was—could only be welcomed in the United States. The agreement was especially greeted because it provided for the release of U.S. prisoners of war still languishing in North Vietnamese jails, a sensitive issue that would be exploited politically in the years to come.[50] A renewed domestic consensus, albeit a temporary one, extended to Kissinger's entire grand design and the administration's second sensational accomplishment after the opening to China: the 1972 SALT I agreement with the Soviet Union.

With SALT I the two superpowers consensually defined the numbers and rules of the arms race for the first time. The treaty was divided into two parts: an interim five-year agreement on land- and submarine-based offensive nuclear weapons (intercontinental ballistic missiles, or ICBMs;

and submarine-launched ballistic missiles, SLBMs) and an agreement on anti–ballistic missile defense systems (the ABM treaty). With the ABM treaty, each superpower agreed to deploy only two (soon to be reduced to one) limited, ground-based defensive systems. The United States and the Soviet Union both renounced nationwide defense systems against strategic ballistic missiles in recognition of their implicit offensive value and the subsequent risk of instigating a new arms race. The interim treaty afforded the Soviet Union superiority in the numbers of long-range missiles: 1,618 ICBMs to 1,054 and 740 SLBMs to 656. This numerical advantage, however, was more than overcome by U.S. technological superiority, which was symbolized by MIRV technology (or multiple independently targetable reentry vehicle, allowing each ICBM to carry multiple nuclear warheads), American dominance in nuclear bombers, and a widespread network of forward bases.[51]

SALT I rapidly became the object of bitter domestic controversy, which would erode the laboriously built consensus around détente. Yet, when it was signed, the treaty appeared as the seal of approval for Nixon and Kissinger's bipolar strategy of détente. The fundamental objectives of that strategy—stabilize the bipolar order, legitimize it through Soviet acceptance, and reduce the burden on the United States—had seemingly been attained. The 1972 agreement, Nixon would stress in his memoirs, dramatically increased Soviet "stake…in international stability and the *status quo.*" The United States and Soviet Union were drawn together through explicit recognition of the inescapable strategic interdependence between the two countries. The agreements, Kissinger maintained, had been stimulated by "a certain commonality of outlook, a sort of interdependence for survival between the two" superpowers.[52]

The way in which SALT I was presented and sold to the U.S. public represented one of the most important elements of Kissinger's strategy of domestic consensus (re)building. Only twenty years earlier the possibilities open to the United States were ostensibly unlimited, with just a few opponents of containment, mainly on the Republican Right, questioning America's ability to sustain the growing costs of the Cold War. Military Keynesianism, embraced by the Kennedy and Johnson administrations in particular, had been endorsed by a vast majority of Americans. It had been considered affordable, necessary, and capable of equally distributing the benefits of high public expenditure and federal orders (as well as the jobs deriving from them) in various areas of the country, including the poorest and least developed.[53]

Once the confidence and illusions of the age of consensus began to crumble, however, a new request to reduce military investments emerged. Suddenly it was more popular to appeal for the reduction of defense expenditure than to ask for an increase. The advocates of costly military programs, such as Democratic senators Henry Jackson (Washington state) and Stuart Symington (Missouri), found themselves on the defensive for the first time. Programs like missile defense were questioned, drastically rethought, and sometimes abandoned. The Senate discussed various proposals, such as that of Mike Mansfield (Montana), which called for a reduction in U.S. military commitments and troop deployments overseas. As emphasized by historian Keith Nelson, the hostility of Congress to "military activism" was reminiscent of the famous congressional investigations during the 1930s into the arms industry.[54]

According to Kissinger, these positions were "symptomatic of the bitter and destructive mood of the period and of the substantial breakdown of national consensus," of a "national malaise" that found its quintessential manifestation in the Mansfield Amendment. "The defense budget," Kissinger claimed, had become "the focal point of antiwar pressures, not of thoughtful analysis." This pervasive antimilitary atmosphere could not be discounted, however, when planning a foreign policy strategy whose task was also to fortify the domestic front and that needed the support of a more assertive and undisciplined Congress. The Nixon administration's commitment to reducing military expenditures without sacrificing the security of the country was constantly reaffirmed by the president and his advisors. Some results were indeed achieved. Between 1969 and 1975, defense investments as a percentage of GNP dropped from 8.7 percent to 5.5 percent. Indexed to inflation, the reduction was around 4.5 percent per year in the period 1970–75, although one must obviously also consider the impact of the end of the Vietnam War. Negotiations with the Soviet Union co-opted the United States' adversary to help manage a bipolar system and accept its legitimacy. These agreements, however, were also meant to encourage domestic backing for U.S. foreign policy by simultaneously containing the pressures of those who urged that the United States renounce world leadership and those who advocated renewed global competition with the Soviet Union. "One of the most serious things" the Nixon administration had to face, Kissinger maintained in late 1971, was "the loss of moral support from the American Establishment." On foreign affairs there was "the absence of a feeling...that the nation [was] a unified and functioning entity." "The reintegration of American society" was thus the main challenge for the administration. In order to confront the challenge, it was necessary to define a "new direction in foreign policy—a direction desirable without regard to party affiliation...which would contribute not only to the likelihood of international peace, but also to the unity of the American nation."[55]

By committing themselves to reducing defense spending, Nixon and Kissinger proved receptive to pressure from both Congress and the public. During this phase of crisis and alleged decline, the request to adopt a less ambitious and costly foreign policy was politically popular and difficult to resist. In 1968, 86 percent of Americans favored the preservation of a mighty military apparatus; four years later the number had diminished to just 61 percent. According to polls, in 1964 the main concerns of Americans were the Cold War and the threat of Communism, whereas by 1972 their concerns had shifted to the cost of living, urban crime, and drugs. These new priorities inevitably influenced foreign policy and the discourse through which it was conveyed to the public. The shift reflected a more general transformation that seemed to render Cold War liberal ideology, with its optimistic take on the cost and scope of modernizing interventionism, as impracticable and obsolete. Moreover, confronting the crisis of the Cold War consensus allowed Kissinger to revive, update, and adapt the topoi and slogans that had distinguished his intellectual work.[56]

Above all, the shift from a "discourse of possibilities" to a "discourse of limits" was particularly Kissingerian in that his scholarly works often underlined the realist notion of the limits statesmen must face and overcome. Such emphasis on limits returned even more powerfully during the Nixon years. "When this Administration came to power at the beginning of 1969," Kissinger argued in 1971,

> we found ourselves in a period with the foreign policy capital of the post-war era virtually exhausted. That era was one in which the United States was the sole nation of the non-Communist world with power sufficient to run foreign affairs....During that era, throughout the non-Communist world questions of security and progress depended on answers from the United

States. It came to be the view of the other nations that their security and progress was of more interest to the United States than it was to them themselves. As a reflection of that, foreign affairs for them came to be little more than lobbying efforts in the United States for action by our government. This situation, of course, simply could not last.

Although "the first two decades after the end of the Second World War posed problems well suited to the American approach to international relations," from the mid-1960s the situation began to change and became more complex. The United States' "undisputed strategic predominance," Kissinger claimed, "was declining just at a time when there was rising domestic resistance to military programs, and impatience for redistribution of resources from national defense to social demands." The United States was "no longer in a position to operate programs globally" and "could no longer impose its preferred solution"; it could not offer "remedies" but rather only "contribute to a structure that will foster the initiative of others." The time had come to finally "think in terms of power and equilibrium": "a clearer understanding of America's interests and of the requirements of equilibrium" could "give perspective" to American idealism. This change in the contents and form of United States foreign policy became all the more necessary with the erosion of presidential power, which reached its peak with Watergate and determined, according to Kissinger, "a nightmarish collapse of presidential authority at home and a desperate struggle to keep foreign adversaries from transforming it into an assault on our nation's security and that of other free peoples."[57]

Statesmen—especially the heroic statesmen celebrated by Kissinger—are always obliged to operate within limits and try, when possible, to transcend them. This element represented the second component of détente's strategic discourse: the necessity for statesmen to act swiftly and resolutely in difficult times, freeing themselves from the inhibitory effect, both conceptually and operatively, imposed by the respect of strict bureaucratic procedures. Once in power, Kissinger worked actively to centralize the decision-making process in the hands of the president, subtracting authority from traditional bureaucracies like the State Department. Intellectual conviction, political convenience, and contingent necessity converged in determining and justifying a concentration of power that had few precedents in U.S. history.[58]

On occasion Kissinger complacently justified this concentration of power, which contributed to his fame and popularity, particularly after 1973. "While intelligent, competent, loyal, and hardworking," State Department experts, according to Kissinger, operate in the "conviction that a lifetime of service and study has given them insights that transcend the untrained and shallow-rooted views of political appointees." Locked in routine, impermeable to change, and unable to analyze problems in a sophisticated, conceptual, and unconventional way, bureaucrats, Kissinger argued, almost inevitably preferred habit to anomaly, certainty to risk. Statesmen must instead be willing to take risks during periods of crisis and transformation. Such a problem was compounded by the education, often juridical, of the American politicians leading the diplomatic corp. According to Kissinger, the approach of Nixon's first secretary of state, William Pierce Rogers, was eminently "tactical"; as a lawyer he was trained to deal with issues as they arose "on their merits." In contrast, Kissinger's own approach was defined as "strategic and geopolitical; I attempted to relate events to each other, to create incentives or pressures on one part of the world to influence events in another. . . . I wanted to accumulate nuances for a long-range strategy." Despite his ability, Rogers came to be viewed by Kissinger as "an insensitive neophyte who threatened the careful design of our foreign policy."[59]

Influenced by Weber, Kissinger-the-scholar had on several occasions compared the charismatic, visionary leader with the conformist, obtuse bureaucrat. Out of necessity and desire, Kissinger-the-statesman applied this conviction in a titanic effort to control all the threads of his complex strategic design: it was Kissinger who de facto conducted the SALT negotiations, keeping experts and members of the U.S. delegation in the dark; it was Kissinger who assumed responsibility for managing the opening to China by sidelining the Department of State; it was Kissinger who participated in seemingly never-ending peace talks with North Vietnamese representatives in Paris; and finally, it was Kissinger who undertook a series of exhausting trips in the Middle East (so-called shuttle diplomacy) and managed a complex diplomatic process that would produce a significant alteration of the regional geopolitical order.[60]

Initially this centralization of power was hidden and covered up, but from a certain moment on it was deliberately publicized. In a process that combined Kissinger's unlimited ambition and the conviction that it was necessary to generate greater domestic consensus for U.S. foreign policy, the concentration of power in Kissinger's hands became the object of growing—and often hagiographic—media attention. The secret trip to Beijing and negotiations in Paris placed Kissinger in the spotlight and propelled him to celebrity status. Between 1971 and 1972, the front cover of several magazines and newspapers celebrated Kissinger's feats: *Life* presented him as "the most important n. 2 man in history"; *Newsweek* and the *New York Times* referred to him as Nixon's "Secret Agent"; for *U.S. News and World Report,* "Kissinger's secret mission to Red China" had "few parallels in the annuals of U.S. diplomacy." In spite of Nixon's initial worries and the influence of the pro-Taiwan lobby, the opening to China was well received by a majority of Americans, reviving an old fascination with the exotic world of China and its chimerical market, which had a long tradition in U.S. history. Kissinger's popularity reached new heights in the following years, concomitant with Watergate and the consequent weakened position of Nixon and the presidential office itself. Various Gallup polls revealed that Kissinger was one of the most admired Americans, if not the most. The press, whose members Kissinger cajoled and flattered incessantly, celebrated the achievements of détente and the merits of Nixon's national security advisor on several occasions. Kissinger's diplomatic successes were compared to those of the great statesmen of the past. The equilibrium produced by Kissinger's triangular diplomacy, journalist Joseph Kraft maintained, represented "a diplomatic accomplishment comparable in magnitude to the feats of Castlereagh and Metternich." Journalist (and former CIA covert operator) Tom Braden proclaimed "this little round man with a German accent" an "American hero," capable of rejecting "ideology in favor of ideas, dogma in favor of deed, the inevitable in favor of the inventive."[61]

Kissinger's realpolitik, and its alleged European matrix, was a crucial contribution to the popularity of Kissinger and détente. It was widely believed at the time that the crisis the United States was facing had also been caused by the country's inability to operate within the international system: by an inclination to promote a foreign policy shaped by naïve and liberal progressive tendencies, and the consequent American ignorance of the laws, given and imperishable, governing relations among states. These were all aspects that Kissinger-the-scholar had underlined with gusto and that Kissinger-the-statesman could only deplore and condemn. The willingness of Americans to promote a proactive foreign policy and "to sustain a long drawn-out contest" had always been connected, Kissinger argued, to a tendency to transform policy into a "moral crusade." The United States "possessed neither the conceptual nor the historical framework" for "cold-blooded" policies. The "many different strands that make up American thinking on foreign policy" had "proved inhospitable to an approach based on the calculation of the national interest and relationships of power." The time had come, however, to "face the stark reality" and "learn to conduct foreign policy as other nations had to conduct it for so many centuries—without escape and without respite."[62]

A realist patina thus enveloped the discourse of détente and contributed to its initial popularity. The task of the Nixon administration, Kissinger would later reckon, was "to educate the American people in the requirements of the balance of power." Americans had to stop believing that "tensions and enmity in international relations" were "anomalies" and that "relations between states" were "either friendly or hostile, both defined in absolute terms." The statesman was not only to be visionary and bold in his analysis as well as action, but also pedagogical in his role as educator of a volatile and inflammable public opinion.[63]

To perform this duty as the nation's mentor and guide, Kissinger resorted to two elements that had informed most of his scholarly work: the critique of liberal universalism and the reaffirmation of stability and equilibrium as the main objectives of diplomacy. Ironically, détente with the Soviet Union, the opening to China, and the exit from Vietnam had been supported by important liberal and Democrat politicians and intellectuals. Political adversaries such as William Fulbright, Ted Kennedy, and Mike Mansfield had often endorsed Kissinger's foreign policy; their justifications, however, differed radically from those of Nixon's national security advisor. Democrats and those on the moderate Left considered the late 1960s and early 1970s as a transition period toward a more interdependent world based on (and regulated by) the primacy of international law and an expanding web of political, economic, and cultural exchanges and interactions. Yet Kissinger conceived (and described) it as a new phase in an old script: the international system remained anarchical; the basic units were still the nation states; relationships had to be disciplined even though they remained fundamentally competitive and antagonistic. Détente thus represented "a means to regulate a competitive relationship" and not a way to end the competition.[64] Economic exchanges with the Soviet Union were not meant, as liberals urged, to create a commonality of interests and consolidate an interdependence that would eventually overcome the rivalry and possibly end the Cold War. They were, on the contrary, an additional lever with which Washington was able to influence and condition Soviet choices. Similarly, the opening to China was presented as part of Kissinger's geopolitical design. As such, it was not the prelude to a new relationship that would, in the long term, end Chinese seclusion, render its markets more penetrable, and contribute to its cultural and political transformation.

Just as it could not be overcome through dialogue and integration, the rivalry with Moscow would not end through confrontation and a renewed Cold War as proposed by the Republican Right and, increasingly, some representatives of the Democratic Party soon to be labeled neoconservatives. Kissinger's, in other words, was a vision that rejected the different variants of the homologating and optimistic finalism, which had represented one of the distinctive marks of Cold War liberalism. The competition with the Soviet Union was not destined to terminate, nor could it be won, because it was not the responsibility of the United States to topple or transform the Soviet regime. The domestic sphere had to be separated from the external one, and the United States had to learn to deal with the foreign policy of a country without regard to its domestic features (an axiom Kissinger often applied to justify alliances with, and support of, authoritarian and unsavory regimes). The objective was to assure the stability of the international system and the preservation of the bipolar equilibrium, which was considered the best way to defend and promote the U.S. national interest. Power remained "the ultimate arbiter." "The United States," Kissinger claimed, had to "be true to its own beliefs, or it will lose its bearing in the world. But at the same time it" had to "survive in a world of sovereign nations and competing wills." "A mature sense of means" was needed lest the United States "substitute wishful thinking for the requirements of survival." "Painful experience should" in fact "have taught" America that it "ought not exaggerate" its "capacity to foresee, let alone to shape, social and political change in other societies."[65]

America's duty was to consolidate stability and equilibrium. To achieve this goal it was necessary to recognize and accept national differences as well their influence on the way a state defined national interest and conducted its foreign policy. Global crusades in the name of democracy and freedom were not Washington's responsibility. On the contrary, it was only possible to consensually regulate bipolarism by working hand in hand with the Soviet Union, or even building strategic alliances with another Communist state that was ideologically more radical and doctrinaire than the USSR itself, such as Mao and Chou En-lai's China. The promotion of the national interest, rather than the unfeasible projects of transforming the global order as invoked by liberal Cold Warriors, defined the moral value of foreign policy.

This realist and amoral discourse distinguished Kissinger's narrative of détente and represented the real and radical rupture of the Nixon era. Only few years earlier it had been common to issue calls to arms in the name of freedom and U.S. values, to proclaim unquestioned moral superiority, and to ask Americans to sacrifice for the triumph of Good. Such Manichean and binary rhetoric dominated not only U.S. public discourse but also the way the way in which competition with Moscow was conceived and waged in governmental circles. The crisis of the liberal Cold War consensus also manifested in this rhetorical shift. In the era of détente it became more common to speak of "stability" and "equilibrium" than "liberty" and "democracy." Kissinger never used the notion of totalitarianism, except in the second volume of his memoirs, which was published in 1982 and came out in the midst of the Reagan era.[66]

Kissinger, the "American Metternich," as he was named by the adulatory American press, seemed the most qualified figure to lead America into a new phase of history. He was to teach the United States to adopt and implement the European laws of international relations and power politics, and to educate the public about the reasons for accepting the costs and compromises necessary to defend the national interest. For a few years this message proved immensely successful, transforming Kissinger into a star and contributing to Nixon's electoral triumph in 1972. But what appeared the main assets of Kissinger's new foreign policy grand narrative and effort to reconstruct domestic consensus—his realism, Europeanness, amorality—were instruments that his opponents rapidly turned against him, and used to attack détente and to relaunch certain topoi, albeit modified, of the early Cold War. The main protagonists of this attack were a group of liberal Democrats destined to be known as neoconservatives.

4

The Domestic Critique of Kissinger

The influence of neoconservative intellectuals and advisors on the foreign policy of George W. Bush has, throughout the first years of the new millennium, stimulated renewed attention for neoconservatism: for its origins, its cultural and philosophical foundations, and its evolution. Many scholars and commentators have stressed the radical nature of neoconservatism, particularly the Trotskyist past of Irving Kristol and other fathers of the movement, or the influence of Leo Strauss on some important neocons like former undersecretary of defense and World Bank president Paul Wolfowitz. Some scholars have underlined the connections between neoconservatism and the religious Right, whereas others, more correctly, have emphasized the liberal, and in some instances, libertarian, matrix of neoconservatism. A great majority of these studies, however, have exaggerated the political and cultural homogeneity of the neoconservative movement and, as a consequence, the coherence of its projects and proposals.[1]

The Genesis of Neoconservatism

These studies have generally paid little attention to the crises the United States experienced during the 1960s and 1970s, and to the importance of the period in catalyzing political and cultural reactions that gave birth to neoconservatism. The crumbling domestic consensus, the questioning of liberal Cold War universalism, and the crisis of containment were some of the reasons behind a profound political and cultural realignment in the United States. Of this realignment, neoconservatives were one of the main protagonists and beneficiaries.[2]

Neoconservatism was a response to the crisis of the principles inspiring U.S. foreign policy during the first two decades of the Cold War. It was a reaction to the contestation of the liberal and reformist centrism that had provided the cognitive compass to read the international system and the tools, both analytic and prescriptive, for navigating the turbulent waters of world politics. The crisis of containment was first and foremost a crisis of the certainties and optimism that had marked Cold War liberalism. It was the collapse of a binary vision of the international order, which seemed to offer simple and coherent answers—both morally and strategically—to the challenges the United States had to face. Democracy, freedom, modernization, anti-Communism were just some of the basic terms and formulas of Cold War discourse that had been hegemonic in the United States, particularly among liberal democrats. During the 1960s such terms were increasingly questioned, domestically and internationally. Self-evident Cold War truths were suddenly open to discussion. Previously unquestionable codes were attacked and explicitly derided. Some of the taboos of U.S. foreign policy discourse and ideology were challenged and often shattered. The political and historiographical revisionism of the New Left, for instance, contested one of the most basilar axioms of the post–World War II consensus: the idea that the United States was a country committed to justice, peace, and order, and therefore that it represented a force for good in the international system.[3]

The New Left constituted a heterogeneous and composite movement, as well as a minority one. Its political and intellectual sources of inspiration were multiple and not always complementary. Its political outcomes were diverse in terms of contents, proposals, and, more so, analytical depth. In time, its ability to exert relevant political influence on the broader American Left would reveal itself to be mostly transitory and contingent.[4]

Nevertheless, the impact of this revisionist challenge and the reaction it provoked within the Democratic Party must not be underestimated. Variegated and politically weak, the New Left actually appeared united to its opponents through powerful as well as detestable common denominators: unacceptable cultural relativism; a refusal of the basic principles of U.S. liberalism; and a rejection of the foundations of U.S. foreign policy and belief that it was essential to promote a global containment of Communism.[5] Far from casually, neoconservatism originated from within the Democratic Party as a reaction to the New Left. It was an attempt to promote the "conservation of liberalism" and a conviction that the "raw material" of liberalism, "the fraternal desires for freedom and equality," was "intrinsically expansionist in character." This effort was stimulated by a willingness to reaffirm values and principles that were now disputed and to defend foreign policy choices made by the United States in the previous two decades.[6]

Initially, the (soon to be called) neoconservatives tried to relaunch a form of internationalism modeled on the liberal and Democratic centrism of the early Cold War. One of the core texts of that era, Arthur Schlesinger's *Vital Center,* was exhumed and proposed as an analytic and prescriptive model for disillusioned Democrats. As historian John Ehrman has shown, the main political and intellectual fathers of the neoconservative movement— Irving Kristol, Norman Podhoretz, Daniel Patrick Moynihan, and Nathan Glazer—were all "veterans of the vital center." They were, in other words, intellectuals whose views were formed in the context of a bitter, fraternal conflict within the Democratic Party and trade union movement in the early Cold War years, which ended with defeat for those on the Left who believed it still possible to cooperate with the Soviet Union.[7]

At first, the future neocons responded to the crisis of containment as if it represented an updated replica of the early Cold War. For them, the debate of the late 1960s/early 1970s soon became a new call to arms for the Democratic Party to defend its anti-Communist and classical liberal identity. Its initial political gurus were Senator Henry Jackson (D-Washington) and Daniel Patrick Moynihan, the Harvard and MIT professor appointed counselor for urban affairs by Nixon, who later became U.S. ambassador to the United Nations (1975–76) and a Democratic senator from New York (1977–2001). Jackson and Moynihan were quintessential representations of

U.S. Cold War liberalism and of an interventionist, anti-Communist, and optimistic nationalism, which justified high military investment and had been endorsed by American trade unions (AFL-CIO).[8]

Nevertheless, the domestic and international conditions necessary to relaunch the discourse and policies of the early Cold War were largely absent. Moreover, Democrats now lacked the unity and cohesion of the Truman years. The various factors that provoked a crisis of containment also exasperated divisions within the Democratic Party. The first, and most obvious, fracture was political and generational; although a political minority, young New Leftists primarily challenged the Democratic Party and what they saw as a huge hiatus between rhetoric and policy, particularly on international matters. Furthermore, the New Left repudiated some of the basic axioms of Cold War liberalism, which now appeared as a simple mask for an imperialist design that Vietnam had finally exposed. According to historian William Appleman Williams, one of the icons of the New Left, the Vietnam War represented the "disaster" and "tragedy" necessary to "change the tragic course of American diplomacy." The most important leader of the civil rights movement, the Reverend Dr. Martin Luther King Jr., urged a "declaration of independence" from the war in Vietnam and denounced the incompatibility of foreign interventions, high military expenditures, and necessary domestic reforms, whose inner interdependence had instead represented one of the bedrocks of containment and the Cold War consensus. "I was increasingly compelled to see the war as an enemy of the poor and to attack it as such," King said. According to the *Berkeley Barb,* an antiwar magazine founded in 1965, the Vietnam War was "beyond brutality": it was "obscenity." In those years, a New Left militant proclaimed, "I learned to despise my countrymen, my government, and the entire English speaking government, with its history of genocide and conquest." During the second half of the 1960s a vast antiwar movement began to take form in the United States. It was a heterogeneous and composite movement that drew various elements of the New Left and proved capable of promoting large demonstrations throughout the United States.[9]

The upheaval provoked different reactions from the liberal and Democratic establishment and intelligentsia. Some senior leaders acknowledged the requests of protesters in part, attempted to moderate the demands, and offered the protesters a voice and political representation. This approach, from different political and cultural perspectives, was tried by Democrats such as Eugene McCarthy, Frank Church, William Fulbright, George McGovern, Ted Kennedy, and before his assassination, his brother Robert. Important liberal intellectuals, including Arthur Schlesinger Jr., admitted that early Cold War formulas had become obsolete and stressed the need to adapt American liberalism to the challenges of the time. Accordingly, containment had to be modified, the tragic war in Vietnam terminated, and a real engagement with the Soviet Union attempted.

There were, however, liberals who did not retreat or believe it necessary to alter the course of U.S. foreign policy. For Jackson, Moynihan, and intellectuals such as Podhoretz, Laqueur, and Kristol, the Cold War had not ended, the Soviet monster had not disappeared (rather, militarily it was mightier), and Moscow had not renounced expansionist ambitions or accepted peaceful coexistence with the West. The moral and strategic rationales that had inspired the initial application of containment remained therefore valid. As conservative journalist James Burnham claimed, "an imperial power" was "not allowed to resign." Henry Jackson maintained that "a great power inescapably" bore "the responsibility of great power": some people in the United States, Jackson argued, were "suffering from a case of combat fatigue." The conflict with the Soviet Union was "not made to disappear," however, and the preservation of an advantageous "relationship of forces" vis-à-vis the Soviets was still needed.[10]

The magazine *Commentary,* edited by Norman Podhoretz, provided these liberals and future neocons with a megaphone amid the heated debate about foreign affairs (domestic and social matters were covered by the *Public Interest,* the other important neoconservative magazine). Initially, the neoconservatives' criticism targeted the New Left and the student movement in particular, against whom Podhoretz believed it was necessary to wage "total war." The New Left had to be attacked not just for its opposition to Vietnam (a war that was increasingly difficult to justify, and in 1971 Podhoretz himself called for a unilateral withdrawal of U.S. troops), but for the supposed antiliberalism and antipatriotism it nourished. New Left intellectuals were criticized, first and foremost, for their betrayal of the universal and timeless values of U.S. liberalism. For the neocons, the New Left was anti-American or, even worse, "un-American." It was an alien political, cultural, and moral phenomenon, which had been facilitated by the difficulties the country was undergoing, but now it contributed to the nurturance of such difficulties and further weakened the United States. Neocon political scientist and future U.S. ambassador to the United Nations (1981–84) Jeane Kirkpatrick claimed that the notion that the United States was a "decent and successful—though imperfect—society" was under attack. With his usual witty style, Irving Kristol asserted that American "young radicals" were "far less dismayed at America's failure to become what it ought to be than they [were] contemptuous of what it thinks it ought to be. For them, as for Oscar Wilde, it [was] not the average American who [was] disgusting; it [was] the ideal American." On several occasions, Henry Jackson attacked the "intolerant extremists who have come to despise America and who would destroy the Democratic Party if they took it over." Moynihan, who during his youth had worked as a shoe shiner and had gone "to the City College of New York on the subway," maintained that the young demonstrators were an "elite group," whose members shared an "ignorant, chiliastic, almost insolent self-confidence," while possessing "incredible powers of derision, destruction, and disdain."[11]

This alleged scorn for America, its values, and democratic practices was expressed through a "third-worldist" fascination, which frequently embraced exotic revolutionary forms and political and economic models outside rigid binary Cold War schemes. Such fascinations were not devoid of contradictions and, indeed, cohabited with the exceptionalist idea that a democratic America had been "lost" and betrayed by the unscrupulous internationalism of the Cold War liberals and the interventionist capitalism of giant corporations. As emphasized by sociologist Todd Gitlin, the New Left's "élan and language were utterly American" and "steeped in a most traditional American individualism."[12]

The third worldism of the New Left became the target of neoconservative polemics. It was the symptom of the alienation of the new generation from the American mainstream, but the neocons profiled and interpreted it—out of convenience as well as prejudice—as a betrayal of American principles and interests. The youths who paid tribute to Ho Chi Minh or Ché Guevara were considered emblematic of a more profound and widespread malaise, which had been seen its paradigmatic manifestation in the transformation of the United Nations, an institution long dominated by the United States, and that had embodied the spirit of the early Cold War liberalism.

With the birth of new states from the ashes of European empires during the 1950s and 1960s, the equilibria within the UN had changed drastically. Until then, the United States had exploited the UN General Assembly with considerable success by cajoling a majority of members to approve resolutions that the Soviet Union then regularly vetoed in the Security Council. On more than one occasion, therefore, the United Nations offered Washington a vehicle for gaining the support of world public opinion. This condition did not last because eventually the UN was transformed into a forum in which the United States found itself in the minority and, increasingly, the target of shifting third-world coalitions. On more than one occasion, U.S. allies assumed positions opposite to those supported by Washington (for instance, on the admission of the People's Republic of China to the UN or Portuguese imperialism) and enjoyed a freedom of maneuver that the United States simply lacked. This anti–United States, and sometimes anti-Western, predisposition of the majority of the General Assembly reached its zenith during the 1970s and was denounced forcefully by the neoconservatives.[13]

The most glaring example of the transformation in the United Nations was the approval of General Assembly Resolution 3379, which "determine[d] that Zionism" was "a form of racism and racial discrimination." The resolution, which was approved in November 1975 after heated discussion and various attempts by the United States to block it, had been supported and sponsored by some prominent dictators, including the Ugandan president Idi Amin. For many neoconservatives, who were strongly pro-Israel and considered that country an exemplary model of Western democracy, Resolution 3379 came to symbolize the moral bankruptcy of the United Nations and its fundamental inability to reform itself. Moynihan, who had just been appointed ambassador to the UN, scathingly denounced the resolution and the faulty third worldism that had contributed to its approval. In so doing, he resorted to words normally used against the cultural relativism of the New Left and that revealed the modern and liberal matrixes of neoconservative thought. "The damage we now do to the idea of human rights and the language of human rights could well be irreversible," Moynihan claimed;

> most of the world believes in newer methods of political thought, in philosophies that do not accept the individual as distinct from and prior to the State; in philosophies that therefore do not provide any justification for the idea of human rights and philosophies that have no words by which to explain their value. If we destroy the words that were given to us by past

centuries, we will not have words to replace them, for philosophy today has no such words. But there are those of us who have not forsaken these older works, still so new to much of the world. Not forsaken them now, not here, not anywhere, not ever.

A few months later, Moynihan would call the UN vote "a doubly ominous event" that suggested "a moral callousness in the West, or moral weakness." Moynihan maintained that

> Israel has become a metaphor for democracy in the world. If the Israeli democracy, which persists in the face of the uttermost peril and difficulty, can be discredited, then it can clearly be established that democracy is not a political and cultural system that can survive in a perilous and difficult world. The dustbin of history is for us.[14]

The reaction to the New Left at home made a crucial contribution to the genesis of neoconservatism. Other factors concurred to spur the rise and consolidation of the neoconservative movement. The parable of the divided and quarrelsome New Left was short-lived, although not ephemeral. The 1970s were characterized by the gradual ebb of the movement and by its progressive abandonment of the dream to promote a more participatory democracy. Nevertheless, neoconservatives did not find themselves devoid of enemies. Neoconservative political projects and slogans had been elaborated primarily in oppositional terms, in reaction to challenges put forward by others. This trait remained, and possibly was augmented, in the following years as neoconservative arrows fell upon liberal Democrat "renegades" and, more importantly, Kissinger's détente and its allegedly realist philosophy.

During the early 1970s the primary concern of the neocons was not just with the New Left as such, but with the influence that the political and cultural climate of the period was exercising on the Democratic Party and its internal equilibrium. According to neoconservatives, this influence was pernicious, defeatist, and manifested itself as deep pessimism in the capacity of the United States to face the rivalry with Moscow as well as passive acceptance of a gradual American decline. The Democratic Left was thus accused of betraying the liberal spirit of the party and turning to a morally repugnant and strategically irresponsible form of faint-hearted isolationism. Those accused, especially senators like Fulbright and Mansfield, had denounced the militarization of U.S. foreign policy during the Cold War and urged a consequent reduction in defense-related investment. Jackson and the trade unions strongly opposed these proposals. Fulbright's *j'accuse* against the "arrogance" of U.S. "power," which "tends to confuse itself with virtue" and "to take itself for omnipotence," was considered treacherous by the neoconservatives. The confidence of Democratic doves in opening a constructive dialogue with Moscow was denounced as naïve and perilous. The emphasis placed by many scholars and experts on the rising interdependence of the international system was considered by neocons as a pretext for justifying and accepting further limitations on U.S. autonomy and freedom of action.[15]

These political conflicts intersected and overlapped with other divisions that were lacerating the Democrats. Their most paradigmatic manifestations were intraparty quarrels on defense policy and the resources that had to be allocated to it. High military expenditures were no longer sustainable politically or economically. Nevertheless, Jackson and his allies were extremely reluctant to accept this state of affairs and, instead, continued to lobby for the military-Keynesian policies of the previous two decades. Political belief and the fear of Soviet strategic superiority combined with electoral convenience: Jackson represented the state of Washington, home to the Boeing Corporation and one of the main beneficiaries of federal largesse, thanks to the relentless lobbying of Jackson himself.

The clash between defense hawks and opponents of high military budgets became particularly acute in the late 1960s/early 1970s when immensely expensive anti–ballistic missile programs supported by Jackson were reduced in scope and cost by other influential Democrats. What was at stake for the likes of Fulbright, Ted Kennedy, and Al Gore Sr. was not just a specific defense program, but the general principle of civilian and democratic control over a military behemoth lacking adequate control and supervision, which had often benefited from congressional timidity and acquiescence. The issue was not the Soviet challenge, Fulbright argued, but whether the Senate "would be able to reassert some control over the military department." In the following years, the program was drastically curtailed (missile defense sites were reduced from twelve to two), which enraged Jackson and the neoconservatives, who denounced the duplicity of the administration, further embittering the atmosphere within the Democratic Party.[16]

The discussion on defense issues revealed how these different positions did not stem exclusively from strategic considerations—a trait that returns in the attack by Jackson and the neocons on Kissinger and the most important result of détente, the SALT agreements. To its supporters, an ambitious program of missile defense preserved and strengthened the strategic position of the United States. More important, however, missile defense reflected some original traits of U.S. Cold War liberalism, especially its nationalist and exceptionalist character. The claim that it was possible to defend against nuclear attack implied two interrelated possibilities: that, once again, an end to the Cold War could be brought about by the final collapse of the Soviet enemy; and that the United States could escape the bonds of strategic interdependence and reacquire its lost autonomy, sovereignty, and indeed, exceptionalism.

The missile defense system contained the seeds to the relaunch of a form of nationalist exceptionalism, based on the conviction that the United States was exempt from those laws of history that all other countries had to abide. This exceptionalism, which had deep roots in U.S. political culture, had been challenged and shattered by the crisis the United States was undergoing. Contrary to what Kissinger and Democratic doves—albeit in different ways—argued, neoconservatives believed that not only could the United States operate in the international system as it had since 1945, but that it was necessary, indeed vital, that it do so. For this reason, Henry Jackson argued during discussions on the anti–ballistic missile system, it was crucial to stop and reverse "the accelerating effort to eviscerate the defense position of this nation and of the West, regardless of the consequences to the safety of this nation and to the future of individual liberty."[17]

The struggle within the Democratic Party became particularly bitter during the 1972 presidential primaries. The candidacy of Henry Jackson was intended to prevent a party shift to the Left and to reaffirm the validity of Cold War liberalism. One of Jackson's advisors, the legal scholar and former undersecretary of state Eugene Rostow, urged the senator to season his speeches with "Old Testament fire, eloquence and passion, and some old-fashioned patriotism as well." "The Democrats," Rostow argued, would be "pleasantly surprised by the response … if you offer the American people nothing but blood, sweat, and tears." To prevent a "vote for Nixon next year," it was imperative to avoid "the party from being taken over by mush heads."[18]

It was indeed a "mush head," the senator from South Dakota, George McGovern, who obtained the nomination. McGovern benefited from a change in the rules governing the appointment of delegates at the Democratic convention and offered a pacifist platform distant from traditional Democrat centrism, which was harshly rejected by the electorate. The neoconservatives denounced the choice of McGovern. They claimed—not incorrectly—that Jackson's positions were more in tune with those of traditional Democratic constituencies (trade union members, blue collar workers, Catholic conservatives, and the South), whose support was still necessary to win the presidency. Jackson even popularized a brutal comment by Republican senator from Pennsylvania, Hugh Scott, accusing McGovern of being a triple A candidate: the candidate of "amnesty, acid, and abortion." Jeane Kirkpatrick attributed the defeat of McGovern to "an inability to establish identification with traditional cultural values." Sociologists Seymour Martin Lipset and Erlin Raab claimed that a majority of Americans wanted change but had perceived the candidacy of McGovern as a threat to "social order itself."[19]

In the months following the election, the neocons tried to establish an organizational structure by creating the Coalition for a Democratic Majority. The goal, one of the founders, writer Midge Decter, claimed, was to take advantage of the opportunity offered by McGovern's defeat to "recapture and revivify...the Democratic party and take control of it again, [and] take it back to the good old days of Harry S. Truman."[20]

This goal proved impossible to achieve. The profound domestic and international transformations of the previous two decades made unfeasible a simple return to the conceptual and prescriptive frames of the 1940s and '50s. The Democratic Party had changed and now included components far from the neoconservative line. Neocons seemed to share more with parts of the Republican and conservative world than with the Democrats. Neoconservatives would enthusiastically support Jackson's bid for the presidency in 1976, but they soon grew disillusioned with Carter and vainly tried to convince Moynihan to run for president in 1980. This date represented a fundamental watershed in the history of the neoconservative movement since its most important exponents decided to leave the Democratic Party and support the candidacy of former California governor Ronald Reagan, who emerged as the figurehead of a new Republican Right with which the neocons had established an intense dialogue in previous years. The base of this dialogue was a common aversion to the strategy of détente and its main architect and supporter in the United States, Henry Kissinger.

The Neoconservative Critique of Détente:
The Strategic Dimension

Détente was based on a basic premise: the recognition of strategic interdependence and the elementary commonality of interests it imposed on both Moscow and Washington. The almost 4,000 pages of Kissinger's memoirs constantly refer to this aspect. According to Kissinger, nuclear arms had determined a radical "transformation in the nature of power" and had "destroyed" the "traditional measure" according to which "every addition of power was—at least theoretically—politically useful." "The paradox of contemporary military strength" was "that a momentous increase in the element of power" had "eroded the traditional relationship of power to policy." Statesmen and scholars should take cognizance of the fact that "the evolution of nuclear strategy had been in the direction of the dead end produced by the widening gap between the destructiveness of nuclear arsenals and any political purpose to which they might be put."[21]

This stark reality, Kissinger affirmed, demanded the opening of serious negotiations with the Soviets. Strategic interdependence had to be institutionalized and disciplined through the reciprocal recognition of a set of rules (and numbers) agreed upon by the two superpowers. This reciprocity implied acceptance of quasi-nuclear parity with Moscow and acknowledgment that U.S. vulnerability had become a permanent and inexorable condition of life. It was one of the major paradoxes of deterrence and the atomic age: to achieve security, the two superpowers agreed to put their safety in the hands of another subject, and not just those of a simple other but rather those of the absolute Cold War enemy against whom such immense destructive potential had been created in the first place.[22]

The neoconservatives would never accept this paradox. In their inflexible refusal of the logic behind deterrence it is easy to see a strong ideological component, which combined exceptionalist nationalism (the rejection of the very "normalization" of America that nuclear arms imposed) and anti-Communism (the unacceptability of the idea that U.S. survival depended on Soviet action). "The first priority of American policy," Jackson argued in 1968, was "to maintain a greater nuclear power and strength than the Soviet Union"; in an "uncertain and dangerous world...strategic parity with the Soviet adversary" was simply "not good enough." "The survival" of the United States and its "allies," Jackson maintained, depended "not on a parity of nuclear power but on a margin of advantage in nuclear power for the peace-keepers over the peace-upsetters." U.S. policy should therefore "create and maintain a relationship of nuclear forces favorable to deterrence of adventurism and aggression." "To believe otherwise" required "one [to] place his faith in nothing more tangible than a dream of Soviet self-restraint."[23]

This quintessentially Cold War ideology had to be embellished with at least some strategic rationale. Initially this embellishment was done through support for expensive missile defense programs. These programs, however, were drastically reduced in light of the opposition of many Democratic senators and, moreover, the signing of the ABM treaty in May 1972. Subsequently, the fight against SALT and the idea that it was possible and wise to negotiate with Moscow became one of the distinct causes embraced by neoconservatives. In addition, the fight offered Cold War liberals a bridge across the aisle to the new Republican Right, which had found its champion in Ronald Reagan.

The 1972 interim agreement on offensive missiles granted the Soviet Union a significant quantitative advantage (1,618 versus 1,054 in ICBMs; 740 versus 656 in SLBMs). Yet this superiority was matched by a plurality of other factors, the most important of which was an undisputed U.S. technological superiority: a gap that the USSR would never be able to fill. The SALT treaty had been hastily negotiated by Kissinger, who was anxious to strike an agreement that could be politically and electorally useful for Nixon and himself. This haste induced Kissinger to overlook some provisions of the treaty that were clearly disadvantageous to the United States. In particular, he had paid insufficient attention to the possibility that the Soviets could rapidly develop the MIRV technology and thus greatly expand their offensive potential. In addition, Nixon and Kissinger underestimated the willingness of U.S. legislators to limit the administration's freedom of maneuver with regard to modernization of the U.S. defensive panoply. Nevertheless, "given trends in strategic weapons development over the previous decade," historian John Gaddis has convincingly argued, "SALT I was clearly to the advantage of the United States."[24]

Aside from partially offsetting other asymmetries in Washington's favor, the numerical superiority the interim treaty gave to Moscow actually reflected the impossibility of comparing arsenals that were diverse in terms of composition, numbers, and technological sophistication. For this reason, speaking of "strategic equivalence" or "equal aggregates" made little or no sense, at least in strictly military terms. This interpretation was all the more accurate when one considers that in terms of aggregate nuclear power (i.e., atomic warheads), U.S. superiority remained beyond doubt in 1972. Furthermore, this superiority was complemented by the U.S. system of forward bases in Europe and Asia, and by long-range bombers equipped with nuclear weapons.

Politically, however, it could prove advantageous to claim that the SALT agreements had weakened the United States and thus had to be amended. The assumption of a different stance would be immensely unpopular because no "responsible official or U.S. senator" could indeed "commit to negotiating something that would make the United States 'inferior.'"[25]

This position was the one held by Jackson and the neoconservatives. Jackson reaffirmed his disagreement with any limiting of ABM systems such as the one negotiated by Kissinger. The United States, Jackson maintained, had a technological edge that it should make use of to improve its anti–ballistic missile defense and reduce the first-strike capability of the Soviets. Jackson claimed that a Soviet surprise attack would destroy 90 percent of U.S. ICBMs or even "the entire land-based deterrent force, missiles and bombers" (a pessimistic and unrealistic estimate that would nevertheless leave the United States with significant retaliatory potential). Moreover, Jackson attacked the quantitative asymmetry that the interim agreement provided, which favored the Soviet Union and its arsenal of large land-based, long-range missiles. During Senate discussions, Jackson succeeded in tacking an amendment onto the treaty—the Jackson Amendment—that urged the president to seek an agreement in the next round of negotiations and that "*inter alia,* would not limit the United States to levels of intercontinental strategic forces inferior to the limits provided for the Soviet Union."[26]

Despite the opposition of many Democratic senators, the Jackson Amendment was approved by a large majority (56 to 35). The amendment embodied the idea that the two powers had to have quantitative "equal aggregates" in nuclear forces. It was a popular idea thanks to the "appeal of its simplicity," although for Kissinger it was "both strategically and politically illiterate."[27] Nixon and Kissinger finally accepted the Jackson Amendment, believing that it would put an end to the SALT controversy. Kissinger thought that Congress would sustain further military programs and that the basic assumptions of his nuclear diplomacy—the acceptance of deterrence and strategic interdependence—had finally been recognized and internalized by the public as well as the political world.

Both predictions proved unfounded. Various defense projects were blocked or reduced in scope and ambition by an assertive Congress that did not intend to passively approve new expensive military programs. The administration, soon to be embroiled in the Watergate drama, could not fight back this challenge. The erosion of presidential authority and leadership loosened discipline within the administration itself. Secretary of Defense James Schlesinger, one of the foremost adversaries of Kissinger, supported Jackson and undertook a significant revision of U.S. military doctrine. Such a revision was primarily based on the rejection of deterrence and relaunched the idea that a nuclear war could somehow be waged, thus challenging the political and strategic assumptions underpinning the SALT agreements. The Schlesinger Doctrine once again concentrated on the ability to conduct limited nuclear war and control nuclear warfare "so that if deterrence were to fail...the use of nuclear weapons would not result in [an] orgy of destruction."[28]

In spite of Kissinger's hopes and predictions, attacks on the strategic dimension of détente and its basic philosophy became more frequent and politically incisive. Invoking equality was in fact a way to a reaffirm a strong topos of U.S. strategic discourse and of the ideology that underpinned it: the request, proudly exceptionalist, that the United States maintain (or regain) clear and unquestioned superiority. The step from the instrumental exhortation of preserving parity to urging the return of nuclear primacy proved indeed to be a short one. Soon, Jackson and the neocons (as well as Reagan) would again reason in terms of a "preponderance of power," which they argued was expendable diplomatically as well as strategically.[29]

In their campaign to reclaim lost superiority, Henry Jackson and the neoconservatives found the support of a group of experts and strategists who had been marginalized during the previous years by advocates of deterrence such as Robert McNamara and Kissinger. Paul Nitze, the architect of NSC 68 and one of the experts involved in negotiations with the Soviets, the Harvard Sovietologist Richard Pipes, Eugene Rostow, the nuclear strategist Albert Wohlstetter, atomic physicist Edward Teller, and many others mounted a campaign against the SALT agreements and the strategic concept behind them. The theoretical assumptions underpinning their campaign were to reaffirm the possibility of waging and winning a nuclear war (the issue on which, from an opposite perspective, Nitze had effectively lambasted Kissinger in 1957) and the claim that nuclear superiority still mattered, politically as well as diplomatically. Atomic weapons represented just one of the many variables that defined the bipolar balance of power. Nevertheless, Paul Nitze claimed that "to have an advantage at the utmost level of violence help[ed] play at every lesser level." The aggressor, in fact, "never wants war; he would prefer to enter your country unopposed." "In seeking each specific objective within their global policy," Nitze maintained, "the Soviet rulers use the lowest level of pressures or of violence necessary and sufficient to achieve that objective. The purpose of their capabilities at the higher level of potential violence, all the way up to intercontinental nuclear war, [was] to deter, and if necessary control, escalation by us to such a higher level." According to Nitze, Cold War precedents proved the point: "In the Korean war, the Berlin blockades, and the Cuban missile crisis the United States had the ultimate edge because of our superiority at the strategic nuclear level. That edge has slipped away." A clear nuclear superiority, the neoconservatives and their experts argued, guaranteed additional leverage in the international arena. This edge was particularly true in the relationship with a regime like the USSR, which adhered to a unidimensional vision of power and understood only the language of force.[30]

The campaign against deterrence and the Jackson Amendment hit the Nixon and Ford administrations hard, and inevitably targeted Henry Kissinger. The rigor of its strategic analysis and realist foundations had represented central elements of Kissinger's discourse and strongly contributed to its initial popularity. Through these elements Kissinger had sought to build a new U.S. foreign policy consensus and, in the process, had become a popular and admired political figure. Now, however, the same assumptions and rhetoric were turned against him. The Kissingerian logic, the neoconservatives argued, rested on a dual and naïve underestimation of the intrinsic aggressiveness of the Soviet Union, which had not given up dreams of global dominance, and of America's (and Americans') willingness to bear the sacrifices and burdens demanded to face and ultimately defeat the Cold War enemy.

The alteration of the nuclear equilibrium to Moscow's advantage, Nitze argued, produced inevitable political repercussions. The USSR would not necessarily undertake military action against the United States but would do its best to gain the maximum benefit from the situation. "The Soviet Union," Nitze claimed, "will continue to pursue a nuclear superiority that is not merely quantitative but designed to produce a theoretical war-winning capability." There was "a major risk that, if such a condition were achieved, the Soviet Union would adjust its policies and actions in ways that would undermine" détente, with "results that could only resurrect the danger of nuclear confrontation or, alternatively, increase the prospect of Soviet expansion through other means of pressure." The United States had to take immediate "action to redress the impending strategic imbalance" if it wanted to persuade the Soviet Union "to abandon its quest for superiority and to resume the path of meaningful limitations and reductions through negotiation." Nixon and Kissinger, Jackson argued, lacked the "self-confidence" and the "optimism" necessary to guide the United States through the turbulent waters of world politics. The greatness of the United States had been "best revealed in times of adversity." The diplomatic, political, and economic difficulties encountered during the second half of the 1960s did not constitute a "decline of America." On the contrary, the United States' "capacity for continued greatness as a nation" was "undiminished." For Jackson, there was certainly "no other country in the world that" possessed the "human, cultural and spiritual resources" of the United States. There was "no other country whose revolutionary values of 200 years" earlier had "been taken to heart by so many people—even in places where tyranny inhibit[ed] the free expression of human aspirations." "For Americans," Jackson claimed, "whose basic values" were "shared by so much of mankind, the problems of the present" were "but opportunities for new achievements."[31]

Lobbying by the neoconservatives became more aggressive and effective. They vociferously requested an expansion and upgrade of the U.S. nuclear arsenal, as well as more severe monitoring of the estimates produced by U.S. intelligence, especially those of the CIA. According to the neocons, CIA estimates of Soviet nuclear potential were influenced by the alleged liberal bias of intelligence analysts. In 1975 the new CIA director, George H. W. Bush, capitulated to the pressures that his predecessor, William Colby, had been able to resist: evaluations by the CIA analysts, gathered in a team A, were compared with those of a group of outside experts (team B), who were mostly critical of deterrence and of the SALT agreements. For the competitive exercise to be effective, the members of team B had unprecedented access to highly classified CIA intelligence. Team B was chaired by Richard Pipes. Its final report severely censured an agency that had already been weakened, both politically and institutionally, by the scandals and revelations of the previous years. The report accused the CIA of having provided the U.S. government with subjective and biased intelligence, influenced by the political and cultural prejudice of its experts, that led it to underestimate the real motivations behind Soviet nuclear rearmament and its effective scope. (Although it was not entirely unfounded, the latter critique was vastly exaggerated.) According to Pipes, "the U.S. intelligence community" shared the liberal "outlook of the U.S. academy," was receptive to the "political pressures from the White House," and tended, therefore, to "reason in terms of conventional wisdom." In the end, it offered "surreptitious political judgments disguised as hardware analyses," which were based on "mirror-imaging" and "unproved assumptions about Soviet behavior." For Pipes, "Soviet nuclear strategy had to be seen in the context of 'grand strategy'": the "Soviet leadership did not subscribe to MAD [the doctrine of mutually assured destruction] but regarded nuclear weapons as tools of war whose proper employment, in offensive as well as defensive modes, promised victory." Unlike Nitze, Pipes and the more radical neoconservatives feared not only the political effects of a nuclear imbalance of power advantageous to the Soviet Union, but also the possibility that Moscow would exploit the situation to strike a decisive blow against the United States.[32]

In 1976 Eugene Rostow and Paul Nitze created the Committee on the Present Danger (CPD), a bipartisan organization that aimed to promote debate and discussion on strategic matters and, above all, to serve as a pressure group against détente. The organization's opening statement—which obviously had the unconditional support of Henry Jackson—stated that the "principal threat" to the United States, "to world peace, and to the cause of human freedom" was "the Soviet drive for dominance based upon an unparalleled military build-up." The Soviet Union, the document proclaimed, had "not altered its long-held goal of a world dominated from a single center—Moscow." "Unless decisive steps" were "taken to alert the nation, and to change the course of its policy," U.S. "economic and military capacity" would "become inadequate to assure peace with security." The United States risked finding itself "isolated in a hostile world, facing the unremitting pressures of Soviet policy backed by an overwhelming preponderance of power." U.S. "national survival itself would be in peril," and America "should face, one after another, bitter choices between war and acquiescence under pressure."[33]

The CPD was an "an organization filled with Jackson Democrats and future Reagan Republicans." From an organizational perspective it provided the bridge linking neoconservative Democrats and sections of the new Republican Right, which would contribute to the political and electoral shift that led to Reagan's victory in 1980. The vector that connected the two critical voices of Kissinger's détente was represented by the denunciation of the "window of vulnerability" that the SALT accords had allegedly opened and the consequent exhortation to rapidly close it through a process of massive rearmament.[34]

The CPD and the neoconservatives operated in two directions: they claimed that Soviet nuclear doctrine was not based on the recognition of deterrence; and they denounced the second round of SALT negotiations (SALT II) by the Carter administration (1977–81) as a replica of previous talks and approaches. Both assumptions were wrong. Deterrence, although frequently masked with Marxist rhetorical cosmetics, had become part and parcel of Soviet strategic thinking. The acceptance that a nuclear exchange was impossible had been behind Moscow's choices in the previous years, inducing the USSR to undertake massive rearmament while seeking some sort of accommodation with Washington. The Soviet Union, historian David Holloway has underlined, was aware that it was no longer possible to escape the "mutual vulnerability" imposed by nuclear deterrence: the Soviets were, in other words, conscious that "victory in a global nuclear war would be anything other than catastrophic" for the Soviet Union as well. At the same time, military expansion had become less and less sustainable for the Soviet economy, although the influence of the military apparatus and the intention to enhance its missile potential induced Soviet leadership not to abandon many defense programs already under way.[35]

The neoconservative denunciation of Carter's security policy and SALT II was also instrumental. Carter and his secretary of defense, Harold Brown, had explored various programs that accepted, at least in part, the request to rapidly expand and modernize the U.S. nuclear arsenal. The new domestic political climate facilitated diverse projects from the *Trident* submarine to the B-2 bomber to the technological upgrading of ICBMs. The proposals initially advanced by Carter during SALT II negotiations echoed Jackson's positions, in particular the request to reduce previously agreed upon quantitative ceilings on intercontinental missiles and their MIRV potential. The final treaty, signed by Carter and Brezhnev in May 1979 (and never ratified by the U.S. Senate), was much less ambitious than that originally envisioned by Carter. Nevertheless, it reduced the 1974 limits on ICBMs, which had been harshly denounced by the neoconservatives at the time.[36]

Carter's initiatives disoriented a Soviet leadership already irritated by the emphasis of the American president on the issue of human rights violations in the Soviet bloc. Carter's activism was not sufficient, however, to placate neoconservative criticism and attacks by the CPD. In the Senate, Jackson mounted a campaign against SALT II that would contribute to blocking its ratification. In the public debate, hawkish voices invoking more ambitious military programs than those proposed by Carter, including the relaunch of missile defense, grew louder and politically stronger. These voices found a receptive audience in public opinion and the political world. Most important, these voices benefited from a significant change in the political and cultural atmosphere. The idea that the United States was facing a dramatic crisis and serious decline remained; the conviction that this crisis could be overcome by promoting dialogue with Moscow was instead vanishing. The relationship between the two superpowers once again deteriorated as a result of the damage caused by some risky Soviet actions (particularly in Africa), by the greater influence exercised by neoconservatives, and by the limits of the process of détente as originally conceived by the two sides.[37]

To a concerned and disoriented country, Kissinger and conservative supporters of détente had promised that difficulties would be overcome and problems solved through an amoral and realist approach to international matters. From this perspective, raison d'état justified the abandonment, once and for all, of ancient principles and useless ideological formulas. Jackson and the neoconservatives disputed this assumption; they argued that in the case of the United States, a realist foreign policy could and should be "moral." For them Kissinger's approach and his foreign policy discourse not only corrupted America's ideals and foreign policy practices, but also damaged the security interests of the United States. Morality and interest had to be connected again because the former was said to strengthen the latter. For trade union leader George Meany, a figure close to the neocons, it was indispensable to restore "the sense of moral purpose that ha[d] evaporated" from U.S. foreign policy. In fact, a lack of moral purpose in foreign policy undermined "moral purpose at home." A "moral" foreign policy, based on defense and the promotion of "human rights," represented the best way to "serve" U.S. "national interest," Henry Jackson proclaimed. The attack on the strategic dimension of détente—and the vulnerability allegedly accepted through the SALT accords—was thus complemented by an even more radical and politically powerful denunciation of the moral deficiencies of détente. Some years later, Jeane Kirkpatrick, the political scientist Reagan would appoint as ambassador to the United Nations, once again underlined that "morality" was (and had to be) "inevitably involved in politics." "Nothing," Kirkpatrick maintained, "could be wronger [*sic*] as a point of departure for thinking about foreign policy than this kind of a disjunction, this kind of treatment of power and morality as though they were opposite categories."[38]

The Neoconservative Critique of Détente: The Moral Dimension

The immorality of détente and Kissinger's realism was to be found, above all, in the acceptance of deterrence. On this the neoconservatives anticipated a critique that was adopted, paradoxically, by Reagan and his most bitter opponent, the antinuclear movement that emerged in Europe and the United States in the early 1980s. Neoconservatives, Reaganites, and pacifists shared a belief that the nuclear peace, magnified by realist scholars like Kenneth Waltz and John Gaddis, was based on an assumption—the certainty of global destruction in case of war—that was morally and strategically unacceptable. It was morally repugnant because a peace founded on the notion that the destruction of the planet was theoretically acceptable was a fictitious and militarized peace: a nonpeace, in fact, which preserved permanent high risk. It was strategically unacceptable, Reaganites and neocons argued, because it obliged the United States to place its security, indeed its own survival, in the hands of the enemy: an absolute enemy—in terms of ideology, methods, global reach—as there had never been before in the history of the United States.[39]

This position also embodied a renewed discourse that was simultaneously nationalist, exceptionalist, and universalistic, as well as antithetical to the amoral and realist relativism of the Kissingerian discourse. The exceptionalist representation of the United States and its unique role in the international system relies on a basic premise: that the United States, being at the ultimate stage in the development of history and civilization, is exempt from the historical laws to which other states are subject. From this perspective the exemption represents the *conditio* of the exception. The strategic interdependence of the Cold War—accepted and canonized by the SALT accords—represented an explicit abandonment of such an exceptionalist claim. Far from casually, Kissinger's rhetoric relied on the constant call for the need to "Europeanize" the United States and for the United States to learn great power politics as all others had done in the past. Such a call was unacceptable and execrable for the neoconservatives, who instead wanted to reaffirm the greatness and uniqueness of the United States. The "pressing problems" of the United States, Jackson claimed in 1976, could not "be successfully handled, outside the framework of traditional American values." This proudly exceptionalist "vision of America" was "under assault" by "prophets of doom" like Henry Kissinger. "We invite the erosion of our society if we listen to the voices of cynicism and doom," Jackson maintained. Kissinger's detente was "a body without a soul—a policy indifferent to human rights." It was once again "time for a foreign policy in Washington" that reflected America's "deepest beliefs as a people" and embodied its "democratic and humanitarian heritage."[40]

To achieve this goal it was fundamental for the United States to regain its lost superiority, equipping itself with a defense capability that went beyond deterrence, and along with it, equivalence. To accept equivalence, as Kissinger wished, would mean to normalize the United States and de-ideologize the conflict with the Soviet Union, transforming it into an ordinary interstate antagonism. The acceptance of strategic equivalence, the neocons argued, implied a relativistic acceptance of moral equivalence. It was in these years, neoconservative scholars Tom Donnelly and Vance Serchuck have later maintained, that "'moral equivalence' between East and West slipped into the mainstream of U.S. strategic thought, and so a critique advanced by left-wing dissenters during the Vietnam years was adopted by a right-wing administration in the White House." The comment by Vance and Serchuck, while clearly exaggerated and simplistic, nonetheless high-lights a point of convergence between Kissinger's cultural relativism and the New Left. Kissinger himself recognized this convergence, dissenting, for instance, with Moynihan's attack on students who contested interven-tion in Vietnam and Nixon's foreign policy. For Kissinger, the relativistic skepticism of young New Leftists could in fact become "the bedrock of a critically intelligent and informed citizenry in the '70s and '80s."[41]

Against such relativism and primacy of geopolitics, the neoconservatives attempted to launch a new, liberal universalism. This universalism was entirely political, especially in light of the crisis of modernization theory, which had represented the most progressive element of Cold War liberal internationalism. And it was a universalism that rediscovered one of the political and "intellectual anchor[s] of the Cold War": the ubiquitous cat-egory of totalitarianism. During the early Cold War, the concept of totali-tarianism had represented one of the most used cognitive and rhetorical tools in the United States. In the 1950s and 1960s, totalitarianism progres-sively disappeared from public discourse. The modernist approach of the Kennedy and Johnson years rejected the conviction, intrinsic to the theory of totalitarianism, that Soviet society was inherently dysfunctional and therefore weak. On the contrary, the modernization theories embraced in these years considered Communism "a politically pathological but or-ganizationally effective means of promoting development and achieving modernity."[42]

The crisis in liberal, modernizing universalism had facilitated, as we have seen, the advent of an exclusively geopolitical and relativistic dis-course. The neoconservative embrace and relaunch of totalitarianism as a tool to understand and describe the Soviet Union and its foreign policy updated the "plausible and frightening vision of a Manichean, radically bifurcated world" that had originally offered "the great mobilizing and unifying concept of the Cold War." According to George Meany, it was vital to stop the "transition from a world dominated by imperfect democ-racies to a world dominated by totalitarianisms." Historian Richard Pipes applied the concept of totalitarianism in his works on the Soviet Union. The intellectual father of neoconservatism, Irving Kristol, vulgarized the work of Jacob Talmon, identifying in the principles and utopias of "French-Continental enlightenment" (which he compared negatively to the pragmatic Anglo-Scottish Enlightenment) the "germs of twentieth-century totalitarianism," which had spread in Europe and reached its apogee in the Soviet Union. For Moynihan the "central struggle" of the time was not between North and South, the haves and have-nots, but remained that "between liberal democracy and totalitarian Communism."[43]

Denouncing the Soviet Union as a totalitarian power and presenting any dialogue with it as morally reprehensible allowed the introduction of two further elements of early Cold War discourse, which were still popular and persuasive: references to what classic historical analogies, in particular the 1930s and the "lesson of Munich," taught the United States; and the idea that a strict and inescapable nexus existed between the foreign and domestic policies of the United States as well as of other states. For the neoconservatives, the nature of the Soviet regime—whatever its actions—oriented its behavior abroad, rendering it automatically aggressive and expansionistic. Such nature needed therefore to be modified.

If Communist Soviet Union was a new totalitarian power like (if not greater than) Nazi Germany, then détente was nothing less than a new form of appeasement. Détente was morally and strategically self-defeating, the neocons claimed, because no accommodation was possible with the Soviet enemy. The parallels between the 1930s and the 1970s became constant in neoconservative discourse and were used to denounce the immorality of Kissinger's realism. As emphasized by one sympathetic biographer, "Jackson's admirers and the senator himself saw a parallel between his relentless campaign against détente during the 1970s and Winston Churchill's campaign against appeasement during the 1930s." For Jackson and his acolytes, the emblematic symbol of this new appeasement was the concept of nuclear sufficiency: "an intellectual and moral error" that risked rendering the United States defenseless in the face of the next, inevitable act of Soviet aggression.[44]

Most neoconservative critiques and analyses were based on the assumption that the world was in the midst of a historical turn not dissimilar from the period between the two world wars. U.S. foreign policy, they argued, had forgotten the "lesson of Munich" and the moral and strategic obligation to not satisfy the appetite—by definition insatiable—of totalitarian powers. "*Mutatis mutandis,*" historian Richard Pipes claimed, "the mood behind the present attitude is not unlike that of Britain during the appeasement era of the 1930s: a combination of a dread of a repetition of a world war (only intensified today because of the nature of new weapons), plus admiration for the Germans as a technologically advanced 'young' nation combined with some disgust over Britain as a 'decadent' country." "The history of our time," Moynihan maintained, "is the history of totalitarian advance." "The uprising in Warsaw, the uprising in Treblinka, the defense of Israel, and the protests in Moscow and Leningrad are all of one piece," affirmed Henry Jackson, embracing the cause of dissidents in the Soviet Union: "They are living testimony of man's indomitable desire to be free. And they hold forth the hope that this desire can ultimately prevail." Also under attack, sometimes in populist tones, were the representatives of the U.S. business community who, allured by the intensification of commercial exchanges it promised, supported normalization of relations with Moscow. For the neocons, pro-détente businessmen had fallen prey to a "nihilist" attitude, which was negatively compared with the bold firmness of trade unions, which "did not let any concerns—economic or otherwise—interfere with the all important task of confronting Communists." While "the chairman of Pepsi-Cola or other luminaries of American business with more strategically important goods to sell were rushing to Moscow laden with the 'rope' that Lenin famously predicted the capitalists would provide for their own execution at the hands of Soviet hangmen," Podhoretz claimed in 1981, retrospectively pondering the era of détente, "the AFL-CIO under George Meany and Lane Kirkland was thinking, and voicing, other thoughts and ideas."[45]

For Jackson and the neoconservatives the core issue, aside from the security of Israel, was Europe. On this subject they shared one premise of Kissinger's geopolitical code: its Eurocentrism and belief that it was necessary to avert a Finlandization of Western Europe, which would guarantee the Soviets indirect, but unassailable, dominion on the Continent. This common assumption generated antithetical prescriptions, however, because the neoconservatives approached the issue in a way that paid more attention to modalities of influence that were not exclusively, or one-dimensionally, geopolitical or military. For Kissinger the preservation of the status quo in Europe systemically blocked any further extension of Soviet influence. For the neoconservatives, the status quo Kissinger wanted to uphold and bolster constituted instead a system that rendered America's position weak and vulnerable. In contrast to Kissinger's belief, the U.S. capacity to condition its allies was limited and decreasing. Passively accepting Soviet dominance in central Eastern Europe, the neocons argued, undermined U.S. moral credibility, whereas bipolar U.S.-USSR détente stimulated, instead of placating, centrifugal pressures within the Atlantic Alliance that could lead to its final collapse.

The risk, historian Fritz Stern claimed, was that détente would fuel tendencies already under way, inducing Europe to "succumb to a 'sulky' neutralism, to a collapse of will, to a 'European Buddhism,'" and, in the end, a "particularly pernicious form of nihilism." For many conservative and neoconservative commentators, anti-Europeanism combined with anti-Kissingerism and antirealism. Willy Brandt's Ostpolitik was therefore presented as the latest incarnation of a weak and self-defeating "state of mind and will": nothing more than a "new name for appeasement." The conceptual and operative "Europeanization" of U.S. foreign policy invoked by Kissinger and used as a rhetorical tool to forge a new domestic consensus was explicitly rejected. Instead, it was presented as an admission of weakness that threatened to contaminate the United States and deprive it of its diversity and exceptionality. Kissinger's "Gaullist realism" was explicitly criticized and derided. The Left presented Kissinger as a von Ribbentrop lent to American diplomacy; the neoconservatives and the new Right were less impressed by the realist and Bismarckian credentials of Kissinger's strategy, and critical of the alleged de-Americanization of U.S. foreign policy instead. Kissinger, "the brilliant refugee," could thus be caricatured by the conservative commentator Richard Whalen as an "unassimilated outsider...a European by heritage and cultural choice, a cosmopolitan by circumstance, an American by deliberate (and hazardous) calculation" who "revealed the derivative nature of his national identity in almost pathetic fashion."[46]

For the neoconservatives, the most blatant expression of this moral deficit was the passive acceptance by the United States of constant human rights violations inside the Soviet Union and the Communist bloc. In the 1970s human rights became a central issue in U.S. public debate and international relations. Occupying center stage in world politics, human rights were part of the "moment of...basic political restructuring" that took place during the decade. And it was on the issue of human rights that the neoconservatives identified a potential vulnerability of Kissinger and his foreign policy that, if aptly exploited, could lead to his downfall and the end of détente.[47]

Henry Jackson and his main assistant, the young arms control expert Richard Perle, promoted several anti-détente initiatives whose main focus was the fate of Soviet Jews and political dissidents persecuted by Moscow. U.S. diplomacy had traditionally paid little attention to how the Soviet regime treated its Jewish citizens and, except during the early Cold War, this issue was far from the center of the agenda of bipolar diplomacy. This inattention had also distinguished the first years of the Nixon presidency. At the time, however, there had been a limited, although not irrelevant, liberalization of Soviet immigration policies, with Moscow granting more visas to Soviet Jews wishing to emigrate to Israel; their number increased from 400 in 1969 to around 35,000 in 1973.[48]

Kissinger's cautiousness on the issue had several justifications, and to understand the dilemmas he faced does not necessarily require a discussion of his Jewishness. Aside from his personal conviction and hostility to blatant violations of national sovereignty (at least when great powers were involved), Kissinger was aware that exercising excessive pressure on the Soviet Union risked derailing détente and his ambitious grand design. Involved at the time in a major effort to restructure the geopolitics of the Middle East by inducing Egypt to side with the United States, Kissinger feared that the issue of Soviet Jews' emigration to Israel would open a new front of conflict and, even worse, result in a rapprochement between the Soviet Union and part of the Arab world.

The issue nevertheless exploded in 1972–73, becoming one the hottest problematics in U.S. political and public debate, and badly damaging the prospects of détente. The Senate was debating the ratification of various trade agreements signed by Nixon, which would authorize further subsidized lending to the USSR and provide, among other things, extension of the Most Favored Nation (MFN) clause to the Soviet Union. During the summer of 1972, the USSR decided to levy an education tax on citizens who wished to emigrate—an act justified as a necessary measure to compensate the Soviet state for the free education and training it had provided to the emigrants. The tax, however, hit primarily Soviet Jews, in particular those with skills and professional qualifications, who intended to emigrate to Israel.[49]

Jackson and the neoconservatives, who had long waited for such an opportunity, responded immediately. Jackson introduced legislation binding the concession of MFN status to states with nonmarket economies (such as the Soviet Union) with respect for the right of their citizens to emigrate. Charles Vanik (D-Ohio) introduced a similar bill in the House of Representatives. It was the beginning of a political dispute that would last for more than two years and end with the defeat of Kissinger and the Nixon administration.[50]

In the following months, Jackson succeeded in obtaining the support of the main American Jewish organization (which until then had been cautious on the issue) and the AFL-CIO. The position of the latter was dictated by traditional anti-Communism as much as by a protectionist stance that was challenged by Nixon's agreements with the Soviets and the trade policy of his administration more generally. Many Israeli politicians supported Jackson, although Prime Minister Golda Meir avoided making public statements while Tel Aviv's ambassador to the United States, Simcha Dinitz, tried to help Kissinger and the administration. The Israeli government feared opening another source of tension with the American "special" ally. Uncertain on its ability to absorb new immigrants in the numbers being discussed, Israel preferred to deal with the issue away from the spotlight, as it had in previous years.[51]

Jackson and the neoconservatives, however, did not intend to remain outside the spotlight. They were genuinely horrified by Soviet abuses and violations of human rights and believed that embracing the issue would offer U.S. foreign policy new, and badly needed, morality. Jackson also harbored presidential ambitions for 1976 and believed, correctly, that U.S. public opinion would appreciate and back his anti-Soviet campaign.

In March 1973, the Jackson-Vanik proposal was reintroduced as an amendment to a comprehensive trade bill, the Trade Reform Act, submitted by Nixon after his reelection. Firmly opposed by the AFL-CIO, the Trade Reform Act expanded presidential authority on trade issues by authorizing the president to undertake negotiations on the reduction of tariffs and trade concessions. In addition, the act granted MFN status to the Soviet Union. The Jackson-Vanik Amendment opposed this last aspect. Jackson believed it was necessary to prevent "nonmarket" economies that denied their "citizens the right or opportunity to emigrate," or imposed "more than normal taxes on emigration," from having access to the "benefits" of an "abundant economy" (i.e., "most favored access to" U.S. "markets, credits guarantees, and investment guarantees"). Resorting to liberal and universalistic afflatus, Jackson emphasized that his position upheld a "traditional [American] commitment to individual liberty—a commitment," he claimed, that was "enshrined in the Universal Declaration of Human Rights unanimously adopted by the United Nations" twenty-five years earlier. Jackson was effectively emulating Kissinger's linkage by connecting further progress in U.S.-Soviet relations regarding a specific issue (trade) to the behavior of the USSR on another (emigration). By doing so, however, he justified a form of interference in Soviet domestic affairs that Moscow could not tolerate.[52]

Kissinger initially underestimated Jackson's initiative. At the height of his fame and popularity, and close to being appointed secretary of state, he was victim to his "growing arrogance" and what he himself had defined as the "aphrodisiac of power." He delayed communicating to Congress that the USSR had, under the table, consented to abrogate the emigration tax. He overestimated the U.S. public's support for détente as well as his own capacity to stop Jackson. He did not inform the Soviets of the problems that the administration was encountering. Most of all, he behaved unscrupulously and superficially, exacerbating the personal and political feud with Jackson and the neoconservatives, instead of attempting to settle or at least soften it. As emphasized by historian Noam Kochavi, "by committing himself so completely to the defeat of Jackson-Vanik, Kissinger risked the administration's credibility, as well as his own, well beyond the point of necessity."[53]

In the end Kissinger was not so much the protagonist of the trilateral dispute that emerged as a mediator between Jackson, on one side, and the Soviet government on the other. He was a far from impartial mediator, however, as was evident during the Arab-Israeli War of October 1973, when Kissinger's unscrupulousness possibly reached its zenith. On this occasion Kissinger delayed the provision of badly needed military supplies to Israel, which had been surprised by the Egyptian and Syrian offensive and was facing unexpected difficulties. Kissinger believed that the war offered the United States an occasion to exercise greater pressure on its Israeli ally, forcing it to abandon the illusion that peace could be pursued unilaterally and to open negotiations with Egypt and other Arab countries. Kissinger worked to delay the airlift of supplies also in the hope of trading U.S. military aid for help from the Israeli government and the American Jewish community in stopping Jackson-Vanik. During the October 1973 War, a paradoxical situation thereby developed: the secretary of state of the leading world power (Kissinger) contacted the ambassador of an ally (Dinitz) to ask him to intercede with a U.S. senator (Jackson) to convince him to withdraw a bill under discussion in Congress (the Jackson-Vanik Amendment).[54]

Kissinger's actions steeled Jackson and antagonized even those moderate American Jewish organizations that previously had a lukewarm attitude toward Jackson-Vanik. Richard Perle, the real architect of Jackson's initiative on emigration from the USSR, claimed that the time had come for "educating Kissinger," to teach him that force represented the only language Moscow understood. Jackson's actions provoked division within the Democratic Party in that many, while supportive of détente and critical of Jackson's position on SALT I, were sympathetic to his denunciation of Soviet human rights violations. Jackson-Vanik opened up a dilemma— how to balance defense of the national interest with protection of human rights—that would frequently return in the following years. At the time, Jackson acted with a coherence that his neoconservative disciples would lack in the future. The senator did not miss the opportunity to denounce the repressive practices of several key allies of the United States, such as South Korea and Pinochet's Chile. In 1975 Jackson urged Kissinger "in the most strenuous terms" to "omit Chile" from his forthcoming tour of Latin America: "a visit to Chile at this time would inevitably give the appearance of giving the Administration's endorsement to a regime which has been the object of almost universal condemnation for its violation of human rights." Jackson claimed that there was "no overriding national interest which would justify a personal visit legitimizing a regime whose policies so violate[d] American values and beliefs."[55]

As a result of incessant and effective lobbying, and benefiting from broad support across the political spectrum, the Jackson-Vanik Amendment was approved by the House of Representatives in December 1973. From then on, the administration's problem was not to stop the amendment but to convince the Soviets to accept it. After approval of the amendment, Jackson demanded that the concession of MFN status to the Soviet Union be granted only if Moscow provided a formal guarantee that it would issue 100,000 exit visas per year (the request was later reduced to 70,000). The Soviet Union displayed surprising flexibility: Moscow first proposed a ceiling of 45,000 annual visas and even agreed not to reject more than 1.6 percent of applications. These openings were bound, however, to a Soviet condition that Jackson—already eyeing the 1976 presidential campaign—was not willing to respect: the agreements would not be formalized or made public. For Moscow, doing otherwise would mean admitting to the violation of its sovereignty and therefore recognizing America's right to interfere in Soviet internal affairs.[56]

In the end, Jackson and Kissinger succeeded in negotiating, through an exchange of letters, a compromise that fixed the limit at 60,000 exit visas per year. The figure was informally accepted by Ambassador Dobrynin and Soviet Foreign Minister Andrei Gromyko. Jackson agreed to include a waiver provision in the Jackson-Vanik Amendment that allowed the president to grant MFN status to nonmarket economies for a period of eighteen months. Jackson, however, revealed the terms of the compromise during a press conference just a few days before the 1974 midterm elections, while Perle released the letters exchanged by Jackson and Kissinger. The senator presented the compromise as a moral victory for the United States and the first step in a transformation of U.S. foreign policy, which was destined to open the "age of human rights." The Soviet response was immediate. Approved by large majorities in the Senate (88–0) and House (323–36), the Jackson-Vanik Amendment to the Trade Reform Act was denounced by Moscow as intolerable meddling in its internal affairs. The exchange of letters between Jackson and Kissinger, Gromyko argued, reflected "a distorted picture" of the Soviet position and what he had "told the American side on the matter." Kissinger's mediation had failed, killed by intransigence on both sides. The number of exit visas granted to Soviet Jews diminished drastically in the following years, as predicted by many opponents of the amendment. The Soviet Union rejected the Trade Reform Act and abrogated the bilateral trade treaty previously signed with the United States. A fundamental piece of the frail détente structure was now missing.[57]

On the issue of human rights and their abuse in the Soviet Union, the United States began to articulate a new foreign policy discourse that Reagan would later take to extremes. Such a discourse had strong "moral" (and also "moralistic") content and displayed a capacity for global projection and a hegemonic strength, both domestic and international, that was certainly missing in Kissinger's quasi-realism. The Jackson-Vanik saga represented a fundamental turn in this transformation. It stimulated a new domestic consensus for a remodeled foreign policy founded on old moral and ideological certainties, as expressed in crystalline and bombastic prose very different from the complex, cryptic, and often ambiguous jargon of détente. Yet the Jackson-Vanik position would not have had the same impact had it not coincided with another example of Soviet brutality that revealed, once again, the nature of the Soviet regime and the foolishness of its foreign policy: a new wave of Soviet repression of domestic dissent, the arrest and deportation of several political dissidents, and the dissolution of various associations created to promote democracy and defend human rights in the Soviet Union.

The most famous Soviet dissidents at the time were two different figures: the writer Aleksandr Solzhenitsyn and the physicist Andrei Sakharov.[58] Jackson and the neoconservatives defended Solzhenitsyn and Sakharov and embroiled them, more or less consciously, in the U.S. debate on the morality of American foreign policy in the 1970s. As such, both figures contributed to the crisis of détente.

Jackson and Perle established contacts with several Soviet dissidents and backed committees and associations created in the United States to support their cause. For the neoconservatives, political repression in the Soviet Union offered the paradigmatic example of the totalitarian nature of the Soviet regime and the immorality of Kissinger's policy of dialogue and compromise. Sakharov was living proof that the Soviet Union had not changed and, consequently, that the Soviet threat had not disappeared. Even in the case of dissidents, ideals and interests inextricably merged. Jackson was fully aware that Moscow's intolerance of dissents provoked the indignation of a majority of Americans and could, therefore, be exploited politically and electorally, as had been the case with Jackson-Vanik.

It was in connection with the amendment that the issue of suppression of political freedoms in the Soviet Union powerfully entered American political debate. In September 1973, Andrei Sakharov sent an open letter to Congress, appealing to its members to support the Jackson-Vanik Amendment. The sacred principle of noninterference in the domestic affairs of a sovereign country, Sakharov claimed, did not apply where international law and the most elementary principles of the Universal Declaration of Human Rights were systematically violated. "The abandonment of a policy of principle," such as the one supported by Jackson, would be "tantamount to total capitulation of democratic principles in face of blackmail, deceit and violence." True détente, Sakharov claimed, could not be limited to arms control and power relations. It had instead to foster the opening and liberalization of the USSR and put an end to its "intolerable isolation," because even its "partial preservation . . . would be highly perilous for all mankind, for international confidence and for détente." Once again, Jackson presented Kissinger's indifference to the fate of Soviet dissidents as a moral and strategic error. The "failure to insist upon progress in the area of human rights in the context of the developing détente," Jackson claimed, was not only a "basic betrayal" of America's "highest values," but also "ignore[d] the requirements for a more peaceful world." The "confidence" one could have "in the commitment of the Soviet Union to a genuine era of peaceful East-West relations" could only "be measured by the willingness of the Soviet authorities to accept an increasing measure of individual freedom in the East." Until this acquiescence occurred and "signs of genuine change in Soviet policy of human rights" were visible, it would be impossible to know "whether the 'relaxation of tensions'" was "tactical and ephemeral" or "basic and likely to endure."[59]

In private, Kissinger reacted with contempt to Sakharov's letter, finding solidarity with George Kennan, who had always been hostile to explicit Western interference in Soviet affairs. Hans Morgenthau, on the contrary, justified his endorsement of the Jackson-Vanik Amendment on realist grounds, believing that the Soviet Union was offering too little in return for the trade benefits it had gained as a consequence of the 1972 agreements.[60] For Kennan, instead, the issue of political dissent in the USSR was solely a "hysteria of the Western press." Nothing had "actually happened" to Sakharov and Solzhenitsyn, and "many of the issues" the dissidents had with the Soviet government were "ones that they themselves provoked." It was wrong in every regard for "a great government such as ours," Kennan maintained, "to try to adjust its foreign policy in order to work internal changes in another country." Kissinger concurred, blaming the "total hypocrisy" of the Western media and the irresponsibility of Soviet dissidents. "You know what would have happened to them under Stalin," he caustically remarked during a phone call with Kennan.[61]

Hypocrisy or not, the issue of human rights violations in the Soviet Union was not destined to disappear from the political agenda. Indeed, this concern explains the broad popular support of the campaign launched by Jackson and the neoconservatives. Sakharov's letter made a strong impression in the United States, and the Western media paid increasing attention to his story and campaign for political freedom. An analogous fate awaited

Aleksandr Solzhenitsyn, the other symbol of Soviet oppression. Solzhenitsyn was expelled from the Soviet Union and stripped of his citizenship in February 1974. Kissinger's silence on the episode was again denounced by Jackson, who reemphasized the indissoluble nexus between human rights and détente, whose artificial separation represented the "most dramatic" contradiction of bipolar diplomacy.[62]

After his expulsion Solzhenitsyn and his family moved to Germany and Switzerland before settling in the United States, where a group of Republican senators, attempting to hijack the issue from the Jackson Democrats, proposed granting honorary American citizenship to the great Russian writer. Kissinger found himself criticized by a majority of both parties. The "Solzhenitsyn effect" was fragmenting U.S. conservatism, contributing to the "emergence of a new, radical humanitarianism," and becoming a "potent force in the public life of Western democracies." Before retiring to a monklike existence in Vermont, Solzhenitsyn publicly intervened in support of Jackson: "in our crowded earth," the writer argued, repeating a passage from his prizewinning Nobel lecture of 1970, there were no exclusively "internal affairs left." The external behavior of the Soviet Union could not be separated from its domestic policy. Real détente also imposed a radical change of the Soviet regime itself.[63]

Solzhenitsyn was also the main protagonist of a new crisis that further weakened Kissinger. In the summer of 1975, Gerald Ford followed Kissinger's suggestion and turned down an offer to meet the writer at the White House. Ford and Kissinger decided then not to attend a dinner organized by the AFL-CIO in honor of Solzhenitsyn. Other members of the administration, among them the secretary of defense James Schlesinger and UN ambassador Daniel Patrick Moynihan, did participate. Several senators and representatives from both parties then invited Solzhenitsyn to address members of both chambers. During the meeting, Solzhenitsyn maintained that not only was détente incompatible with combating repression of dissent and dissidence in the Soviet Union, but that it nourished such repression by contributing to the legitimization of the Soviet regime. Détente, Solzhenitsyn claimed, was "a process of short-sighted concessions; a process of giving up and giving up and hoping that perhaps at some point the wolf will have eaten enough." It was time "to slow down the process of concessions and help the process of liberation." For Jackson, Kissinger had gone well beyond acceptable limits: "this country has not prevailed for two hundred years," the senator from Washington state claimed, "only to have its chief foreign policy spokesman side with the Soviet rulers against the American commitment to freedom."[64]

The realist and "European" turn Kissinger had tried to impress upon U.S. foreign policy had been defeated. Both the Democrats and Republicans now rejected it. Among the former, the surprising 1976 presidential nominee, former governor of Georgia Jimmy Carter, uneasily tried to synthesize competing liberal and conservative positions.[65]

Meanwhile, within the multifaceted Republican Party, the rising star was Ronald Reagan. Just like Jackson and Carter, the former governor of California bitterly denounced Kissinger's policies and realist outlook. Reagan challenged the incumbent president, Gerald Ford, during the Republican primaries and won several important victories. During the campaign, Kissinger was relegated to the sidelines in the belief that his participation would not only be useless to Ford but also potentially embarrassing and counterproductive. Reagan did not gain the nomination in 1976, but his campaign obligated Ford to move to the Right and away from détente, which was now unpopular with a majority of Americans. The foreign policy platform adopted at the Republican convention was distinctively Reagan-esque and Jacksonian neoconservative in that it denounced détente, urged that the United States not grant "unilateral favors" in the pursuit of détente, and "recognize[d] and commend[ed] that great beacon of human courage and morality, Alexander Solzhenitsyn." As asserted by Jussi Hanhimäki, "the president's own party…condemned Kissinger and Ford as guilty of a weak and immoral foreign policy."[66]

Despite Carter's election, 1976 produced a further shift Right in U.S. politics and served as a prelude to Reagan's victory four years later. It was a different, and in many aspects more radical, Right compared to that of Nixon and Ford. It was a "New Right" in which former Cold War liberals, also known as neoconservatives, would find a new political home. Foreign policy, especially the attack on détente and Kissinger's "continental realism," was among the basic catalysts of this conservative turn.

Conclusion

The domestic controversy in the United States, which ended with the defeat of Kissinger's vision, was one of the key factors in the crisis of détente, although not the only one and not necessarily the most important. It was relevant, however, because it intersected with other processes that embittered the relationship between the two superpowers and made dialogue more difficult. The Middle East, the third world, and the Soviet Union's policies in its sphere of influence represented other theaters and issues in which the crisis of détente and, along with it, Kissingerism matured and then exploded.

Between 1974 and 1975, Kissinger promoted a brilliant and unscrupulous diplomatic initiative in the Middle East that would determine a profound geopolitical realignment in the region. Egypt, the leader of the Pan-Arabic front and one of the main allies of the USSR throughout the Cold War, switched sides and became a close U.S. partner (as well as one of the main beneficiaries of American military aid). This change drastically altered the regional equilibria. Soviet influence in the Middle East was severely reduced. Despite détente, the battle for global hegemony was not fading, and the two superpowers had not abandoned the competition of the previous phase of the Cold War.

In the Middle East, Kissinger acted with audacity, ability, and cynicism. The same impudence and unscrupulousness was also displayed—albeit with less ability—by the USSR in the third world, where renewed Soviet activism aroused U.S. and Western European diffidence and provided further ammunition to those who opposed détente and presented it as a new form of appeasement. Particularly in Africa, the Soviet Union saw the possibility of extending its influence and altering the global balance of power to its advantage. The Angolan civil war and, later, the clash between Ethiopia and Somalia seemed to offer new opportunities. In Angola, in particular, Moscow offered economic and military aid to the Marxist-inspired party MPLA (Movimento Popular de Libertação de Angola, or Popular Movement for the Liberation of Angola), one of the three factions involved in the bloody power struggle that followed the implosion of the Portuguese empire. Kissinger had frequently presented the Soviet Union as a status quo power, prone to respect the tacit rules of détente. He considered the new Soviet activism as a betrayal of détente, although he once again attributed the main responsibility for U.S. difficulties to domestic opponents, both liberal and conservative, who were unwilling to support friendly forces in Angola (the former) and were committed to a new anti-Soviet crusade that rendered mediation with the USSR impossible (the latter).[1]

Just like Kissinger's policy in the Middle East, unscrupulous Soviet dynamism in theaters that were, until then, peripheral in the bipolar competition contributed to the crisis of détente. Soviet activism questioned the implicit assumptions of the U.S.-USSR dialogue, fueled and exacerbated regional crises that détente was supposed to prevent or consensually settle, and, finally, offered further arguments to those—Jackson, Reagan, and the neoconservatives—who opposed Kissinger's strategy and denounced inherent Soviet expansionism. It is still difficult to reconstruct the discussions that took place within the Muscovite leadership and the real motivation behind actions that were, almost inevitably, destined to damage détente.[2] What is clear is that the USSR once again proved itself unable to promote a farsighted foreign policy and understand—culturally as much as politically—how to relate to the United States.

This deficit was even more manifest regarding the issue of human rights, which by the mid-1970s had fully entered international relations and world politics discourse. The repression of political dissent in the USSR and the Communist bloc caused genuine revulsion in the United States and Western Europe. Moreover, it offered an extraordinary propagandistic tool to opponents of détente. Moscow showed little or no awareness of this dynamic, as was evident by its reaction to Jackson-Vanik and the campaign promoted by Jackson and others in defense of Soviet dissidents. It is still debated whether the Soviet regime could have survived and preserved its sphere of influence if it had abandoned those practices that were characteristic of its relations with the satellite countries. It is evident, however, that in regard to human rights, Moscow behaved crudely and disdainfully, misjudging the political consequences of its behavior and the impact such behavior would have on its relationship with the United States. As a result of this misjudgment, the Soviet Union inadvertently facilitated the crisis of the détente it had assiduously pursued in the previous years, thanks to which the USSR had gained several important advantages, including recognition of strategic parity, the settlement of European borders, and various trade and financial benefits.

Détente had been sought and promoted by the United States and Soviet Union together, and so its crisis and final implosion were in turn caused by the choices, mistakes, and thoughtlessness of both sides. The neoconservatives were not the only ones responsible for the collapse of détente, although they certainly contributed to it and were among the main political beneficiaries of the new deterioration in U.S.-Soviet relations.

The crisis of détente was catalyzed not just by the choices and actions of either side, however. The intrinsic and structural limits of détente itself—of how it had been conceived and then managed by the two superpowers—also played a role. Paradoxically, one could claim that the end of détente was inevitable given its successes and the attainment of its original objectives. By the mid-1970s most of these objectives had, in fact, been accomplished: strategic interdependence had known a first, fundamental regulation with the SALT accords; dialogue and negotiations on arms control—the basic matrix of the commonality of interests between the United States and Soviet Union—had been institutionalized; and the European status quo had been stabilized and, after the Helsinki conference on Security and Cooperation in Europe, legitimized. By 1975 this first phase of détente had reached the end of the line. At that point, the continuation of détente depended on the transformation of its nature and the consequent redefinition of its goals in more ambitious terms. A structuralist and systemic explanation of détente's end can also be advanced by reversing what has been said about its origins: just as a Hubert Humphrey administration would have probably undertaken a policy of détente, its difficulties and, possibly, implosion would have happened even without Kissinger and the neoconservatives.

Nevertheless, the crisis of détente was also the failure of Kissinger and the end of Kissingerism. It was the failure of Kissinger's strategic vision, foreign policy, and deliberate attempt to forge a new domestic consensus around a redefined U.S. internationalism—which is the basic argument of this book. Kissinger's awareness of the strength and solidity of bipolarism induced him to adopt a rigidly bipolar strategy: in the categories he used to read and decrypt the international system; in the kind of diplomatic initiatives he promoted; and in the objectives he set and intended to achieve. Kissinger's approach was simultaneously within and beyond the traditional boundaries of the Cold War. It rejected their ideological and discursive character, replacing them with realist, relativistic, and anti-universalistic principles. But it also exasperated such logic, adopting a "maniacally bipolar" perspective that reduced the capacity to understand the nuances and intricacies of a complex international system in which power was undergoing dramatic transformations. In spite of predictions and third-force utopias, particularly in Western Europe, two subjects—the United States and the Soviet Union—remained superior and unchallengeable during the 1970s. The attempt to systematically impose a bipolar "cage" on the international system, however, particularly through linkage, accentuated a series of problems instead of solving them. It simplified complex realities and problems, impeding their comprehension and solution. Kissinger's bipolarism thus tended to amplify and aggravate regional and local tensions, which were automatically placed within the binary scheme of the now de-ideologized competition with Moscow. Kissinger the pragmatic realist thus overestimated Soviet influence on North Vietnam, not unlike the liberals who had initially supported the intervention in Indochina. He favored and helped the Chilean coup in 1973, just as twenty years earlier a coup in Guatemala had been endorsed and facilitated by the Eisenhower administration. He also adopted a rigid and intransigent position with regard to the evolution of the political system of various U.S. allies, opposing their "opening to the Left" and assuming the same position of those conservative and neoconservative groups that were hostile to his détente.[3]

The entirely bipolar horizon of Kissinger's thought and policies reflected, paradoxically, a deficit of realism. This discrepancy impeded him from dealing effectively with the "particular," which was instead automatically inscribed under the "universal" of bipolarism and competition with the Soviet Union. In addition, this analytical and prescriptive bipolarism nourished tensions and misunderstandings with Washington's allies—the same tensions and misunderstandings Kissinger-the-scholar had often denounced in his works on the transatlantic relationship, attributing paternity to the United States and its congenital inability to listen to junior partners and satisfy part of their requests. Moreover, Kissinger's rigid bipolarism produced a further nonrealist result, which Hans Morgenthau effectively emphasized at the time: overestimation of the effective commonality of interests between the two superpowers and their ability to consensually discipline their power antagonism. On several occasions during the most critical phases of détente, one had the impression that Soviet and U.S. leaders were on the same side, whether against internal opponents of détente—the neoconservatives in the United States, and dissidents in the USSR and Soviet bloc—or those, particularly in Western Europe, who challenged the persistence of a rigidly bipolar structure.[4]

The limits of Kissinger's strategic vision and bipolar foreign policy help explain his failure. But this failure was even more evident on the domestic front, where the most ambitious element of Kissinger's grand design was ultimately defeated. Kissinger's actions had been inspired by the desire to radically alter the practices, rhetoric, and ideology of U.S. foreign policy. He also looked to elaborate and codify a new internationalist discourse popular enough to generate a broad domestic consensus that replaced the discredited discourse of Cold War liberalism. As a scholar as well as a statesman, Kissinger had paid a lot of attention to the domestic dimension: an effective foreign policy, he frequently claimed, had to rely on broad domestic support. Domestic legitimization of foreign policy choices was thus the "acid test" that every statesman—be it Metternich, Bismarck, or Kissinger himself—had to face.[5] Along with the bipolar rigidity of his geopolitical vision, it is on this terrain that we can measure the effective limits of the actions of Kissinger-the-statesman and the thought of Kissinger-the-scholar.

Most scholarly works on Kissinger and détente tend to overlook or minimize this aspect.[6] Historians have invariably preferred to concentrate on Kissinger's diplomacy and considered the domestic dimension as a disturbing, and often irrational, factor in an otherwise coherent, solid, and often agreeable strategy.[7]

Some of the best and most critically incisive analyses of Kissinger and his foreign policy have instead emphasized his lack of attention and interest in the domestic factor, his inability to understand the changes determined by Vietnam and the national trauma it produced, and his scant sensibility for U.S. democracy, its cultural foundations, and modus operandi. All these, it has been argued, rendered Kissinger unprepared to deal with the challenge from Congress and a volatile public opinion, unable to respond to them, and consequently powerless to prevent the irreparable damage to détente and his foreign policy.[8]

This interpretation presents Kissinger as disrespectful of U.S. democratic procedures and unaware of their importance—an argument I do not find persuasive and contest in this book. Kissinger's attention to the domestic dimension—the media, public opinion, and Congress—was obsessive and almost maniacal. Such attention influenced his choices, action, and rhetoric during his years at the White House. His foreign policy was always conditioned by the objective of shaping a new domestic consensus and awareness that it was necessary to find a surrogate to the hegemonic liberal and centrist discourse of the previous twenty years. Initially, Kissinger's geopolitical and quasi-realist discourse seemed to be appreciated and endorsed by a majority of Americans, disillusioned as they were with the costs of containment, anxious to abandon the perennial tensions of the Cold War, and convinced that the time had come to reduce U.S. international exposure. In the debate opened by the crisis of containment, Kissinger's realpolitik—whether real or imaginary—seemed to offer categories and discursive formulas more in tune with the mood of a nation that was simultaneously seeking to reduce military expenditures, assign greater responsibilities to allies, and abandon naïve meliorism and costly global crusades, which corrupted U.S. society by militarizing and "Prussianizing" it. Containment was founded on (and justified by) a claim of innocence that had solid roots in the history and culture of the United States. The crisis of containment was also the crisis of this presumption and of its proudly exceptionalist foundations. Beginning in the 1960s the presumption of innocence turned into its opposite: for the New Left, of course, but also for liberals who began to denounce the "arrogance of American power" and the "imperial" degeneration of the U.S. presidency.[9]

Through a clever and subtle message, Kissinger succeeded in reversing this denunciation. He transformed the crisis into an opportunity, the loss of innocence into the acquisition of maturity, and the end of diversity and exceptionality into the overcoming of naïveté and the attainment of awareness. He did so by drawing on his scholarly work and the fame he had derived from it. To a frightened and preoccupied America, Kissinger offered a way out inspired by the experience, wisdom, but also cynicism and unscrupulousness of Europe. His mistake was not that he overlooked the U.S. domestic dynamic or was disrespectful of democratic procedures, but rather that he overestimated the change under way and the practicability of a radical ideological and discursive transformation of U.S. foreign policy such as the one he offered. As stated by Phil Williams more than twenty years ago, "the move towards a more ambivalent relationship" with the Soviet Union and the rest of the world "was not easy for a nation which had an absolutist and moralistic approach to world affairs. Such a transformation became even harder to accept when it was initiated not out of magnanimity but out of weakness. The Soviet Union as supplicant might have been acceptable; the Soviet Union as equal was not."[10]

Kissinger's acclaimed "Europeanization" of American foreign policy revealed itself unable to generate a new broad domestic consensus. It proved to be a short-term strategy and discourse—a parenthesis, indeed, unable to resist the impact of more solid and venerable foreign policy traditions that Reagan and the neoconservatives were able to resurrect and adapt to the changed circumstances. All the virtues of Kissinger's alleged realism were transformed by its enemies into the typical and quintessential flaws of a European (and thus very "un-American") policy, which was weak and inept in the face of the Soviet challenge just as it had been in the face of Nazism. Cautiousness became passivity; negotiations were presented as capitulation; détente became synonymous with appeasement. Intoxicated with his initial success, Kissinger did not comprehend the strength of his opponents. Neoconservatism and the New Right, soon to unite, relaunched a highly ideological foreign policy discourse. They reaffirmed, without complexity or sense of guilt, the greatness and uniqueness of the United States and the necessity to henceforth reacquire and strengthen the basic prerogatives of American exceptionality, beginning with power pre-ponderance and invulnerability. By doing so, they once more presented the United States and its democracy as a unique model and source of inspiration to the rest of the world. They reasoned, in other words, with ideology and hegemony—categories that Kissinger, entirely concentrated on the geopolitical dimension, had neglected and disregarded. Reagan's discourse would reveal an extraordinary capacity to generate hegemony domestically and, at least in part, internationally. Kissinger's approach, strategy, and vision suffered from several deficits. Among them was the scant hegemonic capacity of a discourse that instead aimed at constructing consensus and underestimated the resilience of a foreign policy tradition—moral, ideological, and messianic—that the crisis of containment had weakened but not destroyed.

These were the limits of Kissinger's realism and some of the causes behind the rise of neoconservatism. When this short book was first conceived and written a few years ago, neoconservatives seemed to have a strong and unassailable hold on the conduct of U.S. foreign policy. According to many, the dramatic failures of George W. Bush's foreign policy, in Iraq and elsewhere, have probably decreed "the end of the neoconservative moment." Time will tell whether this "end" will last or be reversed. History, however, shows how the latest "neoconservative moment" was not just a temporary folly, but the product of a political and strategic culture that remains more in tune with U.S. foreign policy tradition and history than Kissinger's eccentric realism.[11]

NOTES

Introduction

1. McCain-Obama presidential debate, 26 September 2008, Commission on Presidential Debates, http://www.debates.org/pages/trans2008a.html (accessed 17 April 2009).

2. "Kissinger Unhappy about Obama," *Weekly Standard Blog,* 26 September 2008, http://www.weeklystandard.com/weblogs/TWSFP/2008/09/tws_exclusive_kissinger_unhapp.asp (accessed 17 April 2009).

3. Ron Suskind, "Faith, Certainty and the Presidency of George Bush Jr.," *New York Times Magazine* (on-line ed.), 17 October 2004.

4. Madeleine Albright with Bill Woodward, *Madame Secretary: A Memoir* (New York: Miramax Books, 2003), 505; William Kristol and Robert Kagan, "Toward a Neo-Reaganite Foreign Policy," *Foreign Affairs,* July–August 1996, 18–32; Thomas Carothers, *Aiding Democracy Abroad: The Learning Curve* (Washington, DC: Carnegie Endowment for International Peace, 1999), 352.

5. Francis Fukuyama, *America at the Crossroads: Democracy, Power, and the Neoconservative Legacy* (New Haven: Yale University Press, 2006); Coalition for a Realistic Foreign Policy, http://www.realisticforeignpolicy.org/static/000024.php (accessed 17 April 2009); Charles Krauthammer, *Democratic Realism: An American Foreign Policy for a Unipolar World* (Washington, DC: American Enterprise Institute, 2004); Irving Kristol, lecture, 12 February 2004, http://www.aei.org/publications/pubID.19912,filter.all/pub_detail.asp (accessed 17 April 2009); Condoleezza Rice, "Rethinking the National Interest: American Realism for a New World," *Foreign Affairs* (online ed.), July–August 2008; Charles A. Kupchan and G. John Ikenberry, "Liberal Realism: The Foundations of a Democratic Foreign Policy," *National Interest* 77 (Fall 2004): 38–49. Bill Richardson, "A New

Realism: A Realistic and Principled Foreign Policy," *Foreign Affairs* (online ed.), February–January 2008; Michael D. Shear, "McCain Outlines Foreign Policy," *Washington Post* (online ed.), 27 March 2008; "The National Security Strategy of the United States of America," September 2002, http://merln.ndu.edu/whitepapers/USnss2002.pdf (accessed 17 April 2009); Anatol Lieven and John Hulsman, *Ethical Realism: A Vision for America's Role in the World* (New York: Pantheon Books, 2006). Significantly, Barack Obama never mentioned the words "realism," "realistic," or "realist" in his otherwise conventional foreign policy manifesto. See Barack Obama, "Renewing American Leadership," *Foreign Affairs* (online ed.), July–August 2007.

6. Michael Fullilove, "Why Kissinger Should Support Obama," *Daily Beast,* 30 October 2008, http://www.thedailybeast.com/blogs-and-stories/2008-10-30/why-kissinger-should-prefer-obama/ (accessed 17 April 2009); Trudy Rubin, "Worldview: Issues Link McCain to Bush," *Philadelphia Inquirer* (online ed.), 29 October 2009; Ilan Goldenberg, "McCain and the Realists," *Democracy Arsenal,* 2 October 2008, http://www.democracyarsenal.org/2008/10/mccain-and-the.html (accessed 17 April 2009); Fareed Zakaria, "Obama Abroad," *Newsweek* (online ed.), 28 July 2008. A few weeks after Obama's election, the *Washington Post*'s editorialist E. J. Dionne Jr. also proclaimed the new president a "realist" in the vein of George Bush Sr. E. J. Dionne Jr., "Obama's Bush Doctrine," *Washington Post* (online ed.), 28 November 2008.

7. Henry Kissinger, *Years of Upheaval* (London: Weidenfeld and Nicolson, 1982), 1031 and 1050; Kissinger, as quoted in Frank Ninkovich, *The Wilsonian Century* (Chicago: University of Chicago Press, 1998), 234; Tom Braden, "Henry Kissinger: An American Hero," *Washington Post,* 25 May 1974.

8. A partially different view is suggested in Jeremi Suri's brilliant although, in my view, misconceived *Henry Kissinger and the American Century* (Cambridge: Harvard University Press, 2007). Suri offers some useful hindsight on Kissinger's "Americaness" but falls into the trap of buying one of Kissinger's latest arguments: namely, that his conservatism and "skepticism about democracy" were the product of his experience as a young Jew in Nazi Germany. That experience has supposedly proved to him how "demagoguery" can easily develop in a democratic but unstable environment, thus facilitating the rise of political and cultural extremism (31–33). This argument is the sort Kissinger has employed, since his experience in government, to counter neoconservatives' claims that détente was nothing more than a policy of appeasement of the Soviet Union, the new totalitarian monster of the Cold War. By referring to his formative experience in Germany as an inescapable legacy—one that would forever shape his approach to domestic and international politics and his search for order—Kissinger has argued, particularly in *Diplomacy* (New York: Touchstone, 1994), that détente was not a policy of appeasement and, moreover, represented the only way to avoid a repetition of the 1930s. This argument is clever, but it runs counter to what Kissinger said and wrote before his experience in government (in his words of those years it is difficult to find references to the lesson of the 1930s, for the United States and for himself) and what he argued and did during the Nixon-Ford years. Suri's implication that Kissinger held violent and zealous dictators from the Right and the Left in equal disregard is unsupported by the facts. Kissinger got along well with many leaders of authoritarian regimes, such as Portugal's Marcelo Caetano, Spain's Francisco Franco, Chile's Augusto Pinochet, the members of the military juntas in Greece and Argentina, and, one might add, Chou En-lai and Mao Zedong. He seemed to have more problems with democratically elected leaders, particularly those in the U.S. sphere of influence, such as Salvador Allende, Mario Soares, and Aldo Moro.

9. Robert Dallek, *Nixon and Kissinger: Partners in Power* (New York: HarperCollins, 2007).

10. For typical examples, see the following: John L. Gaddis, "Rescuing Choice from Circumstances: The Statecraft of Henry Kissinger," in *The Diplomats, 1939–1979,* ed. Gordon A. Craig and Francis Loewenheim, 564–92 (Princeton: Princeton University Press, 1994); Gaddis, *The Cold War: A New History* (New York: Penguin, 2005); Walter Isaacson, *Kissinger: A Biography* (New York: Simon and Schuster, 1992).

11. Robert David Johnson, *Congress and the Cold War* (Cambridge: Cambridge University Press, 2006), 190–241; Walter Lafeber, "The Constitution and United States Foreign Policy," *Journal of American History* 3 (December 1987): 695–717; Louis Henkin, *Foreign Affairs and the U.S. Constitution,* 2nd ed. (Oxford: Oxford University Press, 1996).

12. On the risk of a "limitationist" reaction to the difficulties the United States was facing, see the report by the NSC staff, *Analysis of Changes in International Politics since World War II and Their Implications for Our Basic Assumptions about U.S. Foreign Policy,* attachment to "Memorandum from the President's Assistant for National Security Affairs (Kissinger) to President Nixon," 20 October 1969, in *Foundations of Foreign Policy, 1969–1972,* vol. 1 of *Foreign Relations of the United States, 1969–1976* (Washington, DC: Government Printing Office, 2003), available at http://www.state.gov/r/pa/ho/frus/nixon/i/20702.htm (Accessed 17 April 2009).

13. Statement by Senator Henry M. Jackson on Kissinger's attack on Alexander Solzhenitsyn, 16–17 July 1975, Henry M. Jackson Papers, University of Washington Libraries, Manuscripts Collections, Seattle, accession no. 3560-6, Speeches and Writings, folder 11. See also Robert G. Kaufman, *Henry Jackson: A Life in Politics* (Seattle: University of Washington Press, 2000), 242–60; John Ehrman, *The Rise of Neoconservatism: Intellectual and Foreign Affairs* (New Haven: Yale University Press, 1995); Dana H. Allin, *Cold War Illusions: America, Europe and Soviet Power, 1969–1989* (New York: St. Martin's Press, 1995), 51–77.

14. Henry Kissinger, "The Process of Détente," statement delivered to the Senate Foreign Relations Committee, 19 September 1974, reprinted in Henry Kissinger, *American Foreign Policy,* 3rd ed. (New York: Norton, 1977), 144.

15. The conservatism of détente is stressed, from different perspectives, also by Jeremi Suri, *Power and Protest: Global Revolution and the Rise of Detente* (Cambridge: Harvard University Press, 2003); Allin, *Cold War Illusions;* Mary Kaldor, *The Imaginary War: Understanding East-West Conflict* (Oxford: Basic Blackwell, 1990).

16. Henry Kissinger, *White House Years* (London: Weidenfeld and Nicolson, 1979), 67; Mario Del Pero, "I limiti della distensione: Gli Stati Uniti e l'implosione del regime portoghese" [The limits of détente: The United States and the implosion of the Portuguese regime], *Contemporanea* 4 (December 2005): 621–50; Roberto Gualtieri, "The Italian Political System and Détente," *Journal of Modern Italian Studies* 4 (December 2004): 428–49.

17. On this topic see, for example, the considerations in Charles Maier, "Consigning the Twentieth Century to History: Alternative Narratives for the Modern Era," *American Historical Review* 3 (June 2000): 807–31; and Maier, *Among Empires: American Ascendancy and Its Predecessors* (Cambridge: Harvard University Press, 2006).

18. Ronald Reagan, "First Inaugural Address," 20 January 1981, http://www.reagan.utexas.edu/archives/speeches/1981/12081a.htm; Reagan, "Farewell Address to the Nation," 11 January 1989, http://www.reagan.utexas.edu/archives/speeches/1989/011189i.htm.

19. Allin, *Cold War Illusions,* 69–70; Henry Kissinger, "Morality and Power," in *Morality and Foreign Policy: A Symposium on President Carter's Stance,* ed. Ernest W. Lefever, 59–68 (Washington, DC: Ethics and Public Policy Center, Georgetown University, 1977).

1. The Crisis of Containment

1. Robert Latham, *The Liberal Moment: Modernity, Security, and the Making of Postwar International Liberal Order* (New York: Columbia University Press, 1997), 4.

2. On Roosevelt's projects for the postwar period and on his optimism for the possibility of continuing to cooperate with the Soviets, see John L. Harper, *American Visions of Europe: Franklin D. Roosevelt, George F. Kennan, and Dean G. Acheson* (Cambridge: Cambridge University Press, 1994), 77–131; and Robert Dallek, *Franklin D. Roosevelt and American Foreign Policy, 1932–1945* (Oxford: Oxford University Press, 1979). On the possibility of a convergence between the Soviet

and the American models, see Warren Kimball, *The Juggler: Franklin Roosevelt as Wartime Statesman* (Princeton: Princeton University Press, 1991), 198–99. See also Justus D. Doenecke and Mark A. Stoler, *Debating Franklin D. Roosevelt's Foreign Policies, 1933–1945* (Lanham, MD: Rowman and Littlefield), 2005.

3. On the uniqueness and peculiarity of the Cold War, see Anders Stephanson, "Fourteen Notes on the Concept of the Cold War," in *Rethinking Geopolitics*, ed. Simon Dalby and Gearóid Ó Tuathail, 62–85 (London: Routledge, 1998). On the similarities between the two Cold War universalisms, see Susan Buck-Morss, *Dreamworld and Catastrophe: The Passing of Mass Utopias in East and West* (Cambridge: MIT Press, 2001); and Kate Brown, "Gridded Lives: Why Kazakhstan and Montana Are Nearly the Same Place," *American Historical Review* 106 (February 2001): 17–48. For a classic realist interpretation of the Cold War, emphasizing its geopolitical stability, see the excellent John Lewis Gaddis, *The Long Peace: Inquiries into the History of the Cold War* (Oxford: Oxford University Press, 1987).

4. Latham, *Liberal Moment,* 137; Anders Stephanson, "The Cold War Considered as U.S. Project," in *Reinterpreting the End of the Cold War: Issues, Interpretations, Periodizations,* ed. Federico Romero and Silvio Pons, 52–67 (London: Frank Cass, 2005), 59; Fred Logevall, "A Critique of Containment," *Diplomatic History* 4 (September 2004): 473–99.

5. George F. Kennan, "The Sources of Soviet Conduct," *Foreign Affairs* 25 (July 1947): 566–82. The text of the Long Telegram can be found at http://www.gwu.edu/~nsarchiv/coldwar/documents/episode-1/kennan.htm (accessed 24 April 2009). On Kennan see Harper, *American Visions of Europe,* 135–232; Anders Stephanson, *Kennan and the Art of Foreign Policy* (Cambridge: Harvard University Press, 1989); and Walter Miscamble, *George F. Kennan and the Making of American Foreign Policy, 1947–1950* (Princeton: Princeton University Press, 1992); Scott Lucas and Kaeten Mistry, "Illusion of Coherence: George F. Kennan, U.S. Strategy, and Political Warfare in the Early Cold War," *Diplomatic History* 1 (January 2009): 39–66.

6. John L. Gaddis, *Strategies of Containment: A Critical Appraisal of Postwar American National Security Policy* (New York: Oxford University Press, 1982), 26; Henry Kissinger, *White House Years* (London: Weidenfeld and Nicolson, 1979), 135.

7. Giles D. Harlow and George C. Maerz, eds., *Measures Short of War: The George F. Kennan Lectures at the National War College, 1946–47* (Washington, DC: National Defense University Press, 1991). On this aspect see also the two volumes of Kennan's memoirs, *Memoirs,* vol. 1: *1925–1950,* and vol. 2: *1950–1963* (Boston: Little Brown, 1967 and 1972, respectively).

8. Walter Lippmann, *The Cold War: A Study in U.S. Foreign Policy* (New York: Harper, 1947). The metaphor had a long history and had already been used by George Orwell in an article published in 1945. It was Lippmann's book, however, that popularized it first in the United States and then in the rest of the world. See David Reynolds, introduction to *The Origins of the Cold War in Europe,* ed. D. Reynolds (New Haven: Yale University Press, 1994), 1–3; and Stephanson, "Fourteen Notes."

9. Lippmann, *Cold War,* 60. On Lippmann see especially Ronald Steel, *Walter Lippmann and the American Century* (Boston: Little Brown, 1980).

10. See James Burnham, *Containment or Liberation: An Inquiry into the Aims of United States Foreign Policy* (New York: J. Day, 1953). On Burnham see the recent biography by Daniel Kelly, *James Burnham and the Struggle for the World: A Life* (Wilmington: Isi Books, 2002). John Foster Dulles presented his critique of containment in a famous article published in *Life* magazine. See John Foster Dulles, "A Policy of Boldness," *Life,* 19 May 1952. On the controversial John Foster Dulles, see Townsend Hoopes, *The Devil and John Foster Dulles* (Boston: Little Brown, 1973), and the different interpretations in Richard Immerman, ed., *John Foster Dulles and the Diplomacy of the Cold War* (Princeton: Princeton University Press, 1990).

11. On the shock and disappointment of Wisner and others regarding the U.S. decision not to intervene in support of Hungarian protestors, see Peter Grose, *Gentleman Spy: The Life of Allen*

Dulles (Boston: Houghton Mifflin, 1994), 435–43. On the Hungarian crisis as a paradigmatic example of the limits and impracticability of rollback, see the thorough Csaba Bekes, "Cold War, Détente and the 1956 Revolution," working paper, 2002, International Center for Advanced Studies, New York University, http://www.nyu.edu/gsas/dept/icas/Bekes.pdf (accessed 24 April 2009). See also Lazlo Bohri, "Rollback, Liberation, Containment, or Inaction? U.S. Policy and Eastern Europe in the 1950s," *Journal of Cold War Studies* 3 (Fall 1999): 67–110; and Christopher J. Tudda, "Reenacting the Story of Tantalus: Eisenhower, Dulles, and the Failed Rhetoric of Liberation," *Journal of Cold War Studies* 4 (Fall 2005): 3–35.

12. Melvin Leffler, *A Preponderance of Power: National Security, the Truman Administration, and the Cold War* (Stanford: Stanford University Press, 1992).

13. Kennan, "Sources of Soviet Conduct," 580–82. On the common objectives (the transformation of the USSR or its demise) but different methods of Kennan and Roosevelt, see Frank Ninkovich, *Modernity and Power: A History of the Domino Theory in the Twentieth Century* (Chicago: University of Chicago Press, 1994), 134–39.

14. On this and on U.S. capacity to exercise for a long period a uniquely consensual form of leadership and hegemony, see Joseph Nye, *Bound to Lead: The Changing Nature of American Power* (New York: Basic Books, 1990); and G. John Ikenberry, *After Victory: Institutions, Strategic Restraint and the Rebuilding of Order after Major Wars* (Princeton: Princeton University Press, 2001).

15. On this, see especially Michael Hogan, *The Marshall Plan: America, Britain, and the Reconstruction of Western Europe* (Cambridge: Cambridge University Press, 1987); and Hogan, *A Cross of Iron: Harry S. Truman and the Origins of the National Security State* (Cambridge: Cambridge University Press, 1998). On the origins of the National Security State, in addition to Leffler, *Preponderance of Power,* see Daniel Yergin, *Shattered Peace: The Origins of the Cold War and the National Security State* (Boston: Houghton Mifflin, 1977) and Douglas T. Stuart, *Creating the National Security State: A History of the Law That Transformed America* (Princeton: Princeton University Press, 2008).

16. On the estimates (and mistakes) of U.S. intelligence, see John Prados, *The Soviet Estimate: U.S. Intelligence Analysis and Russian Military Strength* (New York: Dial Press, 1982). On Soviet nuclear strategy, see David Holloway, *The Soviet Union and the Arms Race* (New Haven: Yale University Press, 1983).

17. Jacques van Ypersele de Strihou, "Sharing the Defense Burden among Allies," *Review of Economics and Statistics* 4 (November 1967): 527–36. For slightly different data, see Gaddis, *Strategies of Containment,* 359. See also Paul Kennedy, *The Rise and Fall of the Great Powers: Economic Change and Military Conflict from 1500 to 2000* (New York: Random House, 1988); and Martin Walker, *The Cold War: A History* (New York: Henry Holt, 1993), 214. Marc Trachtenberg has convincingly argued that until the early 1960s the United States enjoyed a quasi–first strike capability. See Marc Trachtenberg, *A Constructed Peace: The Making of the European Settlement, 1945–1963* (Princeton: Princeton University Press, 1999), 179–82.

18. On the missile gap controversy, see the balanced reconstructions of Gaddis, *Strategies of Containment,* 182–88; McGeorge Bundy, *Danger and Survival: Choices about the Bomb in the First Fifty Years* (New York: Vintage, 1988), 334–52; and Linda McFarland, *Cold War Strategist: Stuart Symington and the Search for National Security* (Westport, CT: Praeger, 2001), 77–96.

19. Teller, as quoted in Walker, *Cold War,* 114. On Eisenhower's fiscal conservatism and aversion to high military expenditures, see Trachtenberg, *Constructed Peace;* and Stephen Ambrose, *Eisenhower: The President* (New York: Simon and Schuster, 1984). See also David L. Snead, *The Gaither Committee: Eisenhower and the Cold War* (Columbus: Ohio State University Press, 1999); and Cristopher Preble, *John F. Kennedy and the Missile Gap* (DeKalb: Northern Illinois University Press, 2004).

20. Data from Kennedy, *Rise and Fall,* 559–64; Wyatt Wells, *American Capitalism: Continuity and Change from Mass Production to the Information Society* (Chicago: Ivan R. Dee, 2003), 27–39.

See also the data available at the Organisation for Economic Co-operation and Development (OECD) massive database, http://stats.oecd.org/WBOS (accessed 24 April 2009).

21. Arnaldo Testi, *Il secolo degli Stati Uniti* [The U.S. century] (Bologna: Il Mulino, 2008), 186–87; Lizabeth Cohen, *A Consumer's Republic: The Politics of Mass Consumption in Postwar America* (New York: Knopf, 2003), 122–24. Charles Maier, "The Politics of Productivity: Foundations of American International Economic Policy after World War II," *International Organization* 31 (1977): 607–33; on the society of mass consumption and its political implications, see the considerations in many of the essays in Alan Brinkley, *Liberalism and Its Discontents* (Cambridge: Harvard University Press, 1998). On Europe see Tony Judt, *Postwar: A History of Europe since 1945* (New York: Penguin, 2005), 324–53.

22. On this, and more in general on the culture and ideology of modernization, see the pathbreaking work of Michael Latham, *Modernization as Ideology: American Social Science and "Nation Building" in the Kennedy Era* (Chapel Hill: University of North Carolina Press, 2000). See also Kimber Charles Pearce, *Rostow, Kennedy, and the Rhetoric of Foreign Aid* (East Lansing: Michigan State University Press, 2001); and Nils Gilman, *Mandarins of the Future: Modernization Theory in Cold War America* (Baltimore: Johns Hopkins University Press, 2003). The bible of the ideology of modernization was Walt Rostow, *The Stages of Economic Growth: A Non-Communist Manifesto* (Cambridge: Cambridge University Press, 1960).

23. On U.S. exceptionalism, see Anders Stephanson, *Manifest Destiny: American Expansion and the Empire of Right* (New York: Hill and Wang, 1995); Daniel Rodgers, "Exceptionalism," in *Imagined Histories: American Historians Interpret the Past,* ed. Anthony Molho and Gordon Woods, 21–40 (Princeton: Princeton University Press, 1998); and Ian Tyrrel, "American Exceptionalism in the Age of International History," *American Historical Review* 4 (October 1991): 1031–55.

24. David Calleo, *The Imperious Economy* (Cambridge: Harvard University Press, 1982); and Calleo, *Beyond American Hegemony: The Future of the Western Alliance* (New York: Basic Books, 1987). See also Charles Maier, "Consigning the Twentieth Century to History: Alternative Narratives for the Modern Era," *American Historical Review* 3 (June 2000): 807–31.

25. Herman Van Der Wee, *Prosperity and Upheaval: The World Economy, 1945–1980* (London: Penguin, 1987), 48–56.

26. NSC 68, *United States Objectives and Programs for National Security,* 14 April 1950, consultable at http://www.fas.org/irp/offdocs/nsc-hst/nsc-68.htm (accessed 24 April 2009). On the genesis and importance of the document, see Ernest May, ed., *American Cold War Strategy: Interpreting NSC 68* (New York: St. Martin's Press, 1993).

27. Ironically, one of the main authors of the document and of this passage in particular, John Paton Davies, later became a victim of McCarthyism and lost his job at the State Department. See Anders Stephanson, "Liberty or Death: The Cold War as U.S. Ideology," in *Reviewing the Cold War: Approaches, Interpretations, Theory,* ed. Odd Arne Westad, 98 (London: Frank Cass, 2000); Ellen Schrecker, *Many Are the Crimes: McCarthyism in America* (Boston: Little Brown, 1998), 240–51.

28. David Engerman, "American Knowledge and Global Power," *Diplomatic History* 4 (September 2007): 599–622. The literature on "Americanization" and the American model is immense. Among many works, see three different approaches and interpretations: Victoria De Grazia, *Irresistible Empire: America's Advance through Twentieth-Century Europe* (Cambridge: Harvard University Press, 2005); David Ellwood, *Rival and the Lodestar: America and the Politics of Modernisation in Europe, 1898 to the Present* (Oxford: Oxford University Press, forthcoming); and Richard Pells, *Not Like Us: How Europeans Have Loved, Hated, and Transformed American Culture since World War II* (New York: Basic Books, 1997).

29. Geir Lundestad, "Empire by Invitation? The United States and Western Europe, 1945–52," *Journal of Peace Research* 2 (1986): 263–77; Lundestad, *The American Empire* (Oslo-Oxford: Oxford University Press–Norwegian University Press, 1990). Charles Maier, "Alliance and Autonomy:

European Identity and United States Foreign Policy Objectives in the Truman Years," in *The Truman Presidency,* ed. Michael J. Lacey, 273–98 (Cambridge: Cambridge University Press, 1989). For an exceptionalist reading of the Atlantic Alliance, see Lawrence Kaplan, *NATO and the United States: The Enduring Alliance* (Boston: Twayne, 1988).

30. On the opposition to the national security state and its violation (real or alleged) of these principles, see the different interpretations in Hogan, *Cross of Iron;* Stuart, *Creating the National Security State;* Michael Sherry, *In the Shadow of War: The United States since the 1930s* (New Haven: Yale University Press, 1995); and Aaron L. Friedberg, *In the Shadow of the Garrison State* (Princeton: Princeton University Press, 2000).

31. On the conservative opposition to the CIA and, more generally, the National Security State, see Rhodri Jeffreys-Jones, *The CIA and American Democracy,* 2nd ed. (New Haven: Yale University Press, 1998), 24–41. On the alternatives to containment and their failure, see Logevall, "Critique of Containment"; and Thomas G. Paterson, ed., *Cold War Critics: Alternatives to American Foreign Policy in the Truman Years* (Westport, CT: Greenwood Press, 1976).

32. For a sympathetic view of Stalin's security policy, see Geoffrey Roberts, *Stalin's Wars: From World War to the Cold War, 1939–1953* (New Haven: Yale University Press, 2007). For a balanced, although sometimes anodyne, account, see also Melvyn Leffler, *For the Soul of Mankind* (New York: Hill and Wang, 2007), 11–83. On the ancient matrixes of American anti-Communism, see Michael Heale, *American Anticommunism: Combating the Enemy Within* (Baltimore: Johns Hopkins University Press, 1990). On Stalin's search for a total security, see many of the essays in Francesca Gori and Silvio Pons, eds., *The Soviet Union and Europe in the Cold War, 1943–53* (New York: St. Martin's Press, 1996); and Vojtnech Mastny, *The Cold War and Soviet Insecurity: The Stalin Years* (Oxford: Oxford University Press, 1996). The exclusive responsibility of the USSR for the inception of the Cold War is maintained in John Lewis Gaddis, *We Now Know: Rethinking Cold War History* (Oxford: Oxford University Press, 1997). For an opposite interpretation, see Carolyn Eisenberg, *Drawing the Line: The American Decision to Divide Germany, 1944–49* (Cambridge: Cambridge University Press, 1996).

33. The neutrality acts approved in the second half of the 1930s made it virtually impossible for the United States to trade with belligerent countries. The acts symbolized the abandonment of the United States' historical claim, constantly reaffirmed throughout history, of the right of neutral countries to continue trading with all other countries even in times of war.

34. Campbell Craig, "The Not-So-Strange Career of Charles Beard," *Diplomatic History* 2 (Spring 2001): 251–74. More generally, see Justus Doenecke, *Storm on the Horizon: The Challenge to American Intervention, 1939–1941* (Lanham, MD: Rowman and Littlefield, 2000); and the classic volume by Manfred Jonas, *Isolationism in America, 1935–1941* (Ithaca: Cornell University Press, 1966).

35. On Cold War culture and the phobias it produced, see the excellent Stephen J. Whitfield, *The Culture of the Cold War,* 2nd ed. (Baltimore: Johns Hopkins University Press, 1996); and Lisle Abbot Rose, *The Cold War Comes to Main Street: America in 1950* (Lawrence: University Press of Kansas, 1999).

36. Dwight D. Eisenhower, "Address Accepting the Presidential Nomination at the Republican National Convention in Chicago," 11 July 1952, http://www.presidency.ucsb.edu/ws/index.php?pid=75626 (accessed 24 April 2009).

37. Ninkovich, *Modernity and Power;* and Frank Ninkovich, *The Wilsonian Century: U.S. Foreign Policy since 1900* (Chicago: University of Chicago Press, 1998).

38. This contradiction is particularly striking in NSC 68, which constantly emphasizes the strength of the USSR and of Communism, while reaffirming the superiority of the United States and its capacity to meet the challenge.

39. Henry Jackson, "What It Means to Be a Liberal," commencement address, University of Puget Sound, 14 August 1970, Henry M. Jackson Papers, University of Washington Libraries,

Manuscripts Collections, Seattle, accession no. 3560-6: Foreign Policy and Defense Issues, Speeches and Writings, folder 8.

40. "Memorandum of Conversation," meeting between Henry Kissinger and representatives of the Business Council, 1 December 1971, in *Foundations of Foreign Policy, 1969–1972,* vol. 1 of *Foreign Relations of the United States, 1969–1976* (Washington, DC: Government Printing Office, 2003), available at http://www.state.gov/r/pa/ho/frus/nixon/i/20705.htm (accessed 24 April 2009); Jussi Hanhimäki, *The Flawed Architect: Henry Kissinger and American Foreign Policy* (New York: Oxford University Press, 2004), 30.

41. George Kennan, Senate Committee on Foreign Relations, Hearings on Détente, 20 August 1974 (Washington, DC: Congressional Printing Office, 1975), 64. McNamara's quote is in Bundy, *Danger and Survival,* 546. For extraordinary research on the antinuclear movement, see Lawrence S. Wittner, *The Struggle against the Bomb,* vol. 1: *One World or None: A History of the World Nuclear Disarmament Movement through 1953* (Stanford: Stanford University Press, 1993), and vol. 2: *Resisting the Bomb: A History of the World Nuclear Disarmament Movement, 1954–1970* (Stanford: Stanford University Press, 1997).

42. Kennedy and Khrushchev, as quoted in Jeremi Suri, *Power and Protest: Global Revolution and the Rise of Détente* (Cambridge: Harvard University Press, 2003), 42. On the importance of the Test Ban Treaty, see the convincing analysis of Trachtenberg, *Constructed Peace,* 352–402.

43. The United States would nevertheless have preserved a vast retaliatory potential. See Raymond L. Garthoff, *Reflections on the Cuban Missile Crisis,* 2nd ed. (Washington, DC: Brookings Institution Press, 1989).

44. Michael D. War and David R. Davis, "Risky Business: U.S.-Soviet Competition and Corporate Profit," in *The Political Economy of Military Spending in the United States,* ed. Alex Mintz, 65–101 (London: Routledge, 1992). On the technological limits of Soviet rearmament, see Pavel Podvig, "The Window of Vulnerability That Wasn't: Soviet Military Buildup in the 1970s—A Research Note," *International Security* 1 (Summer 2008): 118–38. See also Holloway, *Soviet Union and the Arms Race,* 57–60; Wilfried Loth, *Overcoming the Cold War: A History of Détente* (Basingstoke, UK: Palgrave, 2002), 85–89; and Richard C. Thornton, *The Nixon-Kissinger Years: The Reshaping of American Foreign Policy,* 2nd ed. (St. Paul, MN: Paragon House, 2001), xv–xxi, who exaggerates, however, the political utility of the Soviet nuclear arsenal.

45. This aspect is strongly emphasized by Calleo, *Imperious Economy.* Lovett, as quoted in Gaddis, *Strategies of Containment,* 94.

46. Walker, *Cold War,* 142; Wells, *American Capitalism,* 69–74.

47. Bundy, as quoted in Gaddis, *Strategies of Containment,* 272. On the impact of the Vietnam War on the federal budget, see Michael Eldestein, "War and the American Economy in the Twentieth Century," in *The Cambridge Economic History of the United States,* vol. 3: *The Twentieth Century,* ed. Stanley L. Engerman and Robert E. Gallman, 378–79 (Cambridge: Cambridge University Press, 2000).

48. For some useful data, see the rich OECD database at http://stats.oecd.org/WBOS/ (accessed 24 April 2009). Kennedy, *Rise and Fall,* 543–64; Thornton, *Nixon-Kissinger Years,* 7–10; Walker, *Cold War,* 141–43; Van Der Wee, *Prosperity and Upheaval,* 264–66; Peter H. Lindert, "U.S. Foreign Trade and Trade Policy in the Twentieth Century," in Engerman and Gallman, *Cambridge Economic History of the United States,* 3:407–62.

49. Van Der Wee, *Prosperity and Upheaval,* 472–84; Francis Gavin, *Gold, Dollars and Power: The Politics of International Monetary Relations, 1958–1971* (Chapel Hill: University of North Carolina Press, 2004); Barry Eichengreen, "U.S. Foreign Financial Relations in the Twentieth-Century," in Engerman and Gallman, *Cambridge Economic History of the United States,* 3:497.

50. Henry Kissinger, "Address to the Pacem in Terris III Conference," Washington, DC, 8 October 1973, in Henry Kissinger, *American Foreign Policy,* 3rd ed. (New York: Norton, 1977), 128.

51. For two very different examples, see David Ryan, *The United States and Europe in the Twentieth Century* (London: Longman, 2003); and Geir Lundestad, *"Empire" by Integration: The*

United States and European Integration, 1945–1997 (Oxford: Oxford University Press, 1997). See also the periodization proposed in David Ellwood, "America as a European Power: Four Dimensions of Transatlantic Relationships: 1945 to the Late 1990s," in *Three Postwar Eras in Comparison: Western Europe 1918–1945–1989,* ed. Carl Levy and Mark Roseman, 67–85 (New York: Palgrave, 2002).

52. On de Gaulle and his critique of Cold War Atlanticism, see Gaetano Quagliariello, *De Gaulle e il gollismo* [De Gaulle and Gaullism] (Bologna: Il Mulino, 2003); and Maurice Vaïsse, *La grandeur: Politique étrangère du général de Gaulle, 1958–1969* [La grandeur: The foreign policy of General De Gaulle, 1958–1969] (Paris: Fayard, 1998).

53. Kissinger, *White House Years,* 938–47; Joan Hoff-Wilson, "'Nixingerism,' NATO and Détente," *Diplomatic History* 4 (Autumn 1989): 501–25; Dana H. Allin, *Cold War Illusions: America, Europe and Soviet Power, 1969–1989* (New York: St. Martin's Press, 1995), 29–31.

54. See the detailed reconstruction of Thomas Schwartz, *Lyndon Johnson and Europe: In the Shadow of Vietnam* (Cambridge: Harvard University Press, 2003).

55. Henry Kissinger, A *Troubled Partnership: A Reappraisal of the Atlantic Alliance* (New York: McGraw-Hill, 1965).

56. As we shall see, a similar critique was moved by Kissinger.

57. Suri, *Power and Protest,* 131; on the global character of the protests of 1968, see also Arthur Marwick, *The Sixties: Cultural Revolution in Britain, France, Italy, and the United States, c. 1958–c. 1974* (Oxford: Oxford University Press, 1998); Carole Fink, Philipp Gassert, and Detlef Junker, eds., *1968: The World Transformed* (Cambridge: Cambridge University Press, 1998); Marcello Flores and Alberto De Bernardi, *Il sessantotto (Ninety Sixty-Eight),* 2nd ed. (Bologna: Il Mulino, 2003).

58. David A. Rapkin, William R. Thompson, and Jon A. Cristopherson, "Bipolarity and Bipolarization in the Cold War Era," *Journal of Conflict Resolution* 2 (June 1979): 264. On the mythogenic power of third-world revolutions, and Cuba's in particular, see also Torbjorn L. Knutsen, *The Rise and Fall of World Orders* (Manchester: Manchester University Press, 1999), 234–36.

59. On anti-Communism as a disciplining factor of post-1945 U.S. political discourse, see Heale, *American Anticommunism,* 198–203; and David Campbell, *Writing Security: United States Foreign Policy and the Politics of Identity,* 2nd ed. (Minneapolis: University of Minnesota Press, 1998), 147–60.

60. James Burnham, "Finlandization?" *National Review,* 19 May 1970, 506. On the transformation of the American Right, see Jerome L. Himmenstein, *To the Right: The Transformation of American Conservatism* (Berkeley: University of California Press, 1990), 1–62; and William C. Berman, *America's Right Turn* (Baltimore: Johns Hopkins University Press, 1994), 5–36.

61. Van Gosse, "A Movement of Movements: The Definition and Periodization of the New Left," in *A Companion to Post-1945 America,* ed. Jean-Cristophe Agnew and Roy Rosenzweig (Oxford: Blackwell, 2002), 279.

62. Todd Gitlin, *The Sixties: Years of Hope; Days of Rage* (New York: Bantam Books, 1987); Maurice Isserman, *"If I Had a Hammer…": The Death of the Old Left and the Birth of the New Left* (New York: Basic Books, 1987); Kevin Mattson, *Intellectuals in Action: The Origins of the New Left and Radical Liberalism* (University Park: Pennsylvania State University Press, 2003).

63. John Ehrman, *The Rise of Neoconservatism: Intellectual and Foreign Affairs* (New Haven: Yale University Press, 1995), 33–62.

64. J. William Fulbright, *The Arrogance of Power* (New York: Random House, 1966), 3; Kissinger, *White House Years,* 939. On Mansfield and Fulbright, see the excellent works of Randall Bennet Woods, *Fulbright: A Biography* (Cambridge: Cambridge University Press, 1995); and Gregory Allen Olson, *Mansfield and Vietnam: A Study in Rhetorical Adaptation* (East Lansing: Michigan State University Press, 1995).

65. NSC staff, *Analysis of Changes in International Politics since World War II and Their Implications for Our Basic Assumptions about U.S. Foreign Policy,* attachment to "Memorandum from the

President's Assistant for National Security Affairs (Kissinger) to President Nixon," 20 October 1969, in *Foundations of Foreign Policy, 1969–1972.*

66. Tucker, as quoted in Ehrman, *Rise of Neoconservatism,* 23.

2. Kissinger and Kissingerism

1. For a different interpretation, which stresses Kissinger's search for a moral compass in times of deep moral ambiguity, see Jeremi Suri, *Henry Kissinger and the American Century* (Cambridge: Harvard University Press, 2007). Walter Russel Mead, *Special Providence: American Foreign Policy and How It Changed the World* (New York: Routledge, 2002), 72; Jussi Hanhimäki, *The Flawed Architect: Henry Kissinger and American Foreign Policy* (New York: Oxford University Press, 2004), xxi; Michael Joseph Smith, *Realist Thought: From Weber to Kissinger* (Baton Rouge: Louisiana State University Press, 1986), 193. For a detailed, popular biography of Kissinger that constantly emphasizes his realism, see Walter Isaacson, *Kissinger: A Biography* (New York: Simon and Schuster, 1992).

2. Hans Morgenthau, "Henry Kissinger, Secretary of State: An Evaluation," *Encounter* 5 (November 1975): 57–58. A similar interpretation is offered in one of the first serious historical reconstructions of Kissinger, despite the author not having access to the rich archival sources now available to scholars: Robert D. Schulzinger, *Henry Kissinger: Doctor of Diplomacy* (New York: Columbia University Press, 1989).

3. Bruce Mazlish, *Kissinger: The European Mind in American Policy* (New York: Basic Books, 1976). For a similar, although less hagiographic analysis, see Argyris G. Andrianopoulos, *Western Europe in Kissinger's Global Strategy* (New York: St. Martin's Press, 1988).

4. The best and most detailed reconstruction of this part of Kissinger's life is Isaacson, *Kissinger,* 17–81. See also Suri, *Kissinger and the American Century,* 16–51.

5. Kraemer, as quoted in Isaacson, *Kissinger,* 45 and 57. On Kissinger's experience in the army, see also Suri, *Kissinger and the American Century,* 52–91; Mazlish, *Kissinger,* 36–54.

6. Bruce Kuklick, *Blind Oracles: Intellectuals and War from Kennan to Kissinger* (Princeton: Princeton University Press, 2006), 185, 187. Smith, *Realist Thought,* 197. I have not had the chance to consult the original manuscript, and this reconstruction is based on third sources. Among the many Kissingerists, a few have dedicated most of their research to the study of "The Meaning of History," finding in it the true foundations of Kissinger's realism. See, for example, Peter Dickson, *Kissinger and the Meaning of History* (Cambridge: Cambridge University Press, 1978). See also the useful analyses of Greg Russel, "Kissinger's Philosophy of History and Kantian Ethics," *Diplomacy and Statecraft* 1 (March 1996): 97–124; and Richard Weitz, "Henry Kissinger's Philosophy of International Relations, *Diplomacy and Statecraft* 1 (March 1991): 103–29.

7. Henry Kissinger, *A World Restored: Metternich, Castlereagh, and the Problems of Peace, 1812–1822* (Boston: Houghton Mifflin, 1957).

8. Kissinger, as quoted in Suri, *Kissinger and the American Century,* 129.

9. Kissinger, *World Restored,* 322. Smith, *Realist Thought,* 198; Robert Beisner, "History and Henry Kissinger," *Diplomatic History* 2 (Autumn 1990): 514. See also John D. Montgomery, "The Education of Henry Kissinger," *Journal of International Affairs* 9 (Spring 1975): 49–62.

10. Kuklick, *Blind Oracles,* 189 ("the supremely carried value in the world"); Kissinger, *World Restored,* 1.

11. Kissinger, *World Restored,* 322–23. As was often the case in Kissinger's writings, bombastic statements and sophisticated, brilliant, and baroque prose are not always matched by analytical clarity and precise explanations. In the specific case, Kissinger does not really explain what were the alternative options available to Metternich.

12. Stanley Hoffmann, "America Alone in the World," *American Prospect,* 23 September 2002. Already in 1978, Hoffmann offered a strong and effective critique of Kissinger in *Primacy or World*

Order: American Foreign Policy since the Cold War (New York: McGraw-Hill, 1978). On this topic see also Michael Joseph Smith and Linda B. Miller, "Reflections on an Ideal Influence," in *Ideas and Ideals: Essays on Politics in Honor of Stanley Hoffmann,* ed. M. J. Smith and L. B. Miller, 47–60 (Boulder: Westview Press, 1993). On the fascination of U.S. elites and foreign policy experts with European practices and discourse, see John L. Harper, *American Visions of Europe: Franklin D. Roosevelt, George F. Kennan, and Dean G. Acheson* (Cambridge: Cambridge University Press, 1994).

13. Michael Sherry, *In the Shadow of War: The United States since the 1930s* (New Haven: Yale University Press, 1995), 175; Isaacson, *Kissinger,* 82–90; Hanhimäki, *Flawed Architect,* 8–9.

14. On "massive retaliation" and the controversy it provoked, see John Lewis Gaddis, *Strategies of Containment: A Critical Appraisal of Postwar American National Security Policy* (New York: Oxford University Press, 1982), 146–51; Marc Trachtenberg, *History and Strategy* (Princeton: Princeton University Press, 1991), 161–68.

15. Henry Kissinger, *Nuclear Weapons and Foreign Policy* (New York: Harper and Row, 1957). On the success of *Nuclear Weapons and Foreign Policy,* see Schulzinger, *Kissinger,* 12–14, and Isaacson, *Kissinger,* 88–93. Kissinger had already published two articles on the topic in *Foreign Affairs:* "Force and Diplomacy in the Nuclear Age," *Foreign Affairs* 3 (April 1956): 349–66; and "Strategy and Organization," *Foreign Affairs* 3 (April 1957): 379–94.

16. Kissinger, *Nuclear Weapons and Foreign Policy,* 7, 14, 20.

17. Ibid., 7, 14, 86–87, 242–48; Smith, *Realist Thought,* 203–5 ("reluctance…power"); Hanhimäki, *Flawed Architect,* 8–10 ("risks…opportunities"). On the idea of total victory in U.S. political (and military) culture, see Anders Stephanson, "Fourteen Notes on the Concept of the Cold War," in *Rethinking Geopolitics,* ed. Simon Dalby and Gearóid Ó Tuathail, 62–85 (London: Routledge, 1998); and the classic analysis by Russel Frank Weigley, *The American Way of War: A History of the United States Military Strategy and Policy* (New York: Macmillan, 1973). On Eisenhower's rhetoric of peace at any cost, see Kenneth Osgood, "Form before Substance: Eisenhower's Commitment to Psychological Warfare and Negotiations with the Enemy," *Diplomatic History* 3 (Summer 2000): 405–33; and the rich textual analysis of many of the essays in Martin J. Medhurst, ed., *Eisenhower's War of Words: Rhetoric and Leadership* (East Lansing: Michigan State University Press, 1994).

18. Kissinger, *Nuclear Weapons and Foreign Policy,* 155. See also McGeorge Bundy, *Danger and Survival: Choices about the Bomb in the First Fifty Years* (New York: Vintage, 1988), 348. Lawrence Freedman, *The Evolution of Nuclear Strategy,* 2nd ed. (London: Macmillan, 1989), 106–10.

19. The others were the physicists Edward Teller and Herman Kahn. See Paul Boyer, *Fallout: A Historian Reflects on America's Half-Century Encounter with Nuclear Weapons* (Columbus: Ohio State University Press, 1998), 96–97; Grant Stillman, "Two of the MADest Scientists: Where Strangelove Meets Dr. No; or Unexpected Roots for Kubrick's Cold War Classic," *Film History* 4 (December 2008): 487–500; and Schulzinger, *Kissinger,* 12 ("apocalyptic"). Kissinger, as quoted in Isaacson, *Kissinger,* 92.

20. Schulzinger, *Kissinger,* 13.

21. Campbell Craig, "The Illogic of Henry Kissinger's Nuclear Strategy," *Armed Forces and Society* 4 (Summer 2003): 547–68. Craig offers a convincing and effective critique of Kissinger's reflection on nuclear weapons. Suri finds Craig's account "too dismissive…of Kissinger's strategic thought" but does not elaborate. Suri, *Kissinger and the American Century,* 311.

22. Craig, "Illogic of Henry Kissinger's Nuclear Strategy," 551, 555; Paul Nitze, "Limited Wars or Massive Retaliation," *Reporter,* 5 September 1957, 40–42; Hans Morgenthau, review of *Nuclear Weapons and Foreign Policy,* by Henry Kissinger, *American Political Science Review* 3 (September 1958): 842–44. On the limits of Kissinger's analysis, see also Morton H. Halperin, "Nuclear Weapons and Limited War," *Journal of Conflict Resolution* 2 (June 1961): 146–66.

23. Kissinger, *Nuclear Weapons and Foreign Policy,* 11–12.

24. Hanhimäki, *Flawed Architect,* 11.

25. Frank Ninkovich, *The Wilsonian Century: U.S. Foreign Policy since 1900* (Chicago: University of Chicago Press, 1998), 183–84.

26. Henry Kissinger, *The Necessity for Choice* (New York: Harper, 1961).

27. Ibid., 59, 62.

28. On Kennedy's strategy and its limits, see Lawrence Freedman, *Kennedy's Wars: Berlin, Cuba, Laos, and Vietnam* (Oxford: Oxford University Press, 2000); Gaddis, *Strategies of Containment,* 198–273; Bundy, *Danger and Survival* 488–98.

29. Kissinger, *Necessity for Choice,* 177.

30. Isaacson, *Kissinger,* 106; Hanhimäki, *Flawed Architect,* 13.

31. "The issue," Kissinger maintained, "cannot be settled by comparing our present strength with that of the previous years. Deterrence depends on our strength in relation to that of possible aggressors. Since what has been called *the* Deterrent—the retaliatory power—proved inadequate to deter a vast range of challenges even during the period of nuclear preponderance, there is a serious case for worry when the missile gap approaches" (*Necessity for Choice,* 15).

32. Maxwell D. Taylor, *The Uncertain Trumpet* (New York: Harper, 1960), 131. Kennedy would appoint Taylor chairman of the Joint Chiefs of Staff and later ambassador to South Vietnam. On the work of the Gaither committee, see David L. Snead, *The Gaither Committee: Eisenhower and the Cold War* (Columbus: Ohio State University Press, 1999). On the missile gap controversy, see Cristopher Preble, *John F. Kennedy and the Missile Gap* (DeKalb: Northern Illinois University Press, 2004); and Linda McFarland, *Cold War Strategist: Stuart Symington and the Search for National Security* (Westport, CT: Praeger, 2001), 77–96.

33. Kissinger, *Necessity for Choice,* 1–2, 6, 26.

34. Ibid., 26.

35. Smith, *Realist Thought,* 204–5; and the acute considerations in Stanley Hoffmann, "The Case of Dr. Kissinger," *New York Review of Books,* 6 December 1979.

36. The limits of Kissinger's knowledge of the basics of economics are well known. Later the economist Fred Bergsten would claim that being an economic aide to Kissinger was like being military advisor to the pope; in Thomas W. Zeiler, "Just Do It! Globalization for Diplomatic Historians," *Diplomatic History* 4 (Autumn 2001): 532. See also the considerations of Hedley Bull, "Kissinger: The Primacy of Geopolitics," *International Affairs* 3 (Summer 1980): 484–87.

37. Kissinger, *Necessity for Choice,* 289–90.

38. Michael Latham, *Modernization as Ideology: American Social Science and "Nation Building" in the Kennedy Era* (Chapel Hill: University of North Carolina Press, 2000); Kimber Charles Pearce, *Rostow, Kennedy, and the Rhetoric of Foreign Aid* (East Lansing: Michigan State University Press, 2001); Nils Gilman, *Mandarins of the Future: Modernization Theory in Cold War America* (Baltimore: Johns Hopkins University Press, 2003).

39. "Memorandum of Conversation," meeting of the President's Task Force on Foreign Aid, 2 September 1969, in *Foundations of Foreign Policy, 1969–1972,* vol. 1 of *Foreign Relations of the United States, 1969–1976* (Washington, DC: Government Printing Office, 2003), available at http://www.state.gov/r/pa/ho/frus/nixon/i/20705.htm (accessed 24 April 2004).

40. Kissinger, *White House Years,* 69.

41. Among the many works on transatlantic relations and their tensions during the 1960s, see Geir Lundestad, *"Empire by Integration: The United States and European Integration, 1945–1997* (Oxford: Oxford University Press, 1997), 58–98; Lundestad, *The United States and Western Europe since 1945* (Oxford: Oxford University Press, 2003), 111–67; Wilfried Loth, *Overcoming the Cold War: A History of Détente* (Basingstoke, UK: Palgrave, 2002), 80–102; and Thomas Schwartz, *Lyndon Johnson and Europe: In the Shadow of Vietnam* (Cambridge: Harvard University Press, 2003).

42. Henry Kissinger, *The Troubled Partnership: A Reappraisal of the Atlantic Alliance* (New York: McGraw-Hill, 1965).

43. Ibid., 6, 97.

44. Ibid., 226–27, 235–36, 244, 248. See also Henry Kissinger, "For an Atlantic Confederacy," *Reporter,* 2 February 1961, 16–20.

45. Andrianopoulos, *Western Europe in Kissinger's Global Strategy,* 46, 73; Hanhimäki, *Flawed Architect,* 14.

46. Gaddis, *Strategies of Containment,* 274–308; and John Lewis Gaddis, "Rescuing Choice from Circumstances: The Statecraft of Henry Kissinger," in *The Diplomats, 1939–1979,* ed. Gordon A. Craig and Francis Loewenheim, 564–92 (Princeton: Princeton University Press, 1994).

47. Kissinger, *White House Years,* 105.

48. Kissinger, *Troubled Partnership,* 40–64; Henry Kissinger, "The Illusionist: Why We Misread de Gaulle," *Harper's,* March 1965, 70–77.

49. Kissinger, "Illusionist," 76.

50. Kissinger, *White House Years,* 105.

51. For a synthetic but acute analysis of U.S. hegemony, see Charles Maier, "Alliance and Autonomy: European Identity and United States Foreign Policy Objectives in the Truman Years," in *The Truman Presidency,* ed. Michael J. Lacey, 273–98 (Cambridge: Cambridge University Press, 1989). See also G. John Ikenberry, *After Victory: Institutions, Strategic Restraint and the Rebuilding of Order after Major Wars* (Princeton: Princeton University Press, 2001).

52. This is one of the aspects on which I agree with Suri's ambitious *Kissinger and the American Century.*

53. For a sophisticated analysis of geopolitical discourse, see Gearóid Ó Thuatail, *Critical Geopolitics: The Politics of Writing Global Space* (London: Routledge, 1996); and Gearóid Ó Thuatail and Simon Dalby, eds., *Rethinking Geopolitics* (London: Routledge, 1998). See also David Campbell, *Writing Security: United States Foreign Policy and the Politics of Identity,* 2nd ed. (Minneapolis: University of Minnesota Press, 1998).

54. Gaddis, "Rescuing Choice from Circumstances"; Mark Gismondi, "Tragedy, Realism, and Postmodernity: Kulturpessimismus in the Theories of Max Weber, E. H. Carr, Hans Morgenthau, and Henry Kissinger," *Diplomacy and Statecraft* 15 (2004): 435–63.

55. Henry Kissinger, *American Foreign Policy,* 3rd ed. (New York: Norton, 1977), 79; Robert J. Lieber, *No Common Power: Understanding International Relations* (New York: HarperCollins, 1995), 18, 28; Dana H. Allin, *Cold War Illusions: America, Europe, and Soviet Power, 1969–1989* (London: Macmillan, 1995, 30; Tad Szulc, "Lisbon and Washington: Behind the Portuguese Revolution," *Foreign Policy* 1 (Winter 1975–76): 16; the interview of Henry Kissinger by James Reston is in the *New York Times,* 13 October 1974 (at the time, Kissinger was secretary of state and national security advisor). These examples are purely illustrative. Many others could be added.

56. Osgood talks of "limitationism," in NSC staff, *Analysis of Changes in International Politics since World War II and Their Implications for Our Basic Assumptions about U.S. Foreign Policy,* attachment to "Memorandum from the President's Assistant for National Security Affairs (Kissinger) to President Nixon," 20 October 1969, in *Foundations of Foreign Policy, 1969–1972,* vol. 1 of *Foreign Relations of the United States, 1969–1976* (Washington, DC: Government Printing Office, 2003), available at http://www.state.gov/r/pa/ho/frus/nixon/i/20705.htm (accessed 24 April 2005); Kissinger, *White House Years,* 57.

57. Kissinger, as quoted in Dallek, *Nixon and Kissinger,* 150–51.

58. Ron Robin, *The Making of the Cold War Enemy: Culture and Politics in the Military-Intellectual Complex* (Princeton: Princeton University Press, 2001).

59. A classic case of linkage was represented by the attempt to tie the negotiations between the United States and the USSR, and U.S. economic aid, to progress in Vietnam and North Vietnam's moderation of its requests. This strategy assumed the Soviet Union's ability to influence the choices and behavior of its North Vietnamese ally.

60. Henry Kissinger, "Domestic Structure and Foreign Policy," *Daedalus* 2 (April 1966): 503–29; Kissinger, as quoted in Christopher Hill, *The Changing Politics of Foreign Policy*

(London: Palgrave, 2003), 94; Zeev Maoz, *National Choices and International Processes* (Cambridge: Cambridge University Press, 1990), 54.

61. Hoffmann, "Case of Dr. Kissinger." For a bitter denunciation of the marginalization of the Department of State during the Nixon years, see William Bundy, *A Tangled Web: The Making of Foreign Policy in the Nixon Presidency* (New York: Hill and Wang, 1998). On the U.S. political system, its institutions, and the conduct of foreign policy, see the different interpretations of Michael M. Mastanduno, "The United States Political System and International Leadership: A "Decidedly Inferior" Form of Government?" in *American Foreign Policy: Theoretical Essays,* 2nd ed., ed. John G. Ikenberry, 328–48 (New York: HarperCollins, 1996); John Gerard Ruggie, "The Past as Prologue? Interests, Identity, and American Foreign Policy," *International Security* 4 (Spring 1997): 89–125; and George Kennan, *American Diplomacy* (New York: Mentor Books, 1951).

62. A different interpretation—one that asserts a Judeo-Christian common denominator to transatlantic Cold War elites (of which Kissinger was a quintessential exponent)—is in Suri, *Kissinger and the American Century,* 52–91.

63. George Meany, "Foreign Policy Choices for the 1970s and 80s," statement before the Senate Foreign Relations Committee, 8 December 1975, Henry M. Jackson Papers, University of Washington Libraries, Manuscripts Collections, Seattle, accession no. 3560-6: Foreign Policy and Defense Issues, Speeches and Writings Others, folder 23; Isaacson, *Kissinger,* 655–56; Henry Kissinger, "The Moral Foundations of Foreign Policy," in Kissinger, *American Foreign Policy, 197–213.*

64. Anders Stephanson, "Diritto e giuridificazione delle relazioni internazionali da Franklin D. Roosevelt a George W. Bus" [Law and Juridification in International Relations from Franklin D. Roosevelt to George W. Bush] in *Giudicare e punire: I processi per i crimini di Guerra tra diritto e politica* [Try and Punish: The War Crime Trials between Law and Politics], ed. Luca Baldissarra and Paolo Pezzino, 77–105 (Naples: Ancora del Mediterraneo, 2005); on the legalism of U.S. foreign policy and its foundations, see Thomas Knock, *To End All Wars: Woodrow Wilson and the Quest for a New World Order* (Princeton: Princeton University Press, 1992); and Peter Maguire, *Law and War: An American Story* (New York: Columbia University Press, 2001); the Kissinger quote is in Kissinger, *White House Years,* 60.

65. Kissinger, *White House Years,* 61–62. Scholars of international relations have long debated the effective stability of a bipolar system. In favor of the idea of the inherent stability of a bipolar system are Kenneth Waltz, "The Stability of the Bipolar World," *Daedalus* 43, no. 3 (1964): 881–901; and John Lewis Gaddis, *The Long Peace: Inquiries into the History of the Cold War* (Oxford: Oxford University Press, 1987).

66. Kissinger, as quoted in Isaacson, *Kissinger,* 653.

67. See, for example, many considerations in Henry Kissinger, *Diplomacy* (New York: Simon and Schuster, 1994), where, however, Kissinger softens some of his previous positions. A precise critique of the weakness of Kissinger's concept of legitimacy is in Hoffmann, *Primacy or World Order,* 38–40; and Alastair Buchan, "The Irony of Henry Kissinger," *International Affairs* 3 (July 1974): 367–79. See also Stanley Hoffmann, *Janus and Minerva: Essays in the Theory and Practice of International Politics* (Boulder: Westview Press, 1987), 85–121.

68. Kissinger, *World Restored,* 173; Gismondi, "Tragedy, Realism, and Postmodernity," 450.

69. Ninkovich, *Wilsonian Century;* Knock, *To End All Wars;* and Federico Romero, "Democrazia ed egemonia: Woodrow Wilson e la concezione americana dell'ordine internazionale nel '900" [Democracy and hegemony: Woodrow Wilson and the U.S. conception of international order in the twentieth century], *Passato e Presente* 58 (January–April 2003): 17–43.

70. Suri, *Kissinger and the American Century,* 146 ("zealous idealism"); Henry Kissinger, *Diplomacy* (New York: Touchstone, 1994), 46.

71. Norman Graebner, "Henry Kissinger and American Foreign Policy: A Contemporary Reappraisal," *Australian Journal of Politics and History* 1 (April 1976): 6. John L. Girling, "Kissingerism: The Enduring Problem," *International Affairs* 3 (July 1975): 323–43.

3. Kissingerism in Action

1. Melvin Small, "The Election of 1968," *Diplomatic History* 4 (September 2004): 513. See also Lewis L. Gould, *The Election That Changed America* (Chicago: Ivan R. Dee, 1993); and Walter Lafeber, *The Deadly Bet: LBJ, Vietnam and the 1968 Election* (Lanham, MD: Rowman and Littlefield, 2005).

2. Marilyn Young, *The Vietnam Wars, 1945–1990* (New York: Harper, 1991), 232–33; Lieng Hang T. Nguyen, "Cold War Contradictions: Toward an International History of the Second Indochina War, 1969–1973," in *Making Sense of the Vietnamese Wars: Local, National and Transnational Perspectives,* ed. Marilyn B. Young and Mark P. Bradley, 199–249 (Oxford: Oxford University Press, 2008); Robert Dallek, *Nixon and Kissinger: Partners in Power* (New York: Harper-Collins, 2007), 70–75.

3. Richard M. Nixon, "Asia after Vietnam," *Foreign Affairs* 46 (October 1967): 111–25. Michael Lumbers, "The Irony of Vietnam: The Johnson Administration's Tentative Bridge Building to China, 1965–1966," *Journal of Cole War Studies* 3 (Summer 2004): 68–114; William Bundy, *A Tangled Web: The Making of Foreign Policy in the Nixon Presidency* (New York: Hill and Wang, 1998), 99–101. See also the intriguing analysis of Denise M Bostdorff, "The Evolution of a Diplomatic Surprise: Richard M. Nixon's Rhetoric on China, 1952–July 15, 1971," *Rhetoric and Public Affairs* 1 (Spring 2002): 31–56.

4. Melvyn Leffler, *For the Soul of the Mankind* (New York: Hill and Wang, 2007), 84–150; Vladislav M. Zubok, *A Failed Empire: The Soviet Union in the Cold War from Stalin to Gorbachev* (Chapel Hill: University of North Carolina Press, 2007), 94–121.

5. On the year 1963 as a watershed in the history of the Cold War, see Anders Stephanson, "Fourteen Notes on the Concept of the Cold War," in *Rethinking Geopolitics,* ed. Simon Dalby and Gearóid Ó Tuathail, 62–85 (London: Routledge, 1998); Marc Trachtenberg, *A Constructed Peace: The Making of the European Settlement, 1945–1963* (Princeton: Princeton University Press, 1999), 352–402; Rodolfo Mosca, "La distensione come modello di diplomazia reazionaria" [Détente as reactionary diplomacy], *Affari Esteri* 30 (April 1976): 209–28. On economic détente between the two superpowers, see Michael Mastanduno, *Economic Containment: CoCom and the Politics of East-West Trade* (Ithaca: Cornell University Press, 1992), 135–45.

6. Nixon's statement is quoted in many books. See, for example Jussi Hanhimäki, *The Flawed Architect: Henry Kissinger and American Foreign Policy* (New York: Oxford University Press 2004), 192; and Lloyd Gardner, "The Last Casualty? Richard Nixon and the End of the Vietnam War," in *A Companion to the Vietnam War,* ed. Marilyn B. Young and Robert Buzzanco (Malden, MA: Blackwell, 2002), 237. See also Rosemary Foot, *The Practice of Power: U.S. Relations with China since 1949* (Oxford: Clarendon Press, 1997); Robert S. Ross, *Negotiating Cooperation: The United States and China, 1969–1989* (Stanford: Stanford University Press, 1995). On the impact of the cultural revolution on China's external relations, see Barbara Barnouin and Yu Changgen, *Chinese Foreign Policy during the Cultural Revolution* (New York: Columbia University Press, 1998); and Jeremi Suri, *Power and Protest: Global Revolution and the Rise of Détente* (Cambridge: Harvard University Press, 2003), 114–21.

7. For a detailed historiographical discussion on Kissinger and his influence on Nixon, see Jussi Hanhimäki, "'Dr. Kissinger' or 'Mr. Henry'? Kissingerology, Thirty Years and Counting," *Diplomatic History* 5 (November 2003): 637–76. Nixon's attention to international issues is stressed in Franz Schurman, *The Foreign Politics of Richard Nixon: The Grand Design* (Berkeley: University of California Press, 1986); Joan Hoff, *Nixon Reconsidered* (New York: Basic Books, 1994); and Melvin Small, *The Presidency of Richard Nixon* (Lawrence: University Press of Kansas, 1999).

8. William Burr, ed., *The Kissinger Transcripts: The Top Secret Talks with Beijing and Moscow* (New York: Free Press, 1998), 4 ("It is extremely in our interest"); Stanley Hoffmann, "Varieties of Containment," *Reviews in American History* 2 (June 1983): 281 ("maniacally bipolar"). For

a different interpretation—one that stresses Kissinger's alleged multipolar awareness—see John Lewis Gaddis, *Strategies of Containment: A Critical Appraisal of Postwar American National Security Policy* (New York: Oxford University Press, 1982), 274–344; and Gaddis, "Rescuing Choice from Circumstances: The Statecraft of Henry Kissinger," in *The Diplomats, 1939–1979,* ed. Gordon A. Craig and Francis Loewenheim, 564–92 (Princeton: Princeton University Press, 1994).

9. NSC staff, *Analysis of Changes in International Politics since World War II and Their Implications for Our basic Assumptions about U.S. Foreign Policy,* attachment to "Memorandum from the President's Assistant for National Security Affairs (Kissinger) to President Nixon," 20 October 1969, in *Foundations of Foreign Policy, 1969–1972,* vol. 1 of *Foreign Relations of the United States, 1969–1976* (Washington, DC: Government Printing Office, 2003), available at http://www.state.gov/r/pa/ho/frus/nixon/i/20702.htm (accessed 25 April 2009).

10. Ibid.; "Background Press Briefing by the President's Assistant for National Security Affairs (Kissinger)," 14 August 1970, and "Memorandum of Conversation," meeting between Henry Kissinger and representatives of the Business Council, 1 December 1971, both in *Foundations of Foreign Policy, 1969–1972.*

11. "White House Background Press Briefing by the President's Assistant for National Security Affairs (Kissinger)," 16 February 1970, in *Foundations of Foreign Policy, 1969–1972;* and Henry Kissinger, *White House Years* (London: Weidenfeld and Nicolson, 1979), 54–70. Nixon, as quoted in Jeffrey Kimball, "The Nixon Doctrine: A Saga of Misunderstanding," *Presidential Studies Quarterly* 1 (March 2006): 71.

12. Raymond L. Garthoff, *Détente and Confrontation: American-Soviet Relations from Nixon to Reagan,* 2nd ed. (Washington, DC: Brookings Institution Press, 1994), 37.

13. Kissinger, *White House Years,* 66–67.

14. NSC staff, *Analysis of Changes in International Politics since World War II* ("The solid basis of détente…mutual recognition of the need to avoid war"); Dana H. Allin, *Cold War Illusions: America, Europe and Soviet Power, 1969–1989* (New York: St. Martin's Press, 1995), 25 ("heavily militarized *modus vivendi*" and "stalemate"); Garthoff, *Détente and Confrontation,* 36. See also Lawrence Freedman, *The Evolution of Nuclear Strategy,* 2nd ed. (New York: St. Martin's Press, 1989), 359–71.

15. John L. Girling, "Kissingerism: The Enduring Problems," *International Affairs* 3 (July 1975): 325. See also Argyris G. Andrianopoulos, *Western Europe in Kissinger's Global Strategy* (New York: St. Martin's Press, 1988); and Wilfried Loth, *Overcoming the Cold War: A History of Détente* (Basingstoke, UK: Palgrave, 2002), 102–27.

16. The quotation from Kissinger is in "Secretary of State's Staff Meeting," 26 December 1973, National Archives and Records Administration, College Park, MD (hereafter NARA), record group 59, Records of the Department of State (hereafter RG 59), lot file 78D443, transcripts of Secretary of State Henry Kissinger's staff meetings, 1973–1977, folder 1. See also Silvia Pietrantonio, "L'anno che non fu? L'anno dell'Europa e la crisi nelle relazioni transatlantiche, 1973–74" [The year that never was? The year of Europe and the crisis in the transatlantic relationship, 1973–74], Ph.D. diss., University of Bologna, 2008.

17. Among the many collections, see in particular lot file 78D443, containing transcripts of the meetings of Kissinger's staff between 1973 and 1977, as well as transcripts of Kissinger's telephone conversations, chronological file, in the Nixon Presidential Materials. For an example of Kissinger's attention (and even obsession) with the connection between foreign policy and domestic politics, see Noam Kochavi, "Insights Abandoned, Flexibility Lost: Kissinger, Soviet Jewish Emigration, and the Demise of Détente," *Diplomatic History* 3 (June 2003): 503–30. For more in general on the interdependence between domestic and international factors in U.S. foreign policy, see A. Rosati, *The Politics of United States Foreign Policy* (New York: Harcourt Brace, 1993); Melvin Small, *Democracy and Diplomacy: The Impact of Domestic Politics on U.S. Foreign Policy, 1789–1994* (Baltimore: Johns Hopkins University Press, 1996); Paula Stern, *Water's Edge: Domestic Politics and the Making of American Foreign Policy* (Westport, CT: Greenwood Press, 1997).

18. Henry Kissinger, "Domestic Structure and Foreign Policy," *Daedalus* 2 (April 1966): 523 ("to use foreign policy as a means of bringing about domestic cohesion"), reprinted in Kissinger, *American Foreign Policy,* 3rd ed. (New York: Norton, 1977), 9–43. See also Zeev Maoz, *National Choices and International Processes* (Cambridge: Cambridge University Press, 1990), 51–55. The definition "evangelism of fear" is used by David Campbell in his highly original *Writing Security: United States Foreign Policy and the Politics of Identity,* 2nd ed. (Minneapolis: University of Minnesota Press, 1998), 49.

19. Kissinger, "Process of Détente," statement delivered to the Senate Foreign Relations Committee, 19 September 1974, published in Kissinger, *American Foreign Policy,* 153; and Kissinger, *White House Years,* 130. For a generally sympathetic description of Kissinger's linkage, see Richard C. Thornton, *The Nixon-Kissinger Years: The Reshaping of American Foreign Policy,* 2nd ed. (St. Paul: Paragon House, 2001). For a more critical analysis see Garthoff, *Détente and Confrontation.*

20. On Kissinger's Eurocentrism, see the convincing analysis of Hanhimäki, *Flawed Architect.* See also Jussi Hanhimäki, "Ironies and Turning Points: Détente in Perspective," in *Reviewing the Cold War: Approaches, Interpretations, Theories,* ed. Odd Arne Westad, 326–42 (London: Routledge, 2000); and Allin, *Cold War Illusions,* 27–50.

21. Bundy, *Tangled Web,* 238. See also Nancy Bernkopf Tucker, *China Confidential: American Diplomats and Sino-American Relations, 1945–1996* (New York: Columbia University Press, 2001), 226–27. On this topic see also the memoirs of the Soviet ambassador to Moscow, Anatoly Dobrynin, *In Confidence: Moscow's Ambassador to America's Six Cold War Presidents* (New York: Times Books, 1995), 226–38.

22. Burr, *Kissinger Transcripts,* 6. The term "Finlandization" referred to a fate similar to that of Finland, a democracy with limited sovereignty, whose foreign and security policies were strongly conditioned by the Soviet Union. See the considerations of the conservative intellectuals James Burnham, "Finlandization?" *National Review,* 19 May 1970; and Walter Laqueur, *The Political Psychology of Appeasement: Finlandization and Other Unpopular Essays* (New Brunswick, NJ: Transaction Books, 1980).

23. Hanhimäki, *Flawed Architect,* 56–57; Bundy, *Tangled Web,* 104 ("anti-Soviet action"); Kissinger, *White House Years,* 182.

24. Kissinger, *White House Years,* 182; Dallek, *Nixon and Kissinger,* 146–48.

25. On the Sino-American rapprochement, see also Patrick Tyler, *A Great Wall: Six Presidents and China: An Investigative History* (New York: Century Foundation, 1999), 109–79; James Mann, *About Face: A History of America's Curious Relationship with China, from Nixon to Clinton* (New York: Vintage, 1998), 13–52; Foot, *Practice of Power,* 103–13.

26. "Meeting between Mao Zedong and Pham Van Dong," in *77 Conversations between Chinese and Foreign Leaders on the Wars in Indochina, 1964–1977,* ed. Odd Arne Westad, Chen Jian, Stein Tonnesson, Nguyen Vu Tungand, and James G. Hershberg, Cold War International History Project, working paper 22, http://www.wilsoncenter.org/topics/pubs/ACFB39.pdf (accessed 25 April 2009).

27. Hanhimäki, *Flawed Architect,* 108–9; Bundy, *Tangled Web,* 164–66; Kissinger, *White House Years,* 700–703; Walter Isaacson, *Kissinger: A Biography* (New York: Simon and Schuster, 1992), 336–40; Robert D. Schulzinger, *Henry Kissinger: Doctor of Diplomacy* (New York: Columbia University Press, 1989), 81–85.

28. Hanhimäki, *Flawed Architect,* 116. Yafeng Xia, "China's Elite Politics and Sino-American Rapprochement, January 1969–February 1972," *Journal of Cold War Studies* 4 (Fall 2006): 3–28.

29. On the organization of the trip, the absolute secrecy that surrounded it, and the various expedients devised to keep the press (and part of the administration) in the dark, see the detailed and anecdotic reconstruction in Isaacson, *Kissinger,* 341–54.

30. On this topic see especially Jeffrey Kimball, *Nixon's Vietnam War* (Lawrence: University Press of Kansas, 1998), 239–41; Hanhimäki, *Flawed Architect;* and Jussi Hanhimäki, "Selling the

'Decent Interval': Kissinger, Triangular Diplomacy, and the End of the Vietnam War, 1971–73," *Diplomacy and Statecraft* 1 (March 2003): 159–94. See also *China, 1969–1972,* vol. 17 of *Foreign Relations of the United States, 1969–1976* (Washington, DC: Government Printing Office, 2006), 359–436, available at http://www.state.gov/documents/organization/70142.pdf (accessed 25 April 2009).

31. Hanhimäki, *Flawed Architect,* 140. Similar considerations can be found in Bundy, *Tangled Web,* 304–5. The statements by Kissinger are from Kissinger, *White House Years,* 747; and Kissinger, *Years of Renewal* (New York: Touchstone, 1999), 157.

32. See Kimball, *Nixon's Vietnam War,* 296–300; Larry Berman, *No Peace, No Honor: Nixon, Kissinger and Betrayal in Vietnam* (New York: Touchstone, 2002), 104–5; and especially, Qiang Zhai, *China and the Vietnam War, 1950–1975* (Chapel Hill: University of North Carolina Press, 2000), 193–216.

33. Margaret Macmillan, *Nixon and Mao: The Week That Changed the World* (New York: Random House, 2007). Many of these transcripts have been published in Burr, *Kissinger Transcripts.* See also *China, 1969–1972;* and *Documents on China, 1969–1972,* vol. E-13 of *Foreign Relations of the United States, 1969–1976* (Washington, DC: Government Printing Office, 2006), available at http://www.state.gov/r/pa/ho/frus/nixon/e13/index.htm (Accessed 25 April 2009).

34. "Joint Statement following Discussions with Leaders of the People's Republic of China," 27 February 1972, in *China, 1969–1972,* 812–16, available at http://www.state.gov/documents/organization/70143.pdf (Accessed 25 April 2009). On the visit, in addition to Macmillan, see also Hanhimäki, *Flawed Architect,* 194–99; Isaacson, *Kissinger,* 399–407; Tyler, *Great Wall,* 127–45; Richard Nixon, *RN: The Memoirs of Richard Nixon* (New York: Grosset and Dunlap, 1978), 557–72; and Harry R. Haldeman, *The Haldeman Diaries: Inside the Nixon White House* (New York: Putnam, 1994), 410–21.

35. Loth, *Overcoming the Cold War,* 37–41; Allin, *Cold War Illusions,* 102–27; Youri Devuyst, "American Attitudes on European Political Integration: The Nixon-Kissinger Legacy," Institute for European Studies, working paper, February 2007, http://www.ies.be/files/WP_Youri_Devuyst.pdf (Accessed 25 April 2009). A different interpretation, which emphasizes the potential complementarily between the two détentes, is in James A. McAdams, "The New Diplomacy of the West German Ostpolitik," 537–63, in Craig and Loewenheim, *Diplomats, 1939–1979.*

36. Kissinger, *White House Years,* 132; "Memorandum of Conversation: Ford-Kissinger-Moro-Rumor," 1 August 1975, NARA, RG 59, records of Henry Kissinger, 1973–1977, folder 12; "Secretary of State's Staff Meeting," 12 January 1975, NARA, RG 59, lot file 78D443, folder 1.

37. Willy Brandt, *My Life in Politics* (London: Penguin, 2002), 138–285; originally published as *Erinnerungen* (Zurich: Propyläen, 1988); and Egon Bahr, *Zu meiner Zeit* (Munich: Karl Blessing Verlag, 1996), 268–427. Gottfried Niedhart, "The Federal Republic's Ostpolitik and the United States: Initiatives and Constraints," in *The United States and the European Alliance since 1945,* ed. Kathleen Burk and Melvyn Stokes (Oxford: Berg, 1999).

38. Andrianopoulos, *Western Europe in Kissinger's Global Strategy,* 8 ("subordinate the long-standing relationship…its global position"). On this see also Trachtenberg, *Constructed Peace;* Michael J. Sodaro, *Moscow, Germany and the West from Khrushchev to Gorbachev* (Ithaca: Cornell University Press, 1990), 135–225; and the detailed research of Mary Sarotte, *Dealing with the Devil: East Germany, Détente, and Ostpolitik, 1969–1973* (Chapel Hill: University of North Carolina Press, 2001). On the premises of détente and the nexus between international choices and domestic politics, see also Arne Hofmann, *The Emergence of Détente in Europe: Brandt, Kennedy and the Formation of Ostpolitik* (London: Routledge, 2007).

39. Kissinger, *White House Years,* 409.

40. Henry Kissinger, *Years of Upheaval* (London: Weidenfeld and Nicolson, 1982), 146, 144. Hanhimäki, *Flawed Architect,* 87 ("asset…China"). For a conservative comparison between

Ostpolitik and détente, see James Burnham, "How's Your Ostpolitik," *National Review*, 12 January 1971.

41. Andrianopoulos, *Western Europe in Kissinger's Global Strategy*, 102; Bundy, *Tangled Web*, 174–77; Allin, *Cold War Illusions*, 37–41; Pietrantonio, "Anno che non fu." For an intriguing, theoretical comparison between the two détentes, see Kjell Goldmann, *Change and Stability in Foreign Policy: The Problems and Possibilities of Détente* (Princeton: Princeton University Press, 1988).

42. "Secretary of State's Staff Meeting," 12 January 1975 and 1 July 1976, NARA, RG 59, lot file 78D443, boxes 6 and 10. On this topic see Mario Del Pero, "I limiti della distensione: Gli Stati Uniti e l'implosione del regime portoghese" [The limits of détente: The United States and the implosion of the Portuguese regime], *Contemporanea* 4 (December 2005): 621–50; Roberto Gualtieri, "The Italian Political System and Détente," *Journal of Modern Italian Studies* 4 (December 2004): 428–49; Leopoldo Nuti, "Le relazioni tra Italia e Stati Uniti agli inizi della distensione" [The relations between the United States and Italy at the beginning of détente], in *L'Italia repubblicana nella crisi degli anni Settanta, I: Tra guerra fredda e distensione* [Republican Italy in the crisis of the 1970s. I: Between détente and the Cold War], ed. Agostino Giovagnoli and Silvio Pons (Soveria Mannelli: Rubbettino, 2003), 29–62; and Raffaele D'Agata, "L'altra' distensione: Brandt, Berlinguer e la ricerca di un nuovo ordine di pace negli anni '70" [The "other" détente: Brandt, Berlinguer and the search for a new peace order in the 1970s] *Contemporanea* 2 (April 2002): 233–52.

43. Hanhimäki, *Flawed Architect*, 89–90; Bundy, *Tangled Web*, 246–48; and Sodaro, *Moscow, Germany and the West*.

44. The importance of Western Europe in intensifying USSR's dependence on the West and, ultimately, its weakness is convincingly emphasized in Michael Cox, "Another Transatlantic Split? American and European Narratives of the End of the Cold War," *Cold War History* 1 (2007): 121–46; Frédéric Bozo, "Mitterrand's France, the End of the Cold War, and German Unification: A Reappraisal," *Cold War History* 4 (November 2007): 455–78; Federico Romero, Storia della Guerra Fredda. L'ultimo conflitto per l'Europa [History of the Cold War. The Last Conflict for Europe] (Turin: Einaudi, 2009).

45. An effective critique of the strategic foundations of U.S. intervention in Vietnam remains that of Gaddis, *Strategies of Containment*, 237–73. See also the recent research of Gareth Porter, *The Perils of Dominance: Imbalance of Power and the Road to War in Vietnam* (Berkeley: University of California Press, 2005); and, for a convincing and detailed reconstruction of the influence of domestic considerations on Johnson's decision to escalate the war, Fred Logevall, *Choosing War: The Lost Chance for Peace and the Escalation of War in Vietnam* (Berkeley: University of California Press, 1999).

46. In April 1970, U.S. and South Vietnamese troops invaded Cambodia. In February 1971, South Vietnamese troops, supported by U.S. planes, invaded Laos. The first operation did not achieve the expected results. The second turned into a dramatic fiasco. Both helped to destabilize the frail regional equilibria. See Ralph Smith, "The International Setting of the Cambodian Crisis," *International History Review* 2 (May 1996): 303–35; the controversial book by William Shawcross, *Sideshow: Kissinger, Nixon, and the Destruction of Cambodia* (New York: Simon and Schuster, 1979); and Kissinger's vigorous self-defense in *Years of Upheaval*, 335–55. See also Young, *Vietnam Wars*, 245–55; and Dallek, *Nixon and Kissinger*, 194–212, 257–64.

47. Kissinger, *White House Years*, 235; Kissinger, "The Vietnam Negotiations," *Foreign Affairs* 47 (January 1969): 219–20; George Herring, *America's Longest War*, 4th ed. (New York: McGraw-Hill, 2002), 271–76; Kimball, *Nixon's Vietnam War*, 37–60. See also the acute considerations in Frank Ninkovich, *Wilsonian Century: U.S. Foreign Policy since 1900* (Chicago: University of Chicago Press, 1999), 227–31; and Henry Kissinger's disappointing recollection, which relies mostly on previously published materials, in *Ending the Vietnam War: A History of America's Involvement in and Extrication from the Vietnam War* (New York: Simon and Schuster, 2003).

48. Nixon, as quoted in Hanhimäki, *Flawed Architect,* 209. See also Garthoff, *Détente and Confrontation,* 297–98; and Iliya Gaiduk, *The Soviet Union and the Vietnam War* (Chicago: Ivan R. Dee, 1996).

49. Schulzinger, *Kissinger,* 117–19. On the Paris negotiations, see the detailed reconstructions of Hanhimäki, *Flawed Architect,* 228–59; and Kimball, *Nixon's Vietnam War.* On the domestic consequences of the end of the war, see Young, *Vietnam Wars;* Berman, *No Peace, No Honor,* 235–37; and Robert Schulzinger, *A Time for War: The United States and Vietnam, 1941–1975* (New York: Oxford University Press, 1997), 303–4.

50. On this sensitive issue, see Young, *Vietnam Wars,* 274–80; Susan Katz Keating, *Prisoners of Hope: Exploiting the POW/MIA Myth in America* (New York: Random House, 1994); Michael J. Allen, "'Help Us Tell the Truth about Vietnam': POW/MIA Politics and the End of the American War," in Young and Bradley, *Making Sense of the Vietnamese Wars,* 219–49.

51. Garthoff, *Détente and Confrontation,* 335–37; Raymond L. Garthoff, "SALT I: An Evaluation," *World Politics* 1 (October 1978): 1–25; Bundy, *Tangled Web,* 232–37.

52. Nixon, *RN: Memoirs,* 618; "Briefing by the President's Assistant for National Security Affairs (Kissinger) for the Senate Foreign Relations Committee," 15 June 1972, in *Foundations of Foreign Policy, 1969–1972.* "Basic Principles of Relations between United States of America and the Union of the Soviet Socialist Republics," published under "Paper Agreed upon by the United States and the Soviet Union," 29 May 1972, is also published in *Foundations of Foreign Policy, 1969–1972.*

53. Bruce J. Schulman, *From Cotton Belt to Sun Belt: Federal Policy, Economic Development, and the Transformation of the South, 1938–1980* (Oxford: Oxford University Press, 1991); Alain C. Enthoven and K. Wayne Smith, *How Much Is Enough? Shaping the Defense Program, 1961–1969* (New York: Harper and Row, 1971).

54. Keith Nelson, *The Making of Détente: Soviet-American Relations in the Shadow of Vietnam* (Baltimore: Johns Hopkins University Press, 1995), 83 ("military activism"). See also Arnold Kanter, "Congress and the Defense Budget: 1960–1970," *American Political Science Review* 66 (March 1972): 129–43; and Robert Kaufman, *Henry Jackson: A Life in Politics* (Seattle: University of Washington Press, 2000), 200–222.

55. Kissinger, *White House Years,* 939; and Kissinger, *Years of Upheaval,* 259–60. The data on U.S. military expenditures are from *Budget of the United States Government, Fiscal Year 2005: Historical Tables* (Washington, DC: Government Printing Office, 2004), http://www.whitehouse.gov/omb/budget/fy2005/pdf/hist.pdf (Accessed 25 April 2009); and Gaddis, *Strategies of Containment,* 321–59. See also Miroslav Nincic and Thomas R. Cusack, "The Political Economy of U.S. Military Spending, *Journal of Peace Research* 2 (1979): 101–15; Alex Mintz and Alexander Hicks, "Military Keynesianism in the United States, 1949–1976: Disaggregating Military Expenditures and Their Determination," *American Journal of Sociology* 2 (September 1984): 411–17. The Kissinger quotation is from "Memorandum of Conversation," meeting between Kissinger and representatives of the Business Council, 1 December 1971.

56. Data from Nelson, *Making of Détente,* 19–20. See also William L. Lunch and Peter W. Sperlich, "American Public Opinion and the War in Vietnam," *Western Political Quarterly* 32 (March 1979): 21–44. On the crisis of liberal consensus, see Iwan W. Morgan, *Beyond the Liberal Consensus* (London: Hurst, 1994); David Steigerwald, *The Sixties and the End of Modern America* (New York: St. Martin's Press, 1995); and Edward D. Berkowitz, *Something Happened: A Political and Cultural Overview of the Seventies* (New York: Columbia University Press, 2005).

57. "Memorandum of Conversation," meeting between Kissinger and representatives of the Business Council, 1 December 1971; "Briefing by the President's Assistant for National Security Affairs (Kissinger) for the Senate Foreign Relations Committee," 15 June 1972, in *Foundations of Foreign Policy, 1969–1972;* Kissinger, *Years of Upheaval,* xix; Kissinger, *American Foreign Policy,* 93.

58. This aspect is stressed, and severely censured, by two former diplomats: Bundy, *Tangled Web;* and Garthoff, *Détente and Confrontation;* and even more so in Raymond L. Garthoff, *A Journey through the Cold War: A Memoir of Containment and Coexistence* (Washington, DC: Brookings Institution Press, 2001).

59. Kissinger, *White House Years,* 27–31.

60. On the frustration of the American delegates in Helsinki, who were kept in the dark and unaware of Kissinger's back-channel negotiation with Dobrynin, see Garthoff, *Journey through the Cold War,* 267–70; and Gerald Smith, *Doubletalk: The Story of the First Strategic Arms Limitation Talks* (Garden City: Doubleday, 1980). On Kissinger's shuttle diplomacy, see William Quandt, *Peace Process: American Policy toward the Arab-Israeli Conflict* (Berkeley: University of California Press, 1984), 148–82; and Bundy, *Tangled Web,* 429–72. On the 1973 October War and the ingenuous diplomatic initiative of Kissinger, see the rich documentary collection edited by William Burr for the National Security Archive, http://www.gwu.edu/~nsarchiv/NSAEBB/NSAEBB98/ (Accessed 25 April 2009).

61. Tom Braden, "Henry Kissinger: An American Hero," *Washington Post,* 25 May 1974. The quotations from *Life, Newsweek,* the *New York Times,* and *U.S. News and World Report* are in Hanhimäki, *Flawed Architect,* 189–90; and Schulzinger, *Kissinger,* 89; that of Kraft is in Isaacson, *Kissinger,* 501. On the origins of the Chinese myth, see the useful introduction in David Pletcher, *The Diplomacy of Involvement: American Economic Expansion across the Pacific, 1784–1900* (Columbia: University of Missouri Press, 2001). On the scant attention paid by Nixon and Kissinger to Taiwan and its requests, see Nancy Bernkopf Tucker, "Taiwan Expendable?" *Journal of American History* 1 (June 2005): 109–35.

62. Kissinger, *Years of Upheaval,* 1031, 50; Kissinger, as quoted in Ninkovich, *Wilsonian Century,* 234 ("face…respite").

63. Kissinger, *Years of Upheaval,* 50; and Kissinger, "Process of Détente," in Kissinger, *American Foreign Policy,* 146. On this see also the original and acute reflection of Stanley Hoffmann, "The Return of Henry Kissinger," *New York Review of Books* 7, 29 April 1982.

64. Henry Kissinger, "The Moral Foundations of Foreign Policy," in Kissinger, *American Foreign Policy,* 209.

65. Ibid., 203–4. See also Isaacson, *Kissinger,* 658–61.

66. Kissinger, *Years of Upheaval.* On this see also Hoffmann, *Return of Henry Kissinger;* and Abbot Gleason, *Totalitarianism: The Inner History of the Cold War* (Oxford: Oxford University Press, 1995), 190–210.

4. The Domestic Critique of Kissinger

1. Among the many recent studies on neoconservatism, see Corey Robin, "Remembrance of the Empires Past: 9/11 and the End of the Cold War," in *Cold War Triumphalism: The Misuse of History after the Fall of Communism,* ed. Ellen Schrecker, 274–97 (New York: New Press, 2004); G. John Ikenberry, "The End of the Neoconservative Moment," *Survival* 2 (Summer 2004): 7–22; Anatol Lieven, *America Right or Wrong: An Anatomy of American Nationalism* (Oxford: Oxford University Press, 2004); Jonathan Clarke and Stefan Halper, *America Alone: The Neo-Conservatives and the Global Order* (Cambridge: Cambridge University Press, 2004); James Mann, *The Rise of the Vulcans: The History of Bush's War Cabinet* (New York: Viking, 2004); Giovanni Borgognone, *La destra americana: Dall'isolazionismo ai neocons* [The American Right: From isolationism to the neocons], (Rome-Bari: Laterza, 2004); Sergio Fabbrini, ed., *The United States Contested: American Unilateralism and European Discontent* (London: Routledge 2006); Francis Fukuyama, *America at the Crossroads: Democracy, Power, and the Neoconservative Legacy* (New Haven: Yale University Press, 2006).

2. On this aspect and, in general, on the centrality of international matters in the genesis of neoconservatism, the best study remains John Ehrman, *The Rise of Neoconservatism: Intellectual*

and Foreign Affairs (New Haven: Yale University Press, 1995). See also William C. Berman, *America's Right Turn: From Nixon to Bush* (Baltimore: Johns Hopkins University Press, 1994); Alan Brinkley, "The Problem of American Conservatism," *American Historical Review* 2 (April 1994): 409–29; Kevin Mattson, *Rebels All! A Short History of the Conservative Mind in Postwar America* (New Brunswick, NJ: Rutgers University Press, 2008); and Bruce J. Schulman and Julian E. Zelizer, eds., *Rightward Bound: Making America Conservative in the 1970s* (Cambridge: Harvard University Press, 2008).

3. On the New Left, see the different interpretations in Todd Gitlin, *The Sixties: Years of Hope; Days of Rage* (New York: Bantam Books, 1987); Maurice Isserman, *"If I had a Hammer…": The Death of the Old Left and the Birth of the New Left* (New York: Basic Books, 1987); Van Gosse, "A Movement of Movements: The Definition and Periodization of the New Left" in *A Companion to Post-1945 America,* ed. Jean-Cristophe Agnew and Roy Rosenzweig (Malden, MA: Blackwell, 2002), 277–300; Kevin Mattson, *Intellectuals in Action: The Origins of the New Left and Radical Liberalism* (University Park: Pennsylvania State University Press, 2003). On historiographical revisionism and, in particular, the works of William Appleman Williams, see Peter Novick, *That Noble Dream: The "Objectivity Question" and the American Historical Profession* (Cambridge: Cambridge University Press, 1988), 415–40; Paul M. Buhle and Edward Rice-Maximin, *William Appleman Williams: The Tragedy of Empire* (London: Routledge, 1995); and Leo Ribuffo, "What Is Still Living in the Ideas and Example of William Appleman Williams," in *Diplomatic History* 2 (Spring 2001): 309–16.

4. Iwan W. Morgan, *Beyond the Liberal Consensus* (London: Hurst, 1994); David Steigerwald, *The Sixties and the End of Modern America* (New York: St. Martin's Press, 1995); Maurice Isserman and Michael Kazin, *America Divided: The Civil War of the 1960s* (Oxford: Oxford University Press, 2000).

5. On this topic, see in particular Ehrman, *Rise of Neoconservatism,* 33–62; and Alan Brinkley, *Liberalism and Its Discontents* (Cambridge: Harvard University Press, 1998), 222–36.

6. Tod Lindberg, "Neoconservatism's Liberal Legacy," *Policy Review,* no. 127 (2004), http://www.policyreview.org/oct04/lindberg.html.

7. Ehrman, *Rise of Neoconservatism,* 34. See also the detailed reconstruction in Marco Mariano, *Lo storico nel suo labirinto: Arthur Schlesinger Jr. tra ricerca storica, impegno civile e politica* [The historian in his labyrinth: Arthur Schlesinger Jr. between historical research, civic commitment and politics] (Milan: Franco Angeli, 1999), 121–68. See also John P. Diggins, ed., *The Liberal Persuasion: Arthur Schlesinger Jr., and the Challenge of the American Past* (Princeton: Princeton University Press, 1997); Thomas G. Paterson, ed., *Cold War Critics: Alternatives to American Foreign Policy in the Truman Years* (Chicago: University of Chicago Press, 1971); Alonzo Hamby, *Beyond the New Deal: Harry S. Truman and American Liberalism* (New York: Columbia University Press, 1973); J. Samuel Walker, *Henry A. Wallace and American Foreign Policy* (Westport, CT: Greenwood Press, 1976); Fred Logevall, "A Critique of Containment," *Diplomatic History* 4 (September 2004): 473–99; Hugh Wilford, "Playing the CIA's Tune? The New Leader and the Cultural Cold War," *Diplomatic History* 1 (January 2003): 15–34.

8. On Jackson, see the sympathetic biography by Kaufman, *Henry Jackson: A Life in Politics* (Seattle: University of Washington Press, 2000); on Moynihan, see Ehrman, *Rise of Neoconservatism,* 63–96; and Robert A. Katzmann, ed., *Daniel Patrick Moynihan: The Intellectual in Public Life* (Washington, DC: Woodrow Wilson Center Press, 1998).

9. William A. Williams, *The Tragedy of American Diplomacy,* 3rd ed. (1959; reprint, New York: Norton, 1972), 304; Martin Luther King, as quoted in Isserman and Kazin, *America Divided,* 192. The *Berkeley Barb* is quoted in Jeremi Suri, *Power and Protest: Global Revolution and the Rise of Détente* (Cambridge: Harvard University Press, 2003), 169. The young New Leftist is quoted in Bruce J. Schulman, *The Seventies: The Great Shift in American Culture, Society, and Politics* (Cambridge: Da Capo Press, 2001), 16. See also the detailed reconstruction of Marilyn Young, *The Vietnam Wars, 1945–1990* (New York: HarperCollins, 1991), 192–209.

10. James Burnham, "Finlandization?" *National Review,* 19 May 1970; Henry Jackson, "Perspectives on the Atlantic Alliance," speech at the Fifth International Conference in Chicago, 23 March 1968, Henry M. Jackson Papers, University of Washington Libraries, Manuscripts Collections, Seattle (HMJP-UWL-MC), accession no. 3560-6: Foreign Policy and Defense Issues, Speeches and Writings, folder 6.

11. Jeane Kirkpatrick, "The Revolt of the Masses," *Commentary* 55 (February 1973): 58–62; Irving Kristol, "When Virtue Loses All Her Loveliness—Some Reflections on Capitalism and the Free Society," *Public Interest* (Autumn 1970): 21, 4; Henry Jackson, as quoted in Kaufman, *Henry Jackson,* 223. "Memorandum from the President's Assistant for Urban Affairs (Moynihan) to President Nixon," 13 November 1969, in *Foundations of Foreign Policy, 1969–1972,* vol. 1 of *Foreign Relations of the United States, 1969–1976* (Washington, DC: Government Printing Office, 2003), available at http://www.state.gov/r/pa/ho/frus/nixon/i/20702.htm (Accessed 25 April 2009). See also Irving Kristol, *Reflections of a Neoconservative* (New York: Basic Books, 1993). Podhoretz's endorsement of a withdrawal from Vietnam is in Norman Podhoretz, "A Note on Vietnamization," *Commentary,* May 1971, 6–9; he modified his position ten years later in a famous book titled *Why We Were in Vietnam* (New York: Simon and Schuster, 1982).

12. Gitlin, *Sixties,* 107. See also Trevor B. McCrisken, *American Exceptionalism and the Legacy of Vietnam: U.S. Foreign Policy since 1974* (New York: Palgrave Macmillan, 2003), 20–39.

13. Ehrman, *Rise of Neoconservatorism,* 83. See also the considerations in Henry Kissinger, *Years of Renewal* (New York: Touchstone, 1999), 782–83.

14. The text of the resolution can be consulted at http://www.cfr.org/content/publications/attachments/GA3379.pdf (Accessed 25 April 2009). See also Davidson Nicol, "Africa and the U.S.A. in the United Nations," *Journal of Modern African Studies* 3 (September 1978): 365–95. The first quotation by Moynihan is from the partisan book by Mark Gerson, *The Neoconservative Vision: From the Cold War to the Culture Wars* (Lanham, MD: Madison Books, 1996), 172–73; the second is in Daniel Patrick Moynihan, "We Are Sakharov," 5 July 1976, commencement address at Hebrew University, HMJP-UWL-MC, accession no. 3560-6: Foreign Policy and Defense Issues, subject files, folder 37.

15. William Fulbright, *The Arrogance of Power* (New York: Random House, 1966), 3–4; Ehrman, *Rise of Neoconservatism,* 33–61; Randall Bennet Woods, *Fulbright: A Biography* (Cambridge: Cambridge University Press, 1995). See also William Fulbright, *The Price of Empire* (New York: Pantheon Books, 1989).

16. Fulbright, as quoted in Woods, *Fulbright,* 523. See also the different reconstructions of Kaufman, *Henry Jackson,* 238–41; and Kissinger, *Years of Renewal,* 112–19.

17. Henry Jackson, "Statement on the ABM Program," U.S. Senate, 19 June 1968, HMJP-UWL-MC, accession no. 3560-6: Foreign Policy and Defense Issues, Speeches and Writings, folder 6. On exceptionalism, see the original considerations of Ian Tyrrel, "American Exceptionalism in the Age of International History," *American Historical Review* 4 (October 1991): 1031–55; and Daniel Rodgers, "Exceptionalism," in *Imagined Histories: American Historians Interpret the Past,* ed. Anthony Molho and Gordon Woods, 21–40 (Princeton: Princeton University Press, 1998). On the myth of strategic defense as an expression of a nationalist and exceptionalist logic that would find its sublimation with Reagan's Star Wars, see Frances Fitzgerald, *Way Out There in the Blue: Reagan, Star Wars and the End of the Cold War* (New York: Simon and Schuster, 2000).

18. Eugene Rostow to Henry Jackson, 27 January 1971, HMJP-UWL-MC, accession no. 3560-6: Foreign Policy and Defense Issues, U.S. Senate, Government Operations Committee, Permanent Subcommittee of Investigations, General Correspondence, folder 85.

19. Kirkpatrick, Lipset, and Raab, as quoted in Ehrman, *Rise of Neoconservatism,* 58–59. On Jackson using Scott's comment, see Kaufman, *Henry Jackson,* 236. See also Richard Michael Marano, *Vote Your Conscience: The Last Campaign of George McGovern* (Westport, CT: Greenwood Press, 2003), 5–6. On the elections of 1972, see Theodore H. White, *The Making of the President* (1972; reprint, New York: Atheneum, 1973).

20. Midge Decter, as quoted in Ehrman, *Rise of Neoconservatism,* 60. See also Clarke and Halper, *America Alone,* 55–56.

21. Henry Kissinger, *White House Years* (London: Weidenfeld and Nicolson, 1979), 66; Kissinger, *Years of Upheaval* (London: Weidenfeld and Nicolson, 1982), 999; Kissinger, *Years of Renewal,* 116.

22. See the reflections in McGeorge Bundy, *Danger and Survival: Choices about the Bomb in the First Fifty Years* (New York: Vintage, 1988); John Lewis Gaddis, *The Long Peace: Inquiries into the History of the Cold War* (Oxford: Oxford University Press, 1987); and Lawrence Freedman, *The Evolution of Nuclear Strategy,* 2nd ed.(New York: St. Martin's Press, 1989). See also the acute and sophisticated book of Paul Boyer, *Fallout: A Historian Reflects on America's Half-Century Encounter with Nuclear Weapons* (Columbus: Ohio State University Press, 1998).

23. Henry Jackson, "No Time for Rest," draft speech in the Senate, 24 September 1968; and Jackson, "The Strategic Balance and the Future of Freedom," speech at the American Society of Newspapers Editors, 15 April 1971; both in HMJP-UWL-MC, accession no. 3560-6: Foreign Policy and Defense Issues, Speeches and Writings, folders 6 and 8, respectively.

24. John Lewis Gaddis, *Strategies of Containment: A Critical Appraisal of Postwar American National Security Policy* (New York: Oxford University Press, 1982), 324.

25. Jussi Hanhimäki, *The Flawed Architect: Henry Kissinger and American Foreign Policy* (New York: Oxford University Press, 2004), 221.

26. Henry Jackson to Henry Kissinger, 26 October 1970, HMJP-UWL-MC, accession no. 3560-28: Foreign Policy and Defense Issues, folder 2. The passage from the Jackson Amendment is quoted in Dana H. Allin, *Cold War Illusions: America, Europe and Soviet Power, 1969–1989* (New York: St. Martin's Press, 1995), 57. See also Freedman, *Evolution of Nuclear Strategy,* 356–58; and Kaufman, *Henry Jackson,* 256–60. The Jackson Amendment was the idea of Fred Charles Ikle, who worked for the Arms Control and Disarmament Agency, and Richard Perle, a young expert on nuclear issues and close collaborator of Jackson.

27. Allin, *Cold War Illusions,* 57; Kissinger, *Years of Renewal,* 113–16; Hanhimäki, *Flawed Architect,* 220–22.

28. Nina Tammenwald, *The Nuclear Taboo: The United States and the Non-Use of Nuclear Weapons since 1945* (Cambridge: Cambridge University Press, 2007), 277; Gaddis, *Strategies of Containment,* 325–26; Allin, *Cold War Illusions,* 56–58; Kissinger, *Years of Upheaval,* 1011–18. William Burr, "The Nixon Administration, the 'Horror Strategy,' and the Search for Limited Nuclear Options, 1969–1972: Prelude to the Schlesinger Doctrine," *Journal of Cold War Studies* 3 (Summer 2005): 35–78.

29. Melvin Leffler, *A Preponderance of Power: National Security, the Truman Administration, and the Cold War* (Stanford: Stanford University Press, 1992).

30. Nitze, as quoted in Charles Tyroler II, ed., *Alerting America: The Papers of the Committee on the Present Danger* (Washington, DC: Pergamon-Brassy's, 1984), 159–60. See also Allin, *Cold War Illusions,* 65–66; Bundy, *Danger and Survival,* 556–58. On Paul Nitze, see the biographies by Strobe Talbott, *The Master of the Game: Paul Nitze and the Nuclear Peace* (New York: Knopf, 1988); and Paul Callaghan, *Dangerous Capabilities* (New York: HarperCollins, 1990); and the autobiography, Paul Nitze, *From Hiroshima to Glasnost: At the Center of the Decision: A Memoir* (New York: Grove Weidenfeld, 1989).

31. Paul Nitze, "Assuring Strategic Stability in an Era of Détente," *Foreign Affairs* 54 (January 1976): 217; Henry Jackson, "The U.S. and Europe," 25 March 1974, AHEPA banquet, Washington, DC; and Jackson, "Is the U.S. Still Number 1?" undated (ca. 1975); both at HMJP-UWL-MC, accession no. 3560-6: Foreign Policy and Defense Issues, Speeches and Writings, folders 10 and 11, respectively. On this topic see the convincing rebuke of Robert Jervis, "Why Nuclear Superiority Doesn't Matter," *Political Science Quarterly* 4 (Winter 1979–80): 617–33.

32. Richard Pipes, "Team B: The Reality behind the Myth," *Commentary* 82 (October 1986): 25–40; Rhodri Jeffreys-Jones, *The CIA and American Democracy,* 2nd ed. (New Haven: Yale

University Press, 1998), 212–15. See also Anne Hessing Cahn, *Killing Détente: The Right Attacks the CIA* (University Park: Pennsylvania State University Press, 1998); Alastair Iain Johnston, "Thinking about Strategic Culture," *International Security* 4 (Spring 1995): 32–64; Giordana Pulcini, "L'Opposizione al SALT II: Controllo degli armamenti e politica interna negli Stati Uniti, 1974–1980" [The opposition to SALT II: Arms control and domestic politics in the United States, 1974–1980], Ph.D. diss., University of Rome III, 2008.

33. The document is published in Tyroler, *Alerting America, 3.* See also the original Simon Dalby, *Creating the Second Cold War: The Discourse of Politics* (London: Pinter, 1990); and Pavel Podvig, "The Window of Vulnerability That Wasn't: Soviet Military Buildup in the 1970s—A Research Note," *International Security* 1 (Summer 2008): 118–38.

34. Kaufman, *Henry Jackson,* 360; Fitzgerald, *Way Out There in the Blue,* 82–86; Allin, *Cold War Illusions,* 59–62; Michael McGwire, "The Paradigm That Lost Its Way," *International Affairs* 4 (October 2001): 786–92.

35. David Holloway, *The Soviet Union and the Arms Race* (New Haven: Yale University Press, 1983), 179; Craig Nation, *Black Earth, Red Star: A History of Soviet Security Policy* (Ithaca: Cornell University Press, 1993), 245–84; Vladislav M. Zubok, *A Failed Empire: The Soviet Union in the Cold War from Stalin to Gorbachev* (Chapel Hill: University of North Carolina Press, 2007), 242–44.

36. The 1972 agreements had been amended in late 1974 during a summit between Brezhnev and Ford in Vladivostok. On that occasion, respecting the principle of "equal aggregates" imposed by the Jackson Amendment, the two sides had agreed to fix a limit of 2,400 strategic nuclear delivery vehicles (ICBMs and SLBMs), of which only 1,320 could use MIRV technology. Jackson and the neoconservatives criticized the agreement because the limit was still too high, theoretically leaving the Soviets with the possibility to further improve and upgrade their armament, which was primarily based on heavy missiles. SALT II reduced these limits in part, setting the ceiling at 2,250 and defining various limits on the possibility to equip these missiles with MIRV technology.

37. On the many contradictions of détente and the different U.S. and Soviet conceptions of it, the best analysis is still Raymond L. Garthoff, *Détente and Confrontation: American-Soviet Relations from Nixon to Reagan,* 2nd ed. (Washington, DC: Brookings Institution Press, 1994), 27–75.

38. Henry Jackson, "America and Human Rights," speech at the World Affairs Council of Philadelphia, 19 April 1976, HMJP-UWL-MC, accession no. 3560-6: Foreign Policy and Defense Issues, Speeches and Writings, folder 12; George Meany, "Foreign Policy Choices for the 1970s and 80s," statement before the Senate Foreign Relations Committee, 8 December 1975, and speech of Jeane Kirkpatrick at the B'nai Brith International, 7 January 1981, both in HMJP-UWL-MC, accession no. 3560-6: Foreign Policy and Defense Issues, Speeches and Writings, folder 6.

39. See the outstanding Lawrence Wittner, *The Struggle against the Bomb,* vol. 3: *Toward Nuclear Abolition: A History of World Nuclear Disarmament Movement, 1971 to the Present* (Stanford: Stanford University Press, 2003). The stabilizing effect guaranteed by nuclear weapons is emphasized in the classical Kenneth Waltz, *The Spread of Nuclear Weapons: More May Be Better,* Adelphi Papers, no. 171 (London: Institute of Strategic Studies, 1981); and Gaddis, *Long Peace,* 215–45.

40. Henry Jackson, "America and Freedom's Future," 21 January 1976, Alfred M. Landon Lecture, Kansas State University, Manhattan, Kansas, HMJP-UWL-MC, accession no. 3560-6: Foreign Policy and Defense Issues, Speeches and Writings, folder 12. An exceptionalist rhetoric would accompany Reagan's strategic discourse and the invitation to reacquire supposed invulnerability that had been lost.

41. Tom Donnelly and Vance Serchuk, "John Kerry, Reactionary," *Weekly Standard* (online ed.), 19 July 2004; "Memorandum from the President's Assistant for National Security Affairs (Kissinger) to President Nixon," 3 December 1969, in *Foundations of Foreign Policy, 1969–1972.*

42. Nikhil Pal Singh, "Cold War Redux: On the 'New Totalitarianism,'" *Radical History Review* 1 (Winter 2003): 173; Nils Gilman, *Mandarins of the Future: Modernization Theory in Cold War America* (Baltimore: Johns Hopkins University Press, 2003), 156.

43. Meany, "Foreign Policy Choices for the 1970s and 80," statement before the Senate Foreign Relations Committee, 8 December 1975. Abbot Gleason, *Totalitarianism: The Inner History of the Cold War* (Oxford: Oxford University Press, 1995), 1, 193–94. On the use of the category of totalitarianism in the early Cold War, see also Thomas Paterson and Les Adler, "Red Fascism: The Merger of Nazi Germany and Soviet Russia in the American Image of Totalitarianism, 1930s–1950s," *American Historical Review* 2 (April 1970): 1046–64.

44. Kaufman, *Henry Jackson,* 243; Allin, *Cold War Illusions.* On the importance of the "lesson of Munich," see also Ernest May, *"Lessons" of the Past: The Use and Misuse of History in American Foreign Policy* (Oxford: Oxford University Press, 1973); and Mikkel Vedby Rasmussen, "The History of a Lesson: Versailles, Munich and the Social Construction of the Past," *Review of International Studies* 4 (2003): 499–519. Jackson, in his parallel with Churchill, conveniently forgot that the British statesman had supported an early détente with the Soviets in the 1950s. See Logevall, "Critique of Containment"; and Klaus Larres, *Churchill's Cold War: The Politics of Personal Diplomacy* (New Haven: Yale University Press, 2002), 215–38.

45. Richard Pipes to Henry Jackson, 26 February 1971; and Henry Jackson, "Message for the 29th Annual Commemoration of the Warsaw Ghetto Uprising," 9 April 1972; both at HMJP-UWL-MC, accession no. 3560-6: Foreign Policy and Defense Issues, Speeches and Writings, folder 25 and 9, respectively; Moynihan, as quoted in Gleason, *Totalitarianism,* 193; Gerson, *Neoconservative Vision,* 185; Norman Podhoretz, "The Future Danger," *Commentary,* April 1981, 35. See also Carl Gershman, "Selling Them the Rope: Business and the Soviets," *Commentary* 4 (April 1979). Many neocons maintained this position even during the Gorbachev era. For an example, see Rowland Evans and Robert Novak, "Is Trade with the Soviets Just Trade?" *Washington Post,* 8 January 1988.

46. Walter Laqueur, "Kissinger and the Politics of Détente," *Commentary* 6 (December 1973): 46; Fritz Stern, "The End of the Postwar Era," *Commentary* 3 (April 1974):, 35, 28; James Burnham, "How's Your Ostpolitik," *National Review* 1 (January 1971): 26; Richard J. Whalen, "A Foreign Policy without a Country," *National Review* 14 (September 1973): 1005.

47. Kenneth Cmiel, "The Emergence of Human Rights Politics in the United States," *Journal of American History* 4 (December 1999): 1234; Michael Ignatieff, *Human Rights as Politics and Idolatry* (Princeton: Princeton University Press, 2001); Hugh M. Arnold, "Henry Kissinger and Human Rights," *Human Rights Quarterly* 4 (October–December 1980): 51–71; Daniel C. Thomas, *The Helsinki Effect: International Norms, Human Rights and the Demise of Communism* (Princeton: Princeton University Press, 2001); John Shattuck, *Freedom on Fire: Human Rights Wars and America's Response* (Cambridge: Harvard University Press, 2003).

48. Hanhimäki, *Flawed Architect,* 340–42; William Bundy, *A Tangled Web: The Making of Foreign Policy in the Nixon Presidency* (New York: Hill and Wang, 1998), 400–410; Garthoff, *Détente and Confrontation,* 473–83; Keith Nelson, "Nixon, Kissinger and the Domestic Side of Détente," in *Reviewing the Cold War,* ed. Keith Nelson and Patrick M. Morgan (Westport, CT: Praeger, 2000), 129–30. A different position from the one adopted here is in Kaufman, *Henry Jackson,* 266–83. In addition, see the excellent reconstruction in Noam Kochavi, "Insights Abandoned, Flexibility Lost: Kissinger, Soviet Jewish Emigration, and the Demise of Détente," *Diplomatic History* 3 (June 2005): 503–30.

49. Kochavi, "Insights Abandoned," 514; and Kaufman, *Henry Jackson,* 266–67; Zubok, *Failed Empire,* 231–33. See also the reconstruction by the Soviet ambassador to Washington, Anatoly Dobrynin, *In Confidence: Moscow's Ambassador to America's Six Cold War's Presidents* (New York: Times Books, 1995), 268–69. Various explanations of the Soviet decision have been given: their willingness to prevent the loss of skilled and qualified workers; their attempt to improve the difficult relations with the Arab world; and the tensions within the Soviet leadership between moderates and radicals, with the latter having the upper hand on this occasion.

50. The amendment introduced by Vanik denied credits to countries that imposed a fee of $50 or more on emigration. It was quickly discovered, however, that if it were effected, the United States would have obliged to stop providing credits to Israel as well. See Garthoff, *Détente and Confrontation,* 309; and Paula Stern, *Water's Edge: Domestic Politics and the Making of American Foreign Policy* (Westport, CT: Greenwood, 1979), 18–52.

51. On Dinitz's attempts to help Kissinger and his perplexities over Jackson, see Kaufman, *Henry Jackson,* 262–63. Kissinger deals frequently with his relationship with Dinitz in the second volume of his memoirs, *Years of Upheaval.*

52. Jackson, as quoted in Kaufman, *Henry Jackson,* 267–68. The impossibility of the Soviets accepting such interference is emphasized both in Kissinger, *Years of Upheaval,* 250–54; and Garthoff, *Détente and Confrontation,* 346–48.

53. Kochavi, "Insights Abandoned," 517, 515 ("arrogance") and ("aphrodisiac of power"). Less severe with Kissinger and more critical of Jackson instead are Hanhimäki, *Flawed Architect,* 268–79; and Garthoff, *Détente and Confrontation,* 454–56.

54. The frequent phone calls between Kissinger, Dinitz, and Jackson are now available in the collection of transcripts of Kissinger's telephone conversations, chronological file, Nixon Presidential Materials, NARA, folder 23. See also Kochavi, "Insights Abandoned," 519–20; and Zaki Shalom, "Kissinger and the American Jewish Leadership after the 1973 War," *Israel Studies* 1 (Spring 2002): 209–17.

55. Kochavi, "Insights Abandoned," 506 ("educating Kissinger"); Woods, *Fulbright,* 641–45. Jackson's denunciations of human rights violations in Chile and South Korea are in Henry Jackson to Park Chung Hee (president of South Korea), 3 October 1975, HMJP-UWL-MC, accession no. 3560-6: Correspondence, folder 1; and Henry Jackson to Henry Kissinger, 26 March 1975, HMJP-UWL-MC, accession no. 3560-6: Speeches and Writings, folder 11. This coherence would progressively disappear in the following years, reaching its peak with the famous distinction between totalitarian and authoritarian regimes put forward by political scientist Jeane Kirkpatrick, in her article "Dictatorship and Double Standards," *Commentary,* November 1979, 34–45, which was later expanded into the book *Dictatorship and Double Standards: Rationalism and Reason in Politics* (New York: Simon and Schuster, 1982).

56. Hanhimäki, *Flawed Architect,* 366–67; Dobrynin, *In Confidence,* 267–70; on the congressional discussions and attempted mediations, see Arlene Lazarowitz, "Senator Jacob K. Javits and Soviet Emigration," *Shofar: An Interdisciplinary Journal of Jewish Studies* 4 (2003): 19–31; Robert David Johnson, *Congress and the Cold War* (Cambridge: Cambridge University Press, 2006), 199–200.

57. Gromyko, as quoted in Kaufman, *Henry Jackson,* 279–80. See also Hanhimäki, *Flawed Architect,* 366–70, 378–80; Kochavi, "Insights Abandoned," 506; Kissinger, *Years of Renewal,* 255–60; Walter Isaacson, *Kissinger: A Biography* (New York: Simon and Schuster, 1992), 611–20; Garthoff, *Détente and Confrontation,* 457–63.

58. On Sakharov see Marco Clementi, *Il diritto al dissenso: Il pensiero costituzionale di Andrej Sakharov* [The right to dissent: The constitutional thought of Andrei Sakharov] (Rome: Odradek, 2002). Several interesting documents on Soviet repression of political dissent are contained in Jussi Hanhimäki and Odd Arne Westad, eds., *The Cold War: A History in Documents and Eyewitness Accounts* (Oxford: Oxford University Press, 2003), 473–77, 531–32. Sakharov won the Nobel Peace Prize in 1975. Solzhenitsyn was awarded the Nobel Prize for Literature in 1970.

59. Sakharov's letter and Jackson's speech are both in Proceedings of the 93rd Cong., 1st sess., *Congressional Record* 119 (17 September 1973). See also Kaufman, *Henry Jackson,* 272–73; Abraham Brumberg, "Dissent in Russia," *Foreign Affairs* 4 (July 1974); Richard N. Dean, "Contacts with the West: The Dissidents' View of Western Support for the Human Rights Movement in the Soviet Union," *Universal Human Rights* 1 (January–March 1980): 47–65; Joshua Rubenstein

and Alexander Gribanov, *The KGB File of Andrei Sakharov* (New Haven: Yale University Press, 2005), 158–59.

60. Hans Morgenthau, "Henry Kissinger, Secretary of State: An Evaluation," *Encounter* 5 (November 1975): 57–61; Benjamin M. Mollow, "Jewry's Prophetic Challenge to Soviet and Other Totalitarian Regimes According to Hans J. Morgenthau," *Journal of Church and State* 3 (Summer 1997): 561–75.

61. Telephone call from George Kennan to Henry Kissinger, 14 September 1973, 8.55 p.m., Hak-Telecons, NPM, NARA, folder 22; Kennan to Kissinger, 19 September 1973, NPM, NARA, National Security Council, Country Files, folder 722.

62. Henry Jackson, "Solzhenitsyn and Détente," 15 February 1974, HMJP-UWL-MC, accession no. 3560-6: Speeches and Writings, folder 10; "Jackson attacks Nixon Stance on Solzhenitsyn," *Los Angeles Times,* 4 March 1974.

63. Aleksandr Solzhenitsyn, undated [1975], HMJP-UWL-MC, accession no. 3560-6: Speeches and Writings, folder 9; Alexander Solzhenitsyn, "Schlesinger and Kissinger," *New York Times,* 1 December 1975. The other quotes in the paragraph are from Robert Horvath, "'The Solzhenitsyn Effect': East European Dissidents and the Demise of Revolutionary Privilege," *Human Rights Quarterly* 29 (2007): 879, 881.

64. The text of Solzhenitsyn's address, titled "America: You Must Think About the World," is in Alexander Solzhenitsyn, *Détente: Prospects for Democracy and Dictatorship* (New Brunswick, NJ: Transaction Books, 1976), 7–38. Statement by Henry M. Jackson on Kissinger's attack on Alexander Solzhenitsyn, 16–17 July 1975, HMJP-UWL-MC, accession no. 3560-6: Speeches and Writings, folder 11. Kaufman, *Henry Jackson,* 291–93; Hanhimäki, *Flawed Architect,* 433–35; Isaacson, *Kissinger,* 657–58; Kissinger, *Years of Renewal,* 648–52.

65. On Carter and his foreign policy, see Gaddis Smith, *Morality, Reason and Power: American Diplomacy in the Carter Years* (New York: Hill and Wang, 1986); Olav Njøltad, *Peacekeeper and Troublemaker: The Containment Policy of Jimmy Carter, 1977–1978* (Oslo: Institut for Forsvarsstudier, 1995); Robert A. Strong, *Working in the World: Jimmy Carter and the Making of American Foreign Policy* (Baton Rouge: Louisiana State University Press, 2000); Robert Alexander Kraig, "The Tragic Science: The Uses of Jimmy Carter in Foreign Policy Realism," *Rhetoric and Public Affairs* 1 (Spring 2002): 1–30; Burton Kaufman and Scott Kaufman, *The Presidency of James Earl Carter Jr.,* 2nd ed. (Lawrence: University Press of Kansas, 2006).

66. Hanhimäki, *Flawed Architect,* 447; Robert D. Schulzinger, *Henry Kissinger: Doctor of Diplomacy* (New York: Columbia University Press, 1989), 229. The text of the platform adopted at the convention can be found at http://www.presidency.ucsb.edu/ws/index.php?pid=25843 (accessed 26 April 2009). See also Sean Wilentz, *The Age of Reagan, 1974–2008* (New York: Harper-Collins, 2008), 26–71.

Conclusion

1. Henry Kissinger, *Years of Renewal* (New York: Touchstone, 1999), 791–833. In defense of the Soviet Union, it has been claimed that Soviet intervention in Angola was in many ways a reaction to South African intervention and motivated by defensive or idealistic reasons rather than a willingness to extend Soviet influence in Africa. More recently, the historian Piero Gleijeses has maintained, in his extraordinarily researched *Conflicting Missions: Havana, Washington and Africa, 1959–1976* (Chapel Hill: University of North Carolina Press, 2002), that the USSR was somehow dragged into Africa by Cuba, which was promoting a highly idealistic (and ideological) foreign policy in the region with the main goal of advancing socialism. Gleijeses's is a well-argued, documented, and partially convincing interpretation that tends to underplay the geopolitical matrixes of the USSR's African policy. On this topic, see Odd Arne Westad, "Moscow and the Angolan Crisis, 1974–1976," *Cold War International History Project Bulletin,* working paper 8, 1996–97, 21–32;

Westad, *The Global Cold War: Third World Interventions and the Making of Our Times* (Cambridge: Cambridge University Press, 2005), 207–86; and Witney W. Schneidman, *Engaging Africa: Washington and the Fall of Portugal's Colonial Empire* (Lanham, MD: University Press of America, 2004), 187–223.

2. The first two serious attempts are Westad, *Global Cold War;* and the important book by Vladisdlav M. Zubok, *A Failed Empire: The Soviet Union in the Cold War from Stalin to Gorbachev* (Chapel Hill: University of North Carolina Press, 2007), 227–63.

3. Stanley Hoffmann, "Varieties of Containment," *Reviews in American History* 2 (June 1983): 281 ("maniacally bipolar"). The case of Italy was paradigmatic. In contrast to many opponents of the so-called historical compromise and participation of the Italian Communist Party in a government of national unity, Kissinger recognized the possibility that Italian Communists could be truly independent from Moscow, but believed it made them even more dangerous because they were free from the bipolar discipline guaranteed by Soviet control. Kissinger's reflection on this aspect is evident in two meetings of his staff on 12 January 1975 and 1 July 1976, both in NARA, RG 59, lot file 78D443 (transcripts of Secretary of State Henry Kissinger's Staff Meetings, 1973–1977), folders 6 and 10, respectively. On the Chilean drama, on which we now have a significant mass of documents, see the reconstructions of Peter Kornbluh, *The Pinochet File: A Declassified Dossier on Atrocity and Accountability* (New York: New Press, 2003); and Jonathan Haslam, *The Nixon Administration and the Death of Allende's Chile: A Case of Assisted Suicide* (London: Verso, 2005).

4. John L. Girling, "Kissingerism: The Enduring Problem," *International Affairs* 3 (July 1975): 325. See also Argyris G. Andrianopoulos, *Western Europe in Kissinger's Global Strategy* (New York: St. Martin's Press, 1988); Mary Kaldor, *The Imaginary War: Understanding the East-West Conflict* (Oxford: Blackwell, 1990); Wilfried Loth, *Overcoming the Cold War: A History of Détente* (Basingstoke, UK: Palgrave, 2002), 102–27; William Bundy, *A Tangled Web: The Making of Foreign Policy in the Nixon Presidency* (New York: Hill and Wang, 1998).

5. Henry Kissinger, *A World Restored: Metternich, Castlereagh, and the Problems of Peace, 1812–1822* (Boston: Houghton Mifflin, 1957), 325.

6. Important exceptions are Noam Kochavi, "Insights Abandoned, Flexibility Lost: Kissinger, Soviet Jewish Emigration, and the Demise of Détente," *Diplomatic History* 3 (June 2003): 503–30; and Jeremi Suri, *Henry Kissinger and the American Century* (Cambridge: Harvard University Press, 2007).

7. For a typical example see John Lewis Gaddis, "Rescuing Choice from Circumstances: The Statecraft of Henry Kissinger," in *The Diplomats, 1939–1979,* ed. Gordon A. Craig and Francis Loewenheim, 564–92 (Princeton: Princeton University Press, 1994).

8. This critique is common among commentators and scholars with different historiographical and political backgrounds. For some examples, see Gabriel Schoenfeld, "Was Kissinger Right?" *Commentary* 5 (May 1999): 55–60; James Chace, "The Kissinger Years: A Gravely Flawed Foreign Policy," *New Republic,* 9 November 1974, 30–33; Stanley Hoffmann, "The Case of Dr. Kissinger," *New York Review of Books,* 6 December 1979; and Hoffmann, "The Return of Henry Kissinger," *New York Review of Books,* 29 April 1982; Norman Podhoretz, "Kissinger Reconsidered," *Commentary* 6 (June 1982): 19–28; Robert Beisner, "History and Henry Kissinger," *Diplomatic History* 2 (Autumn 1990): 511–27; Robert D. Schulzinger, *Henry Kissinger: Doctor of Diplomacy* (New York: Columbia University Press, 1989).

9. William Fulbright, *The Arrogance of Power* (New York: Vintage, 1966); Fulbright, *The Price of Empire* (New York: Pantheon Books, 1989); Arthur Schlesinger Jr., *The Imperial Presidency* (Boston: Houghton Mifflin, 1973).

10. Phil Williams, "Détente and U.S. Domestic Politics," *International Affairs* 3 (Summer 1985): 437. See also Phil Williams and Mike Bowker, *Superpower Détente: A Reappraisal* (London: Royal Institute of International Affairs, 1988).

11. This argument is also the one I have put forward in my last book, *Libertà e impero: Gli Stati Uniti e il mondo, 1776–2006* [Empire and liberty: The United States and the world, 1776–2006] (Rome-Bari: Laterza, 2008). On the end of the neoconservative moment, see G. John Ikenberry, "The End of the Neoconservative Moment," *Survival* 2 (Summer 2004): 7–22; and Francis Fukuyama, *America at the Crossroads: Democracy, Power, and the Neoconservative Legacy* (New Haven: Yale University Press, 2006).

INDEX